TH   THORN

THE IRON THORN

The Defeat of the British by the Jamaican Maroons

by

Carey Robinson

Parts of this volume were originally published as The Fighting Maroons
of Jamaica, by William Collins and Sangster (Jamaica) Ltd., 1969
© 1969 by Cary Robinson

© 1993 by Cary Robinson
First edition 1993

Published by LMH Publishing Ltd.
7-9 Norman Road, Kingston CSO
Email: henryles@cwjamaica.com

ISBN 976-610-159-0

Cover illustration by Marlon Cunningham
Typeset by Lazertec Limited
Printed by Lightning Print

CONTENTS

ILLUSTRATIONS

Between pages 34 and 35:

Map of Jamaica (c. 1684)
Map of Jamaica (1771)
Map of Jamaica, showing the main areas of the
* Trelawny and Windward Maroons*
Map of the Cockpit Country and surrounding
* districts*

Between pages 98 and 99:

A Maroon warrior
A Mosquito Indian
Governor Robert Hunter (1729-34)
Cudjoe of the Maroons
Philip Thicknesse
An artist's impression of Trelawny Town

Between pages 162 and 163:

Colonel William Fitch
Maroon ambush of Colonel Sandford's force, which
* took place between the Old Town and the New*
* Town*
Map of the Cockpits, drawn by J. Robertson in 1803,
* showing the area of the Maroon War in 1795-6*
Details of the Cockpits, based on J. Robertson's map
Privates of the 17th Lancers (Light Dragoons)
Major-General George Walpole
Colonel Skinner

Between pages 258 and 259:

Leonard Parkinson, one of the Maroon captains
The Earl of Balcarres, Governor of Jamaica at the
* time of the Second Maroon War*
Cuban chasseur with dog
Map of Maroon transportation: from Port Royal to
* Halifax, Nova Scotia, in 1796; thence to*
* Freetown in 1800*
Halifax citadel, Nova Scotia

SOURCES OF ILLUSTRATIONS

The Institute of Jamaica is the source of most of the illustrations used in this book. *Governor Robert Hunter, Philip Thicknesse* and *The Earl of Balcarres* are reproduced courtesy of the National Library of Jamaica, *A Mosquito Indian* belongs to the National Library of Scotland, and the Nova Scotia Information Service is to be thanked for the photograph of the *Halifax Citadel*. The modern maps of *Jamaica, The Cockpit Country, Details of the Cockpits* and *Maroon Transportation* are reproduced from *The Fighting Maroons of Jamaica*, published by William Collins and Sangster (Jamaica) Ltd., 1969.

INTRODUCTION

One result of Columbus' voyages to the "New World" and his visits to Jamaica, was the establishment in 1509 of a small Spanish colony called New Seville, on the north coast of Jamaica. This led to the extinction of the Arawaks, the original inhabitants, and to the introduction of Africans to work under conditions of bondage.

When the British invaded Jamaica in 1655 they thought they had won an easy victory. But Spanish militants and their African servitors began a struggle to recover the island which lasted five years. The Africans fought as if the country belonged to them and their morale and determination grew, even while the chances of success diminished.

At the outset of the struggle some of the Africans established separate camps under their own chosen leaders. It was as if the right moment had arrived to shrug off their bondage to the Spaniards.

Comparatively speaking, that bondage was not a heavy one. The small size of the Spanish colony and its vulnerability to attack obliged the settlers to place a high value on the support of the Africans, who had become an indispensable and irreplaceable part of the workforce. Their real but unofficial status was exemplified by two of their number who were especially mentioned in the records at the time of the British invasion. One was a priest from Angola who acted as a peace envoy between the British and the

Spaniards and was hanged by militant Spaniards. The other was Diego Pimienta, a heroic hunter, born in Jamaica, who fought the British with great courage and skill at the battle of Caobana.

In August 1655, a British force pushed westwards to get at Spanish ranches beyond the Caobana (Mahogany) river (known today as the Black River). The Caobana had strong currents, was lined on either side by wide swamps and abounded in crocodiles. There were two fords which were about five feet deep. One led to the Caobana ranch and the other to the Jaquatabo ranch. Both were guarded by breastworks.

The British tried to cross at the Caobana ford but were beaten back with a loss of forty men. Early in September they returned with reinforcements and, after attempting to divert the attention of the Spanish defenders, again plunged into the Caobana ford. During the more than four-hour battle, Diego Pimienta, the black hunter, was outstanding. Every time he was ready to shoot he would say: "That Englishman drops now"; and down would go a soldier as he fired.

The English built rafts under cover of the battle, crossed the river and forced the Caobana garrison to withdraw; but by then, Diego Pimienta had become a hero. An officer, Julian de Castilla, in a written report to Spain, said:

> Diego Pimienta (a creole) showed how greatly does
> virtue adorn the individual, and how diversity of colour
> is no obstacle to nobility of blood and worth.

In the five years of warfare the Africans became the most valuable element in the Spanish force. The British began to woo them, realizing that if they abandoned the fight, the Spanish cause would collapse.

As the conflict neared its end, a disillusioned section of the Africans defected to the British on the promise of land

and status. The rest, purged of this compromising element, pledged themselves to a life of freedom and independence. Many years later, this group, and others who embraced their way of life, were called Maroons; which could be interpreted to mean:

> "Fugitives whose spirit could not be broken; living in the wilderness and dangerous to encounter".

The early Maroons lived in a world which had no great appreciation of freedom. Aggression and oppression were taken for granted. Adventurers who raided the possessions of foreign countries, and ruthlessly plundered and terrorized their populations, were openly praised as sound policy in the maintenance of the status quo. Capturing people, selling them into slavery and degrading their humanity, was a legitimate business activity.

In the midst of this world of bondage, a handful of defiant people emerged in Jamaica and rejected servitude. They had two choices if they were to remain in the island after the conquest. Either place themselves under British rule, as some did, or embark on the difficult and dangerous road of freedom and independence. They chose the latter. It was a wise choice; for under the developing slave regime in the West Indies and the Americas, the humanity of people of African origin was violently assaulted and they were forced to evaluate themselves by criteria laid down by their masters, which were always to their disadvantage.

The early Maroons, on the other hand, existing resolutely outside the net of colonial power, laid down their own criteria. They converted the mountains and forests into natural fortresses of tremendous strength. They learned to live off the land in the most inhospitable places; making pathways where none existed, and finding food and water where none appeared to be. They moved faster, endured longer and skillfully camouflaged themselves with leaves ʔ twigs. They developed a type of warfare which canr out the enemy's advantage in numbers and fire-power, and fashioned a system of communication by means of their Abengs (cow horns), which was effective over long distances. They dug deeply into their inner resources; creating, innovating, inventing, initiating, making maximum use of the natural environment; and they faced the gilded British forces without fear; fighting on their own terms with unparalleled audacity.

The Maroons of Jamaica made their demand for freedom long before Simón Bolivar conceived his plan for the liberation of Latin America; before the Haitian Revolution and the French Revolution, before the American War of Independence. Fearing that their continued success would inspire the slave population into island-wide revolt, the British were finally obliged to make peace with them in 1739, and to guarantee their freedom. Perhaps the most important clauses in the peace treaties were those which required the Maroons to suppress or destroy all rebels throughout the island and to return all runaways. The use of slaves against them during the war paved the way for the acceptance of these clauses.

Nevertheless, in the days after the treaties, the Maroons rescued and hid many a runaway, absorbed into their ranks many an unwilling slave, and were even known to "go slow" in the destruction of rebel bands. Their flouting of the treaties became so outrageous that the Colonial Government was forced to pass a law, making the inveigling of slaves from their masters or the harbouring of runaways a crime punishable by transportation. Maroons found guilty of this offence could be sold as slaves to people in other Caribbean islands or on the American continent.

At a time when the self-worth of people of African descent was being undermined, the Maroons stood proudly on the summit of their physical and cultural heritage. Their lofty, confident bearing was a phenomenon wonderful to behold in the dread days of bondage. Wherever they went, they inspired a feeling of awe. Their long fight for freedom was the great Jamaican epic and it strongly influenced the character of the Jamaican people.

CHAPTER 1

THE BEGINNING

Driven off course by contrary winds during his fourth voyage to the New World, Christopher Columbus gave up trying to reach Hispañiola and headed for Jamaica. His men were forced to pump day and night, to keep the wormeaten ships afloat. On June 25th, 1503, at high tide; he coasted into Santa Gloria (St. Ann's Bay), which was the name he had given the north coast harbour when he first saw it in 1494, nine years before.

He grounded the sinking ships in shallow water and built palm leaf shelters on the decks, in which he lived with his crews for a little over a year. Using a convenient eclipse to claim that his god had the power to make the moon disappear, Columbus intimidated the Arawak inhabitants of the island into feeding his men. He was rescued on June 28th 1504, having survived among other things, a mutiny.

Jamaica left an indelible impression on Columbus. With the consent of the Spanish crown, it became a part of his family holdings, and after his death in 1506, his son Diego ordered a settlement to be established on the island. In November 1509, Captain Juan de Esquivel, a seasoned soldier who had served with distinction in Hispañiola, landed at Santa Gloria with a small force of men supported by fierce dogs, and commenced the subjugation of the Arawak.

The Arawaks began to die out almost immediately. European diseases, against which they had no resistance, hastened their demise — in 1520, an epidemic killed many. It is said they also committed mass suicide by drinking the poisonous cassava juice, rather than endure the domination of the Spaniards.

To solve the problem brought about by the diminishing supply of "Arawak" Indian or "Mosquito" Indian, the Spaniards began importing Africans to work as slaves. The first Africans for the Jamaican labour force arrived between 1513 and 1517. For the most part they appeared to have been body servants. As the Arawaks diminished, the Africans began to play an increasingly significant role in the development of the colony.

However, when the Spaniards could find no gold they stopped importing Africans. Spanish settlers no longer came to the island, and many who were already living in the country migrated to New World territories where gold had been found. Those who remained devoted themselves primarily to ranching and farming.

Jamaica became a base from which to supply men, horses, arms and food for the conquest of Cuba and the American mainland. Her farms and ranches produced bread, cassava, corn, salted beef and bacon for the troops. But it was the livestock industry which was the mainstay of the infant Spanish-Jamaican community.

Pigs, goats and cattle were imported and multiplied rapidly, roaming in vast herds over the grassy plains. Each year there was a big hunt in which hundreds of cattle, swine and goats were killed and stripped of their hides and fat. The meat was left behind to decay but the precious hides and fat were exported to Cuba and the Spanish American mainland.

One of the significant things arising from the livestock business was the use of Africans as cowboys, herdsmen and hunters. The slaves used in this way had the opportunity to live a semi-free existence on the wild southern plains and in the hills. They became familiar with the thickly wooded terrain of the interior.

In 1589 the African population was increased by 155 Angola slaves who had been left by Frenchmen at Oristan (Bluefields) and were sold by public auction for 31,192 pesos. By this time there was a certain intermingling of Spaniards, Arawaks and Africans. It was said that some Africans slew surviving Arawak men to gain possession of their women.

The Spanish colony in Jamaica was poor and badly governed. There were several scattered settlements but only one real town, Villa de la Vega (Spanish Town) with houses of wood and tiles. Francisco Marques de Villalobos, appointed Abbot of Jamaica in May 1581, said that the Governors were seldom present (they apparently spent most of their time in Santo Domingo) and refused the pleas of the settlers for the redress of wrongs. Many settlers became discouraged and deserted the island. In 1596, it was reported that there were only about 130 Spanish inhabitants in Jamaica.

During the governorship of Fernando Melgarejo de Cordova (1597-1606), the population appears to have been increased by the arrival of migrants chiefly from Puerto Rico. To protect the island from the constant raids of Dutch, French, English and Portuguese pirates, Melgarejo raised four companies of soldiers, one of them made up of Indians and free Mulattoes (men of mixed African and Spanish descent). With these men he fought off pirate raids from Negril to Yallahs and in 1603 defeated the great English freebooter, Christopher Newport, in a rousing battle less than a mile outside of Spanish Town.

In 1611, another Abbot of Jamaica (a successor to Abbot Villalobos who died in August, 1606) noted the number of confessions that he had ordered to be made with particular care that year. From this form of census he estimated that there were 1,510 persons of all classes and conditions in Jamaica; 523 Spaniards including men and women, 173

3

children, 107 free Negroes, 74 Native Arawak Indians, 558 slaves and 75 foreigners. He mentioned that the Spanish families were so closely mixed by marriage that they were all related.

"This causes many and grave incests to be committed by which the country is remarkably stained". The Abbot's figures testify eloquently to the fact that the Arawaks, between 60,000 or 100,000 strong, had almost disappeared. By the early seventeenth century the Jamaican community was a decidedly Spanish-African one, liberally laced with Arawak Indian blood.

Captain Jacinto Sedeno y Albornoz, Commissioner of Accounts, who arrived in Jamaica on May 2nd, 1649 to investigate charges against his predecessor, Pedro de Caballero, ran into plenty of trouble. He blamed his misfortunes on the wickedness and malice of one Don Francisco de Leyba Yzazi. He condemned him "as a man who though married has had intercourse with a coloured woman for more than sixteen years." Leyba Yzazi was certainly not the only Spanish Jamaican with a coloured or black mistress.

Sedeno also made reference to another of his enemies, Juan de Chabres Bejarano the grandson of a man who was hanged, drawn and quartered in the island "for attempting to raise a rebellion among the Negroes." This is one of the first indications in Jamaica of a collective revolt among the Africans against the conditions of slavery.

The gentle, peace-loving Arawaks, witnessing the destruction of their culture and unable to organize a successful physical resistance, lost the will to live. The Africans, however, displayed a tougher disposition.

Sedeno described Jamaica of the 1640s and 50s as:

> More important...than any other (island), as it is more fertile and abundant than all those they have settled in the Indies. Cuba and Hispañiola are indeed much larger,

but Jamaica in its entirety is more plentiful than those,
for it has much horned stock and herds of tame swine
and wild ones in great numbers, from the hunting of
which every year is obtained a quantity of lard that
serves instead of oil for cooking.

Likewise there is a large number of horses, donkeys
and mules, fisheries of turtle and dainty fish, a very
fine climate from its healthy airs and waters, many
copious rivers, pleasant valleys and plains most suitable for plantations of cocoa, which in any other part of
the Indies would be highly esteemed; a great quantity
of wood for ship-building and of such superior quality
that it surpasses all that has been seen so far in these
regions, good as they are, for the shipworm (broma)
does not injure or enter the woods of this island.

In like manner there are different sorts of woods especially mahogany, cedar, basil wood and red ebony which
is not found elsewhere and all in abundance, and in the
same way lots of trees of the pepper called 'Tobasco'
that is used to put in chocolate.

The displaced Africans seemed to renew their spirits in
the island. Amid the poverty of the Spanish community
there is a suggestion that they lived vigorously; hunting
the wild cattle, finding pathways in the virgin wilderness,
and relearning the arts of the warrior in desperate skirmishes with pirates.

Sedeno wrote partly of them in his reports:

I have heard with much concern many conversations
with regard to colonising this island and fortifying two
ports, one on the north side and one on the south. I
always told them that there was a garrison of ten companies of infantry stationed by the King, our master,
besides three in the town and two of mounted
Mulattoes and free Negroes armed with hocking knives
and half moons, (a scythe-like weapon) of whom they
are much afraid.

5

. Later on he said:

> Nearly 450 men bear arms, including the hunters and
> country folks, all of whom are labouring people, strong
> and suitable for war by reason of their courageous spir-
> its; if indeed lacking in military discipline.

This was the state of Jamaica at the time of the English
invasion in 1655. The island was badly defended, poverty
stricken, underdeveloped and underpopulated; the
Government officials corrupt or weak and ineffective. The
inhabitants were indolent and demoralized, money was
scarce and trade was falling off. Nevertheless, in the midst of
the small, enervated population there existed a hard core
made up of hunters, labourers, slaves and a few of the better-
off Spaniards: black, white and brown men who loved the
country and were capable of fighting and enduring hardships.

On May 10th, 1655, an English force under Admiral
Penn and General Venables arrived in 38 ships. About
8,000 men were landed. The Spaniards abandoned both
the port defences and the town of Villa de la Vega and fled
to the mountains with their families. Except when governed by a strong man like Melgarejo this retreat into the
mountains had for some time been their normal practice
whenever threatened by raiders. Their present Governor,
Juan Ramirez de Orellana, was old and sick and could give
no leadership. But unlike other raiders in the past, the
invading force had come to stay. They occupied the town,
and the Spanish Governor surrendered. The English provided the Spaniards with ships to leave the island. Most of
them went but elements of the hard core remained.

The ailing Governor Ramirez died on shipboard. The
head of the military forces, Francisco de Proenza, old and
almost blind, handed over command to Christoval Arnaldo
de Ysassi, a Jamaican-born Spaniard. Ysassi was not a
trained soldier but he was determined to fight to regain the
island.

Some of the Africans who had not remained with their Spanish masters, took to the hills on their own. They followed those of their number who had been hunters and herdsmen and who had learned the secret paths into the wilderness of the interior. They were to become the original Maroons of Jamaica.

The origins of the word 'Maroon' are not well-established. According to the historian Long, the name 'Maroon' probably comes from the Spanish 'marran', a sow or young hog. The name was first given to hunters of wild hogs to distinguish them from the buccaneers, who hunted wild cattle and horses. Others believe that 'Maroon' is a corruption of the Spanish 'cimarron', meaning "wild" or "unruly". The French word for a runaway slave is 'marron'. Whatever its derivation, it is a name to be proudly borne and a word deeply rooted in the history of Jamaica.

CHAPTER 2

THE AFRICAN CONTINGENT

After the English conquest of the island, Don Christoval Arnaldo de Ysassi took over leadership of the Spanish resistance movement and began to shape it. He roamed the hills and forests of the interior gathering his tiny force and making plans to strike at his enemy. At first, disease helped him in his cause, as the English soldiers died by the hundreds from fever and starvation. Three of the English Commissioners of the island, Fortescue, Sedgewick and Brayne, perished one after the other.

Ysassi had two main problems. One was to get sufficient reinforcements and supplies to enable him to confront the English openly, and the other was to secure the help of the Africans who had escaped into the bush and keep them loyal to the Spanish cause. Until reinforcements arrived, his plan was to harass the English by guerrilla warfare, but without the Africans as active allies, he could not hope to do this successfully. A few of the Africans had remained loyal to their Spanish masters, but the vast majority, with a strong show of independence, set up their own camps in the bush.

A large number of them collected in the mountains of Clarendon under a leader called Juan Lubolo, who later became known as Juan de Bolas. No one knew whether they would finally decide to help their late masters, go over to the English or just stay out of the fight and mind their own business. Ysassi was to spend a good deal of time and energy trying to keep them out of the hands of the English.

Africans were present in just about every one of the raids, ambushes, skirmishes or battles which marked the long struggle between the Spaniards and the English in Jamaica. They were present as scouts, hunters and foragers, and they also fought shoulder to shoulder with the Spanish infantrymen. But they were of greatest value as suppliers of food. Without them the Spanish reinforcements would have been defeated by hunger alone.

They fed the Spaniards who had remained behind in the north, after the bulk of the colonists had fled, they hunted the wild animals in the interior; and established extensive cultivations in the Lluidas Vale area.

Rambling throughout the southern countryside, they killed any English soldiers who fell into their hands. Major General Sedgewick, one of the Commissioners, writing in 1656 to Secretary Thurloe, predicted that they would become a thorn in the side of the English. He bemoaned the fact that they gave no quarter to his men, but destroyed them at every opportunity, and he reported that as his own soldiers grew more confident and careless, the Africans became more enterprising and bloody minded. Once they even launched a night attack on the English in their quarters in the capital town, Villa de la Vega, and set fire to some of the houses in which the soldiers were lodged.

Sedgewick was baffled by their ruthless, hard-hitting methods. He expressed his dilemma with the Africans in these words:

> Having no moral sense, and not understanding what the laws and customs of civil nations mean, we know not how to capitulate or treat with any one of them. But be assured they must either be destroyed or brought in, upon some terms or other, or else they will prove a great discouragement to the settling of the country.

9

Towards the end of 1656 the English managed to do them some small damage, but they immediately retaliated by cutting off and slaughtering forty soldiers who had carelessly wandered away from their camp. A detachment was hurriedly sent after them and succeeded in killing seven or eight before they escaped.

Meanwhile, Ysassi moved south with his Sargento Mayor, Captain Don Christoval de Leyba, and a few of the Africans. He joined the handful of Spaniards who still remained in the south and made a camp at a place called Guatibacoa, about twenty-four miles from Spanish Town. He had some two thousand head of cattle and a few beasts of burden in the vicinity of the camp, but his force numbered only about fifty, black and white included.

Ysassi's position was excellent. His camp was so located that he could obstruct enemy movements between Spanish Town and Negril in the far west. Whenever the hungry English attempted to cultivate the land or to establish posts, Ysassi's guerillas ambushed them, killing many, taking prisoners and capturing valuable baggage. He reported that every day he captured or killed troops.

For his services rendered in the defence of the island, Ysassi was appointed Governor by the King of Spain in 1656. The King also directed that reinforcements, arms and provisions be sent to Jamaica from Santo Domingo, Cuba and Puerto Rico. Later Ysassi was advised by the Duke of Albuquerque, Viceroy of Mexico and the leading Spanish Governor in the Indies, that he was to promise freedom to runaway slaves who would return to help fight the English.

In July, 1657, reinforcements landed at Ocho Rios. About 200 of them were Spanish-Jamaicans who had fled to Cuba on the arrival of the English. Leaving some of the troops at Ocho Rios to guard the provisions, Ysassi set out with most of the reinforcements for the south side, meaning to attack the English in force. After a few days of marching through the rough countryside they ran out of food. The two senior officers of the contingent, Reyes and da Silva, afraid of the venture and resentful of Ysassi whom they regarded as an amateur, asked to be allowed to return to the coast with their men. Ysassi let them go with the greater number of troops, after directing them to remove the provisions from where they were hidden and store them in a stronger place.

With his reduced force, Ysassi reached his camp in Upper Clarendon. No longer able to attack the English in force, he proceeded to harass them, destroying their provision grounds, driving off their cattle and wiping out their scouting parties and foragers. Then the rains came down, day and night, and he was forced to call a halt to his operations. Food was scarce but the captured cattle and the foraging of the African hunters kept them from starving.

In all of these months Ysassi had been able to persuade most, if not all, of the Africans to join him in the fight against the English. He ordered a pardon to be published in the name of the King to all runaways, with the promise of freedom for those who distinguished themselves in his service. He acknowledged their great importance in a report to Albuquerque in which he said:

> It has been no small success to have reduced them (the runaway Africans) on account of their knowledge of the island, and, if they wanted to do mischief, could have done us very much harm.

Juan de Bolas had emerged as the most powerful chief among the Africans. A born leader, de Bolas was an expert hunter and had acquired a vast knowledge of much of the wild country in the interior of the island. He gave active help to Ysassi who came to value his assistance and depend upon his skill.

General William Brayne, one of the English Commissioners died on September 2nd, 1657, and was succeeded by Edward D'Oyley who began to govern by court-martial. Tougher than his predecessors, D'Oyley survived the diseases and the hardships and set himself to drive Ysassi from Jamaica.

At about the time of the rains, Ysassi received a couple of severe setbacks. The English learned that he had only a handful of men and sent a party of 500 soldiers to find him. Ysassi reported in September that he left his camp and marched to meet them with only 80 men. According to him he destroyed them in an ambush and captured all the baggage they were carrying. Nevertheless, because his whereabouts had been discovered he was forced to move on to Oristan (Bluefields, in Westmoreland).

Shortly afterwards he learned that the men he had left at Ocho Rios to guard the baggage had been attacked and defeated, the camp overrun and the provisions seized. Reyes and da Silva had disobeyed his orders to leave the exposed site where the camp had been set up and withdraw to Baycani where their flanks would have been secure. The English landed six miles away, brushed aside a weak ambush and charged the camp. They fired two volleys into the shallow trench and stockade that served as a fortification and drove out the defenders. The defeated men were without proper clothing or food. Ysassi sent one of his lieutenants to rally them and two parties of hunters to supply them with food. Presently, Reyes and most of the men returned to Cuba in canoes and thus ended the first attempt to launch a major attack on the English.

Undaunted, Ysassi asked for more reinforcements, provisions, arms and medical supplies. He had many enemies among his own countrymen, one of the chief of whom was the Governor of Cuba who delayed the supplies which he desperately needed.

The second relief contingent arrived in May, 1658 and landed at Rio Nuevo on a Saturday morning. It was made up of about 560 badly-armed Spaniards, Negroes,

Mulattoes and Indians. They did not immediately find Ysassi; but discovered one of the African settlements about 18 miles away, with the huts burnt down and other signs that indicated a defeat. Eight days after their arrival Ysassi turned up.

On May 28th, the contingent fought off three English ships and two days later beat off another attack by five ships. After this the Spaniards began completing a fort on a hill overlooking the bay which had been started by Ysassi. The fort was not quite finished when on June 25th, an English fleet appeared carrying a body of picked troops commanded by D'Oyley himself. A strong party of men was landed on the beach. From his small, crowded, unfinished fort Ysassi sent two Spanish captains with seventy soldiers and twenty Africans under their own captain to oppose the landing. In the encounter nearly all of them died fighting.

The warships pounded the Spanish defences, more troops were landed and at the end of three days of continuous fighting the fort was taken. Most of the Spanish force was killed or wounded and some sources say that the last man to leave the fort was Ysassi. It took him four or five days to gather what remained of his scattered forces.

Don Francisco de Leyba, the Spanish Lieutenant-General to Jamaica, said that when he left the island after the defeat at Rio Nuevo, Ysassi remained with 120 men consisting of Spaniards, Negroes, Indians and Mulattoes, most of them being former Inhabitants of Jamaica. Along with these, de Leyba left his own slaves so that they might feed the survivors by hunting. Ysassi eventually sent most of the survivors back to Cuba and remained in Jamaica himself with about 50 men.

In August, he wrote a report to the Spanish King in which, for the first time, he appeared to have misgivings about his ability to hold the Africans. Writing of them Ysassi said:

> The Negroes, sir, who have remained fugitives from
> their masters who have abandoned the island and your
> Majesty's arms, are more than two hundred strong but
> many have died. I have not done a small thing in con-
> serving them, keeping them under my obedience when
> they have been sought after with papers from the
> enemy.
>
> I have promised their chiefs freedom in your Majesty's
> name but have not given it until I receive an order for
> it.

Don Francisco de Leyba echoed Ysassi's fears in
stronger terms when he later recalled the situation as it
existed at the time. He said that besides those who
remained with Ysassi,

> ... there are in three settlements about two hun-
> dred and fifty black men and women who govern them-
> selves although they are obedient to the Governor
> (Ysassi) who keeps them in this way so that they may
> separate themselves from His Majesty's service. I do
> not know if these Negroes seeing the English prevail in
> the island will subject themselves to their government
> as they have many times solicited.
>
> The Governor has impeded it by kind words, offering
> the loyal ones freedom and His Majesty'sprotection.

Continuing, de Leyba said that 50 to 60 men together
with the Negroes in the settlements would be enough to
maintain a footing in the island until a fleet could be sent.
A small force could better hide and feed itself than a large
one, provided the men were sent clothing and given some
recognition for their services.

De Leyba also suggested that an order be sent to Ysassi
"to give liberty to the Negroes who deserve it." This was
especially important as the English had also offered them
liberty, saying that they would allow them to settle where
they liked, provided they agreed to live under English law.

CHAPTER 3

JUAN DE BOLAS, THE GREAT TRAITOR

The English were quick to realize the value of the African auxiliaries and launched a determined campaign to woo them away from the Spaniards by promising land and instant freedom. In this respect, they had the advantage of Ysassi, who had to wait until he received an order from his King before he could confirm freedom. Up to the time of the Rio Nuevo defeat this order had not come through. The English posted notices written in Spanish upon the trees, offering passage to Spanish ports to any Spaniards who would surrender, and urging the Africans to desert to them.

The Africans were aware of the insubordinate behaviour of Reyes and da Silva which resulted in the Ocho Rios defeat. Against the strong, fairly disciplined ranks of the English, they must have contrasted the untidy ranks of raw, confused, ill-armed, ill-clad men who made up the relieving forces. They also knew of the official hostility and shabby treatment Ysassi received from some quarters, especially from Don Pedro de Bayona, Governor of Cuba. Inevitably they must have asked themselves if a cause represented by such men, who even in adversity sought to destroy each other, was worth supporting.

It is possible that Ysassi never quite understood the change that had taken place in the Jamaican-Africans. He seemed not to have realized that the rickety Spanish colony had crumbled and that the ex-slaves had seen how ineffectual it had been. The Africans had not only lost respect for their former masters, but had developed a great deal of confidence in themselves.

Ysassi's and de Leyba's reports confirm that there were three distinct groups amongst the Africans in Jamaica: the free men who fought with the Spanish-Jamaicans as men defending their homeland against attack; the slaves who remained loyal to their Spanish masters; and the runaways and hunters who took to the bush after the invasion and set up settlements under their own chiefs.

Despite all the opposition, the setbacks and the uncertainties, Ysassi refused to give up. On September 23rd, 1659, Oliver Cromwell, Lord Protector of England, died, and the English forces in Jamaica went through a period of great insecurity. They received no suppplies from home and did not know what would happen to them when Charles II was restored to the throne. Realizing their demoralized state, Ysassi seized the opportunity to attack them as hard as he could. But somewhere between the end of the year and February, 1660, Juan de Bolas went over to the English and from that time Ysassi realized that his days in Jamaica were numbered.

In a letter to the King he admitted that the loss of Bolas was:

> very serious because... the Negroes are capable and experienced on the roads, mountains, remote places (and) are hunters handy for everything.

Bolas had one of the biggest settlements and he took all his people when he went over to the English. But it was not only the number of people who went with Bolas that distressed Ysassi, it was the loss of Bolas's skill and the knowledge which he carried of the whereabouts of all the Spanish camps and hiding-places.

On February 22nd, 1660, Ysassi held a Council of War

and it was decided that under the circumstances it would be best to abandon the island. As the notary, Captain Francisco de Belensuela, put it:

> All the Captains present were of the opinion that the island should be abandoned as the Negroes are so experienced and acquainted with the mountains that no success could be obtained there, but that (we) were all exposed to the unknown risk of being murdered without escape, considering the few troops (we) had and the number of the enemy.

The Council of War decided that until the ship arrived from Cuba with supplies, the camp should be removed to another place. But not even this move was able to save them. On February 26th, 1660, leading a detachment of English under Colonel Edward Tyson and accompanied by his own men, Juan de Bolas tracked the Spaniards to their new camp and they were routed.

On February 27th, Colonel Tyson wrote a letter in which he mentioned that when his men overran the Spanish camp they had been "accompanied by the Negroes of Governor Juan Lubolo." He also requested the Spaniards to surrender at Ocho Rios, promising to give them passage to Cuba or to any other place to which they desired to go. He gave them seven days to reply, warning that if he did not hear from them at the end of that time he would seek them with all rigour "in the remotest parts of the island accompanied by the Negroes."

In his reply, Ysassi asked safety for the lives of all who were with him and free passage for all infantry and other troops of any rank and condition who had served him "without excepting any person provided they be not people from a settlement." From this it seems that he had lost all confidence in the African settlements and was prepared to abandon them. This may have been due to de Bolas' betrayal, but it may also have resulted from the Philip Starkey incident.

Philip Starkey, a rash over-confident British soldier, set out to find an African settlement at Los Vermejales; governed by a powerful leader named Juan de Serras, a man as well known and respected as Juan de Bolas. It seemed that his intention was to persuade de Serras to surrender, for the position of the Spanish force now seemed hopeless. Starkey entered the settlement of de Serras under a flag of truce, believing that this would ensure his safety. He was slain, despite his flag of truce.

The British commander, Edward D'Oyley, angrily demanded that Ysassi punish de Serras and his men; but Ysassi explained that the men he was being asked to punish were "the heads of that settlement who have governed themselves like the others, with a slight submission (to his authority)." He no longer had any control over them. D'Oyley would not accept Ysassi's explanation and threatened to reject his peace proposals unless he agreed that only Spaniards would be permitted to leave the island.

Unfortunately, the greater part of the Spanish force that remained in Jamaica was made up of Indians, Blacks and Mulattoes, not counting slaves and coloured domestic servants, and Ysassi was determined not to leave behind even the meanest of those who had served him. He refused therefore to comply with the request to surrender. The deadline for capitulation came and went but Ysassi did not appear. Instead he took to the bush on the north coast near Rio Nuevo and waited for a ship from Cuba to take his men off.

Two months passed. The English returned to Spanish Town by sea and land. Finally, when it seemed that no ship would get through to him, Ysassi built two canoes. He managed to squeeze 76 of his men into them, and set off for Cuba on May 9th, 1660, leaving behind 36 men under a captain. His departure marked the end of Spanish resistance in Jamaica.

Juan de Bolas and his followers were granted lands by

the English, and it was declared by proclamation that they should enjoy all the liberties and privileges of Englishmen. On January 30th, 1663, de Bolas was appointed Colonel of a black regiment of militia. He was also made a magistrate over the Africans with the power to decide all cases except those of life and death.

He had been given a magnificent reward for his services and the English hoped that this would encourage the others to come down from their settlements. But they would not budge.

The most outstanding of the Afro-Spanish Maroon leaders who remained opposed to the British was Juan de Serras. Unlike Juan de Bolas, de Serras could not be persuaded to surrender his hard-won freedom and independence for high rank and status under British rule. He and his people were aiming for something much larger: to create a society in which they would be their own masters. Though just a handful of survivors from a lost cause, they were attempting to carve out an independent destiny in the hinterlands of an island which had been taken over by a numerically and technologically superior force; poised for growth and with virtually unlimited access to supplies and support.

When Juan de Bolas switched sides he immediately attacked de Serras' camp before the latter even knew he had defected. De Serras moved from Los Vermejales into the Cave Valley area. But his new camp was discovered, stormed and destroyed. His band was scattered but most of them found their way back to him. Again and again the British offered to make peace, promising freedom, citizenship and status; but de Serras refused.

In 1663, when de Bolas was made a colonel of black militia and a magistrate, and his followers were granted the full rights of citizenship, every male over the age of eighteen in his community received the regular settler allotment of thirty acres. In exchange, the children were required to learn English and de Bolas was committed to search out and destroy all Africans who refused to submit to the British.

Martial Law, under which Jamaica had been governed since the invasion, came to an end in 1663; and Lieutenant-Governor Sir Charles Lyttleton once more offered a full pardon, with land and freedom from all manner of slavery to Maroons who surrendered. De Serras and all the others scorned the offer.

The promise of land meant nothing. They had all the territory of the interior to hunt, farm and roam about in as they wished; and the individual ownership of land was not a social or economic imperative in their way of life.

The British were now thoroughly outraged by what they saw as an unreasonable refusal to accept their generous proposals. They ordered Juan de Bolas, who had proven to be effective instrument of destruction, to wipe out the Maroon menace once and for all. He went out on his mission of destruction, but was caught in an ambush, perhaps set by de Serras himself. His force was cut to pieces, and the great Colonel Juan de Bolas was killed.

Juan de Serras and his people were declared outlaws; but in a sense this was an empty gesture, for they had never been a part of the British colony. A reward was offered to anyone who killed de Serras or his second in command. There is no record that anyone ever collected that reward.

CHAPTER 4

CUDJOE, THE MOUNTAIN LION

The defeat and death of the formidable Juan de Bolas hardened the resolve of the Maroons and increased their confidence. There was now no thought of turning back from the road on which they had set themselves; but it was also becoming increasingly obvious that the English were in Jamaica to stay and that their numbers would grow.

Over the years raids and ambushes became so severe that the English soldiers, now turned settlers, were greatly discouraged from cultivating the land. This helped bring on the famines which, in addition to the severe epidemics, threatened the very existence of the colony in the early years.

However, new settlers began to arrive; first from Nevis, and then from Barbados, New England, Bermuda and Surinam. After Ysassi's departure military rule was discontinued. Civil Government was set up and Jamaica was on the way to becoming a stable British colony.

At first the pattern of settlement was of many small farms on which a number of food products was grown. But in 1668 when the inferior local cane was supplanted by cane of superior quality from Barbados, the pattern began to change. Many of the food crops dropped out of cultivation and sugar became the foremost commodity. Small-holdings were swallowed up and sugar estates grew to giant proportions. But sugar cane grown on a large scale required plenty of workers, and since Europeans could not be induced to engage voluntarily in this kind of work, the English began to bring Africans to Jamaica to work as slaves.

Most of them came from West Africa and were of many different types. There were Iboes from the Bight of Benin, Mandingoes from the south coast of Sierra Leone, Coromantees (Akim, Ashanti and Fanti peoples) from the Gold Coast (the area which includes modern Ghana), Papaws from Whiddah, and some from the Congo and Angola. But among all these different types it was the Gold Coast Coromantees who stood out.

According to slave owners and slave buyers of the time, the Coromantees were strong, bellicose and virile. Almost every slave revolt was inspired or led by Coromantees, and the planters were divided between admiration of their superior strength and activity, and apprehension of their fierceness.

It was during the 20 years following the death of Juan de Bolas that the buccaneers began to flourish. Port Royal became famous and men like Henry Morgan attained considerable prominence. Morgan sacked Porto Bello, plundered and burnt Panama, was knighted and twice made Lieutenant-Governor of Jamaica. The exploits of Morgan and the buccaneers are recorded in history books as one of the most colourful periods in the Jamaican story, but to reluctant slaves like the Coromantees they meant little or nothing; neither did the peevish struggles between the House of Assembly and the Crown, in which the slaves naturally had no part. Their great source of constant inspiration was the rebel Maroons, the presence of whom meant hope.

The first big recorded slave outbreak under the British took place in 1684 and was followed by another in 1686. It was not until 1690, however, two years before the destruction of Port Royal by an earthquake, that a really dangerous insurrection occurred. It took place on Sutton's Estate near Chapelton in the parish of Clarendon and is believed to have been caused by brutal treatment. The slaves killed the man in charge and seized the arms and ammunition with which most estates were well supplied. The next day they were overwhelmed and their ringleaders captured and executed. Some eluded capture, however, and escaped into the Clarendon hills. Among them was a Coromantee boy named Cudjoe and his two brothers, Johnny and Accompong.

The survivors of the 1690 Sutton outbreak did not head for the old Spanish-African Maroon settlements which appeared to be in the north and east of the island. They remained instead in the Clarendon hills which was the old haunt of Juan de Bolas. Along with other rebel-runaways they formed small gangs and began raiding the farms of outlying settlers.

Proof that fugitives from Sutton's had survived, was obtained in 1729, nearly forty years after the outbreak. On July 31st of that year, the Assembly recorded that Captain Varney Philip, Commander of the regiment in Clarendon and Vere, had empowered Captain Simon Boothe to raise and lead a voluntary party for the purpose of pursuing and destroying a group of 'Rebellious Negroes' who had come into Porus in Clarendon. In a clash with these rebels, Boothe and his party killed one man and four women. The man and two of the women were found to have been branded with the mark 'TS, with a heart'. This was old Colonel Sutton's mark. They had escaped during the 1690 outbreak and had been 'out' all that time.

Four adult rebels and seven children were also captured by Boothe. They included a man belonging to Colonel Philip, who had been 'out' for two years; a woman of Rippon's, 'out' seven years; a woman of Wright's, 'out' over two years, and an old woman, who bore the TS and heart mark of Colonel Sutton, and had been 'out' since 1690.

The rebel runaways kept in constant touch with the slaves on nearby plantations, many of whom were old friends or even relatives. In lean times they were supplied with food from the provision grounds of the slaves. One result of this constant communication was that the run-aways could be warned whenever armed parties of militia or soldiers were moving against them.

During the decades of guerrilla activity between 1690 and 1720, Cudjoe emerged as a 'gang' leader. He became a tough, aggressive raider, and stories of his exploits began to be told throughout the area.

At first the rebel bands were content to kill and carry off cattle, but gradually their raids became more formidable. They plundered the houses of isolated settlers, destroyed or drove away their cattle and carried off their slaves. They so harassed the country round about their hide-outs that the development of that particular part of Jamaica was greatly retarded.

Some of the tougher farmers held on doggedly and man-aged to develop their estates, but they lived in constant expectation of attack. Their houses were planned to serve both as dwellings and forts, and were built on commanding positions from which they could overlook the plantation works and buildings, and the group of huts where the slaves lived. On either side of the house were flanking structures with loopholes through which attackers could be fired upon. Almost every house had its stand of arms and was amply supplied with powder and shot. The American frontiersman settled on the edge of hostile Indian country lived no more perilously than his Jamaican counterpart.

Under the almost ceaseless pressure of rebel raids, the planters and farmers in the region grew more and more desperate. They complained bitterly to the Government and sent frequent delegations and representations to the House of Assembly. Consequently, the Government con-centrated armed detachments in the area and brought in

Indians from the Mosquito coast to help.

To combat this move the rebels in Western Jamaica joined forces and chose Cudjoe to lead them. On assuming command, he appointed his two brothers, Accompong and Johnny, as captains under him. The Hon. John William Fortescue, author of *The History of the 17th Lancers*, described Cudjoe as a man of genius, ..."By whose efforts the various wandering bands were welded into a single body, organized on a quasi-military footing, and made twice as formidable as before. The Maroons of the north (original Spanish Maroons) who from the beginning had never left their strong-holds joined him and enlisted under his banner".

With Cudjoe as their leader, the Western rebels defied all attempts to subdue them and began to pursue "a more regular and connected system of warfare".

Obtaining arms and ammunition was always a problem for the rebels. They got weapons from soldiers and militiamen who fell in battle against them, or who threw down their arms in wild flight from the scene of some ambush. Sometimes they would be supplied by friends who purchased arms and powder under pretence of being hunters and fowlers. Occasionally they would go down from the hills on market day carrying a few fowls and baskets of food, looking no different from the crowd of slaves that thronged the market-place. They would make discreet purchases of munitions and return without arousing any suspicions.

One result of the difficulty in obtaining powder and shot was that the rebels were much more careful than the troops sent against them, and seldom threw away a shot ineffectually. They knew how to bide their time and shoot only when they were fairly certain of hitting the mark. Even whilst hunting they learnt to bring down wild animals on the run with a single shot. Of their ability and skill as trackers, the historian Long wrote:

> They are remarkable, like the North American Indians,
> for tracking in the woods; discerning the vestige of the
> person, or party, of whom they are in quest, by the turn
> of a dried leaf, the position of a small twig, and other
> insignificant marks, which an European would over-
> look.

Long also described the terrible cutlass fights that sometimes developed when slave companies and Maroons
clashed with each other. After the first volley, if both sides
stood their ground, cutlasses would be drawn. In the use of
this weapon...

> ... they are surprisingly active and skilful, using either
> hand alternately, as they see occasion... Sometimes...
> they will fight very desperately, and stand to it with
> the insensibility of posts, till they almost hack one
> another to pieces, before either will surrender".

The Maroons observed the ways in which the English
soldiers manoeuvered, but wisely avoided imitating them.
Cunningly camouflaged by leaves and branches, they used
trees, rocks and uneven ground for cover. Their attacks
from ambush were frighteningly sudden and devastating.
The confusion of such attacks on the dim forest trails, combined with expert shooting, usually brought quick victory.

Sometimes, however, troops under attack were unusual-
ly well led and had nerves of steel. Such men might recover from the first surprise, fight back hard and force the
Maroons to give ground. In such cases the Maroons would
vanish into the bush and the soldiers, encouraged by what
they thought to be a victory, would push forward with
vigour, only to fall into another ambush.

One of the exercises which the Maroons developed was
described by the historian, Long, in 1764, when they gave a
peaceful demonstration to entertain the Governor. Long
noted that:

> With amazing ability they ran, or rather rolled through
> their various firings and evolutions. This part of their
> exercise indeed more justly deserves to be stiled evolu-
> tion than any that is practiced by regular troops, for
> they fire stooping almost to the very ground, and no
> sooner are their muskets discharged than they throw
> themselves into a thousand antic gestures, and tumble
> over and over, so as to be continually shifting their
> place; the intention of which is to elude the shot as well
> as to deceive the aim of their adversaries which their
> nimble and almost instantaneous change of position
> renders extremely uncertain.

These were indeed sensible tactics for an outnumbered
and poorly supplied people, but European armies were not
to learn such life-saving methods until the best of their
young men had been slaughtered in the terrible battles of
World War I. In the eighteenth century Englishmen could
not help looking down on the guerrilla system of
stratagems, partly because they could not cope with it and
had therefore to assure themselves of its inferiority.

The soldiers were almost never successful in surprising
the Maroons, for they kept sharp-eyed lookouts at strategic
places in the vicinity of their camps and settlements.
Whenever these lookouts spotted an enemy they signalled
by blowing on an abeng — a cow horn with a hole at the tip
and blow-hole at one side. The sound of the abeng could
carry over many miles and enable isolated bands to contact
each other quickly. Skilled signalers could blow a wide
variety of calls on the horn and summon each member of a
gang from afar by blowing the code signal for each individual's name.

During this period, official documents referred to the
Maroons as "Wild Negroes, Rebellious Slaves, or Slaves in
Rebellion." Their life was hard and full of danger. Often
their camps and towns were overrun by troops and their
provision grounds destroyed. During such periods they
faced starvation and the breakup of their communities.

The women and children were caught up in every crisis, and were ravaged by the trauma of displacement and pursuit. Many times, when they were forced out of their towns, they burnt their houses themselves, and the woods and hard rocks became their habitations. But the majority never gave up, for, to them, the most perilous kind of freedom was preferable to the safe, fetid barracks of bondage.

CHAPTER 5

THE INVINCIBLE WINDWARD MAROONS

On September 22nd, 1703, thirteen years after Cudjoe's escape from Sutton's, Colonel Peter Beckford (Lieutenant-Governor of Jamaica in 1702), reported that he had sent four parties in pursuit of "Rebellious Negroes... who have been a great body for these ten years past". Beckford said they had settled in the mountains between "the North and South-east point" of the island, and had a town and over one hundred acres of land well-planted with provisions. This had been their 'nest' for several years.

The town was burnt by Beckford's men. One party occupied the site, while the other three pushed on to seek out and destroy the fugitives. Beckford vowed that he would not rest until the rebels were totally destroyed or reduced. He wrote:

> I take this thing to be as much consequence as any I
> can think of at present. These rascals have destroyed
> some of the out settlements... and if not quelled, may
> prove more dangerous.

Beckford was right about the dangerous nature of the problem, but he failed to either destroy or reduce the rebels. They grew stronger and more dangerous. Twenty-five years after Beckford wrote his report, rebels in the north-east (the Windward Maroons) were locked in a desperate conflict with soldiers, sailors, militia, volunteer

companies and contingents of armed slaves called Black
Shots. So formidable were the attacks of the Windwards
and so stout their defences that the British felt they were
receiving help from Spaniards in Cuba, and expected a
Spanish attack.

At a Council of War held in St. Jago de la Vega on
Tuesday, April 29th, 1729, it was resolved that a proclamation be issued promising freedom to white indentured servants and slaves who distinguished themselves against the
rebels. It was also agreed to build three roads to link the
settled areas of the South with the 'isolated' North Coast.
The roads were to run from Plantain Garden River to Port
Antonio; from Clarendon through Old Woman's Savannah
to St. Ann; from the Cave in Westmoreland to Montego
Bay.* The North Coast was the weakest part of the island,
and Port Antonio was felt to be the most threatened point,
primarily because of its proximity to the chief strength of
the Windward rebels.

Port Antonio was the capital of the recently created
parish of Portland, named after Henry Bentinck, Marquis
of Titchfield and Duke of Portland. The Duke was appointed
Governor of Jamaica in September 1721. He arrived on
December 22nd, 1722, and the following year the House of
Assembly put into force a law for settling the north-east
section of the island. The Government purchased 30,000
acres for the purpose and the new parish of Portland was
formed out of part of St. George and part of St. Thomas in
the East. The Titchfield lands of Port Antonio were named
after the Duke's second title. The Duke died in Spanish
Town on July 4th, 1726 at the age of forty-four.

During the turbulent years between 1729 and 1734,

---

* *The Militia of the five North-side parishes (St. James, St. Ann, St. Mary, St. George and
Portland) consisted of only one regiment. It was divided into two, and a Council of War
decided that command should be given to Major Thomas Orgill, Captain John Orgill,
Captain Jasper Ashworth, Alexander Brooks and Captain John Brooke, all of St. Mary
and St. George. Huts and barracks for 500 men were built at Port Antonio.*

Robert Hunter Esq. Major General of His Majesty's forces, was "Captain General and Governor in Chief of Jamaica and the territories thereon depending, and Vice Admiral of the same". Descended from an ancient Scottish family, Hunter had taken part in the battle of Blenheim in 1703, as a major in Brigadier-General Ross' Dragoons (the 5th Royal Irish Dragoons). He was brevetted Lieutenant-Colonel by the British Commander, the Duke of Marlborough, with whom he appeared to have been personally acquainted.

Hunter was Governor of New York and New Jersey from 1710-19. He brought to America a number of refugees from the Rhine Palatinate who had fled their war-torn homeland, and settled them on the Hudson River. During the War of the Spanish Succession between Britain and France, he was active in the defence of the French/Canadian border. He was thought by many to be the "best-loved and most able of the Royal Governors of Colonial New York".

Hunter arrived in Jamaica in 1729 when the Spaniards were again threatening the island, and when the conflict with rebel slaves was about to reach crisis proportions; he wrote to Thomas Pelham-Holles, Duke of Newcastle and Secretary of State, in September 1729, complaining that the militia was made up chiefly of hired or indentured servants who were mostly Irish. He said their backwardness, mutinous behaviour and desertions had destroyed his hopes of making good use of them in the defence of the island.

Hunter cited an instance when Captain Loughton of the *Plymouth* was standing at the door of a punch house in Port Antonio which was full of Irish militiamen, and overheard them saying that they had no quarrel with the Spaniards and would not fight them. Hunter said that if a Spanish attack came he would station a reserve of black men in the rear of the militia, to knock down anyone who tried to desert or fly from his rank. He wrote:

31

"The Irish here, of which our servants and lower ranks
of people chiefly consist, are a lazy useless people, who
come cheap and serve for deficiencies. Their hearts are
not with us".

Under Hunter's administration the war against the
rebels escalated and numerous war parties were sent out
against them. Their towns were stormed, and burnt or
occupied, but new towns sprang up and old towns were
often recaptured. Time after time the parties were
ambushed and driven back to base, or prevented from
reaching their objectives by heavy rains and flooded rivers,
particularly in the north-east part of the island in the
newly-created parish of Portland.

The provision grounds of the rebels were sometimes discovered and destroyed. Those beaten out of their towns
had a terrible time. Their women and children were
always with them and suffered greatly as they wandered
through the mountains and forests, seeking food and new
homes. But the rebels never gave up, and preferred death
to surrender.

The slaves were divided between those who opposed the
rebels and those who supported them. The larger section
was jubilant at the militancy and repeated success of the
rebels. A few joined them and most yearned to do so. The
section opposed to the rebels threw in their lot with the
British in the hope of gaining freedom and financial
reward.

In 1730, a Grand Party sent against the Windward
rebels, under the command of Captain Brooke, failed miser-
ably "due to the want of conduct or resolution in the commanding officer". He was a member of the Assembly and
had been recommended by them to command. Brooke and
his officers were prosecuted before a Court Martial and, for
his failure, Brooke was fined all the pay due to him for the
time he had served.

An Act was passed to raise another party, to be called the Country Party. In November 1730, the House resolved that if sufficient volunteers did not come forward, men should be drafted from the regiments of horse and foot. The House felt that "Negroes and Mulattoes" might be the most suitable if they were properly disciplined and under white commanders. It was therefore recommended that three-quarters of the party be made up of "Negroes and Mulattoes".

The shortage of British man-power had for some time forced the authorities to turn increasingly to non-whites for the defence of the country, just as the Spaniards had been obliged to do over a hundred years before. In 1726 when the fleet stationed at Jamaica was short of seamen, Admiral Hosier was empowered by the Council to impress half the sailors on each ship in Kingston Harbour. In addition, free Negroes, Indians and Mulattoes in the militia regiments were sent aboard his flagship, the *Bredah*. The next year, free Negroes fled to the bush rather than serve aboard the warships *Superb*, *Rippon*, *Dragon* and *Leopard*.

No volunteers offered to join the Country Party so men were drafted from the regiments. While the Party was being assembled and equipped in Kingston in January 1731, Tudor, the commander, was arrested for a Petty Debt. This was contrary to the law as he was a Freeholder. He was taken to the Marshal's house where he was killed by a shot from behind when his men apparently attempted to rescue him. Two of his party were also killed and others wounded near the door of the house. The Marshal and his men were arrested on a charge of wilful murder.

Governor Hunter, on the recommendation of the Assembly, chose Thomas Peters to replace Tudor as commander of the Country Party. On February 1st, 1731, the Party, consisting of about 180 men, set sail from Port Royal for Port Antonio. They managed to surprise the chief Rebel settlement in the neighbourhood of Port Antonio, and got in

33

with the loss of only two killed and a few wounded. The rebels set fire to part of the town and under cover of the smoke withdrew to nearby mountains. The Party did not pursue, but lingered in the town for three days. On the fourth day they burnt the town, which had 106 houses, and returned to Port Antonio, contrary to orders. They had not taken even one prisoner. Peters' excuse was that his men would not stay longer nor allow him to send for provisions.

Hunter was furious. In his report to the Duke of Newcastle, telling of the repeated failures and the precarious condition of the island's defences, he said that the rebels were so numerous and well provided with arms and ammunition that he was persuaded they must be receiving encouragement from either within or outside the country.

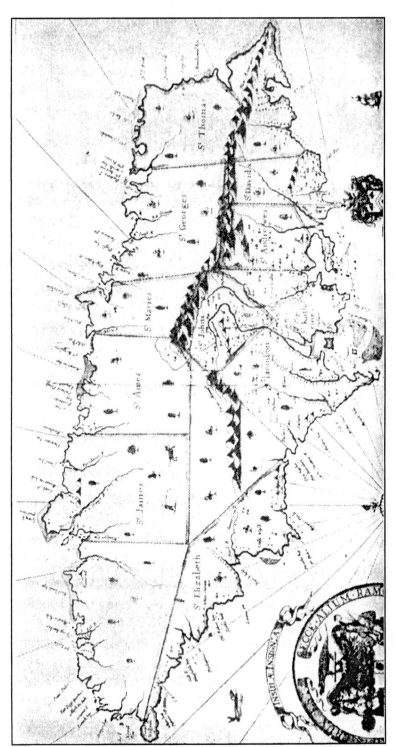

Map of Jamaica (c.1684)

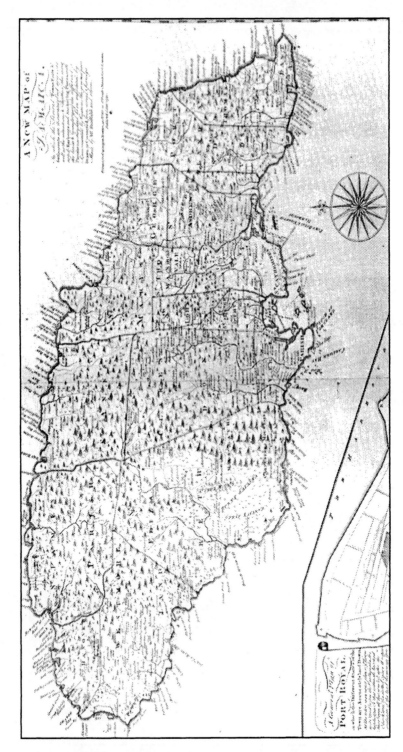

Map of Jamaica (1771)

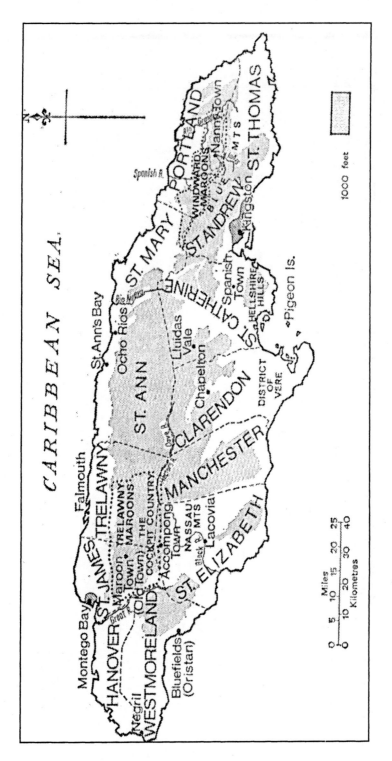

Map of Jamaica showing the main areas of the Trelawny and Windward Maroons

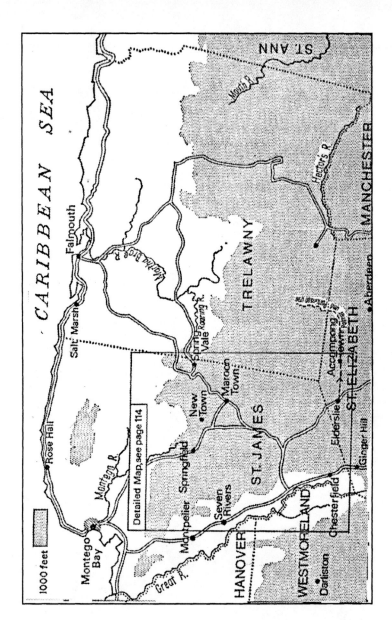

Map of the Cockpit Country and surrounding districts

CHAPTER 6

REINFORCEMENTS AND RUM

Hunter reported that Jamaica was in such a weak and defenceless state that it was not unlikely that the colonists might one day become prey to their slaves. He said that the Mosquito Indians, imported to help destroy the rebels, were utterly unfit for service in the rocks and mountains. Their own country was a place of marshes and bogs, and their expeditions there had been carried out mostly in canoes.

The Duke of Newcastle, responding to Hunter's pessimistic reports, wrote from Windsor Castle to say that His Majesty was extremely concerned about the defenceless condition of the island, and approved of the care he had taken for defence and security.

> "But considering the ill success that the attempts to reduce the Rebellious Blacks have lately met with, and the small number of white men on the Island,* His Majesty had been pleased to order the two Regiments of Foot, commanded by Brigadier Newton and Colonel Hayes, which are now at Gibraltar, to be forthwith sent from thence, which you are, upon their arrival, to take under your command and make the best provision you can for their reception and subsistence in Jamaica".

---

* A population census taken in 1731 estimated that there were:
  - Whites (men, women, children) 7,648
  - Black slaves 74,525
  - Rebellious Negroes 2,000

The King did not doubt that his subjects in Jamaica would receive the Regiments in a proper manner, and readily contribute whatever was necessary for their support and maintenance over and above their established pay.

Two transports carrying the first of the soldiers from Gibralter arrived on February 4th, three days after the Country Party under Peters left Port Royal on their expedition against the Windward maroons. Four other transports arrived on February 7th. The officers and men were in good health, but tents and clothing for Colonel Hayes' Regiment had not yet come. The Assembly voted money to keep the regiments for six months, after the provisions they brought were expended. Ten pounds were to be paid to officers and soldiers for every rebel slave killed or taken alive.

Twenty-two houses provided for temporary accommodation at Port Royal proved inadequate, so the troops were ordered to remain on the transports for awhile. When they began to sicken, however, they were landed, and those in excess of what the houses at Port Royal could accommodate were sent to Kingston.

Barracks were built, and the regiments were broken up into companies and sent to various quarters where it was thought they might be of most use. In places where the barracks were not finished they were quartered by the parishioners.

The privates at first continued in good health but the officers soon began to die. Major Brandrett and Captain Malloy of Colonel Hayes' Regiment, and Captain Ballender of Colonel Cope's Regiment were the first to die. Colonel Hayes died in Port Royal on March 19th, and in April, Lieutenant Thomas Parker and Ensign Emmanuel Kencham of Hayes' Regiment died. Lieutenant Colonel Townsend and Captain Close of Copes' Regiment died in May. In addition to the deaths, three Captains and seven subalterns had not turned up with the regiments.

The private soldiers also began to suffer casualties.

Malaria and yellow fever took a dreadful toll, but rum was chiefly to blame. Excerpts from Hunter's reports described the rapid deterioration.

> **April 2nd, 1731,** the Companies are all marched or transported to their several quarters – the private men in good condition and health, and I hope may continue so, if we can keep them from rum.

> **April 10th, 1731,** the men are in good health and condition; ... (But) if I cannot... get some law passed to restrain the abuse in the retail of rum, the companies in the town will be very thin in a little time.

> **May 29th,1731,** the Companies are all at their respective quarters... well barracked or lodged and pretty healthy, and might be kept so were it not for the rum.

> **June 5th, 1731,** the soldiers in the country have suffered least, being further from rum than those in towns.

> **September 29th, 1731,** the regiments here are in a woeful state, some companies having lost more than half their complement of men, chiefly owing to drunkeness. The remote quarters have buried fewest.

> **October 8th, 1731,** the two regiments are reduced to a woeful number fit for service, by death and sickness. Of the officers there are eighteen dead since their arrival.

On June 5th the Assembly resolved to pay for the regiments' subsistence for another six months. The following month Hunter ordered a 'Grand Party' of four Regular companies, 80 armed blacks and 80 baggage carriers to march from Port Antonio in yet another attempt to crush the Windward rebels. However, sickness had so reduced the companies that the commanding officer said he had less than twenty men to march.

Reinforcements were sent by sea from the south. Stormy weather overtook them and the ship was "beat back" by lightning and contrary winds. Several men were killed. A fresh detachment was sent by another ship, the *Tartar*; but heavy unseasonable rains further held up the expedition.

On November 13th, 1731, Hunter reported that rebels had been active in different sections of the island. The Black Shots had built a barrack (called the Breastwork) almost half-way on the road to the chief Windward rebel town, and a garrison had been stationed there. A road had also been cleared from the barracks to Port Antonio. In spite of this, rebels had boldly raided the area, and struck the parish of St. David, south of Portland. Others had descended on the north-west parish of St. James, where two soldiers who had strayed from their barracks were slain. Twenty slaves from Colonel Nedham's north-side estate had joined the rebels.

CHAPTER 7

THE FLIGHT OF DE LA MILLIÈRE

The 'Grand Party' was finally assembled on November 26 1731, and left Port Antonio for the Breastwork, which was the last outpost for troops entering the wilderness where the towns of the Windward rebels lay. The Party was commanded by Captain de la Millière. The Overseer of the Pioneers (the group which cleared pathways and threw up fortifications) was Thomas Peters, who had led the country party and taken a rebel town earlier in the year, and then, contrary to orders, abandoned it after three days. Peters would try to redeem himself on this expedition.

The 'Grand Party' left Breastwork on November 30th. They marched "into the back river of Grandy" (up the Rio Grande) over steep rocks and through deep, rapid rivers. The advance guard consisted of Sergeant William Gibbons, a Corporal, six white soldiers, and six Black Shots. With them was Thomas Ascraft, a guide. Behind the advance guard were the contingent of Black Shots and the baggage carriers, followed by Captain de la Millière at the head of the white soldiers.

On Saturday December 4th, at four o'clock in the afternoon, Thomas Ascraft, the guide, called for de la Millière. He told him they were approaching the place where the rebels had been accustomed to lie in ambush.

"We mustn't go near that place then," said de la Millière. "Let us cut our way over, through the woods".

"That would take two or three days," Ascraft replied. "I think we should march on towards the river".

"I believe we should cut another way," the Captain insisted; but Ascraft was confident that the better way was towards the river.

"There is no danger," he said.

Against his better judgement de la Millière gave in, and resumed the march along the river route. He took the precaution however of ordering the men to "draw their guns and fresh load".

After a while they came to the river.

"We are past all danger here," said Ascraft.

De la Millière assembled as many men as he could on a small beach by the river.

"Keep very close together," he told them.

There was a steep rock about three yards high in front of them and, beyond it, stretched the river. Because they had to climb over the rock the men were not able to keep as close together as was necessary, and there was further straggling as they went through the water.

The advance guard and the Black Shots crossed the river and moved forward into the country beyond. Just as de la Millière emerged from the river a shot rang out in front of the advance guard, and another in front of the soldiers. Then there was a full volley from what sounded like about two hundred guns. Accompanied by Peter La Fountaine, Edmond Lee, Thomas Peters and two or three others, de la Millière raced towards the advance guard. As he turned a corner he met the Black Shots coming back in full flight. They ran down upon the men who were crossing the river. De la Millière shouted as loud as he could:

"Stop, stop, turn back;" and to the men in the water he
yelled, "Advance, advance!"

The Black Shots kept going across the river and most of
the baggage carriers threw down their loads and ran. The
soldiers were floundering in the water. De la Millière ran
up to the advance guard. Sergeant Gibbons had been
killed. Three soldiers and a Black Shot were also lying
dead. Peter La Fountaine's arm was broken by a slug,
Edmond Lee was wounded by a slug in the head, and
Thomas Peters received a swan shot in the thigh. Thomas
Ascraft, the guide, ran off.

"Turn back, turn back, the front is all cut off," shouted
de la Millière.

The soldiers still in the water were thrown into greater
confusion. Some fell in the water, others threw themselves
from the big rock on which they had climbed. Several men
dropped their guns as they fled. None stayed to assist their
Captain, who suddenly found himself alone in the midst of
enemy fire, except for the wounded Thomas Peters and
Edmond Lee, and a man named Hargraves. All four now
ran for their lives. Peter probably had to limp along
because of the wound in his thigh. As he himself said later,
in a letter to Governor Hunter:

As to my own part I leave it to Captain de la Millière
and the rest of the men, of my management in the
engagement, which I believe they can give no slender
character of me, for, as I may say, their lives being
saved was owing to myself... The engagement (lasted)
about four or five minutes. There was but the Captain
and five or six more, with myself, who fought at that
time.

De la Millière and his three companions crossed the
river and reached the woods in safety, probably because the
enemy's fire, after the first big volley, had become scattered
and sporadic. In the woods he found the men in complete

41

disorder. He drew them up. Eight were missing.

Most of the arms and ammunition were wet, and just about all the baggage was gone. The advance could not be resumed even though at first de la Millière had thought of doing so. It would be pointless trying to cut another way through the woods past the ambush, since he had no provisions with which to continue the journey. So he turned back.

The party marched to the huts where they had camped the night before, and, the next day, set off for Breastwork. De la Millière gave orders to the officer in the rear not to leave a man behind. However, Jack Diamond, of Colonel Cornwall's company, fell ill with an ague, and dropped behind. When it was discovered that he was missing frequent halts were made to give the rear time to come up. Black Shots were sent back twice to bring in Diamond, but he was never found. He had been lost about ten miles away from Breastwork.

The party arrived at Breastwork on Monday, December 6th. De la Millière reinforced the small guard there to bring it up to thirty men, and set out the next day for Port Antonio. When they reached the Rio Grande the water was rising; only some of the contingent were able to get across. The rest were ordered back to Breastwork until the river subsided.

At Port Antonio a weary de la Millière sat down to write his report to Governor Hunter. He was concerned that enemies he had made since he first arrived at Port Antonio would now attack him; so he begged the governor to:

> Order a General Court Martial, to examine and enquire into my conduct and behaviour, where I may vindicate my character, if innocent, or suffer the just punishment they shall inflict, if guilty.

He explained to the Governor that he had lost a little trunk in which he kept his journal and other "necessaries", so he was unable to submit the required copy of the journal. "My fatigue has been so great", he wrote "that I am scarce able to hold my pen. But as soon as I am a little recovered I shall... send your excellency a particular account of our march, going and coming".

De la Millière had special praise for Edmond Lee and Thomas Peters, whose courage, he said, was "very remarkable" on the day of the fight. As he was finishing his letter, the rest of the party who had been left at Breastwork because of the swollen Rio Grande, came in. Among the wounded in the fight were Thomas Weakley, who took five swan shots in the back; Hercules, a slave belonging to Mr. Robinson, who was shot in the arm, and Tower Bill, a slave of Colonel Dawkins, who got a swan shot in the back.

There was speculation as to why the rebels had not followed up their advantage while the soldiers were floundering in the river, and had not pursued them in the woods. It was concluded that they must have been short of ammunition as their fire had been much "thinner" after the first volley.

De la Millière's defeat became a major reference point in the relentless struggle with the Windward rebels. It prompted a serious enquiry into the reasons for the repeated defeats and the failure to hold towns when they had been captured. Subsequent expeditions calculated their progress by way of "marks" left by de la Millière notably his huts and his ambush.

The defeat also "increased the fearful apprehensions of the out-settlements of the parishes of St. George and Portland". More slaves began to desert their plantations. Companies of soldiers in remote places were drawn into barracks at Port Royal and Port Antonio, so they could be on hand for any emergency. The Governor was advised to increase and maintain the guard at Breastwork, especially as the rebels were now in possession of arms and ammunition that had been lost by the Grand Party.

CHAPTER 8

NO QUARTER

Lieutenant-Colonel Cornwallis (who had succeeded Hayes), Lieutenant-Colonel Fountain and Major Sloly conducted an investigation to determine the cause of the repeated failures in the East. In his report de la Millière said that on the trail he had taken, there were a hundred different places where ten resolute men would be sufficient to stop one thousand.

The military investigation disclosed that in the four or five days march from Breastwork, the men had to go along the course of a river and cross the fords more than twenty times in one day; and near as often every day. The water in most places was breast high and huge rocks were often encountered. To scale these, the men had to climb on each other's backs and hand up their arms, ammunition and baggage.

On every side were thick woods and mountainous ground. A few men lodged above on either side of the river could, without exposing themselves, destroy any number crossing the fords. Men had been wounded fifteen yards from the enemy without catching sight of them. The practice of the enemy was to fire, lie down, load and constantly keep under cover. Rapid currents, high rocks and narrow defiles where two men could not march abreast, were only part of the difficulties.

Cornwallis, Fountain and Sloly said that the only effective

way of dealing with the problem was to use slaves to cut and clear roads to allow at least six to march abreast; and to find alternative routes when it was impossible to widen the trail. Narrow defiles should be avoided.

They told Hunter that it would be impossible to follow his orders to keep guards in captured towns unless proper access roads were cut to facilitate the supply of provisions. They also recommended that men from the two Gibraltar regiments which were soon to depart, be encouraged to join the independent companies and remain in Jamaica. One hundred and twenty-six soldiers and two sergeants joined up before the survivors of the regiments left for Ireland on March 16th and 17th, 1732.

The colony was reeling from the blows delivered by the rebels. It was further dispirited by the desertion of slaves to join the rebels, the decrease of public credit and trade, and the consequent diminution of the number of European colonists.

In March 1732, a distraught Governor Hunter, pleading poor health and fatigue, applied for six months leave to go to England. He badly needed to get away, not only from the problems caused by the slaves in rebellion, but also from the clique of planters and attorneys who were obstructing the measures he sought to put into place for the safety of the island, and from such unreliable elements as the Irish indentured servants whom he said were "a drawback" on the strength of the colony. He told the Council that there never was a time which more required their attention to the safety of the island than the present.

> "Your slaves in rebellion, animated by their success, and others ready to join them on the first favourable opportunity; your Militia very insignificant, the daily decrease in the numbers of your people and the increase of rebel slaves: these circumstances must convince you of the necessity of entering upon more solid measures... for your security, all former attempts

against (the rebels) having been either unsuccessful or
to very little purpose.

It has been suggested at home to His Majesty's
Ministers and the Lords Commissioners of Trade, that
a treaty with the Rebels, by which they are to agree to
be transported to some of the Bahama Islands, or the
employing again of Mosquito Indians against them may
be of use."

In the hope of erasing the de la Millière disaster, a party
of soldiers and Black Shots marched from Liguanea.
Another powerful contingent of two hundred and seventeen
soldiers and Black Shots with sixty-one baggage carriers,
commanded by Henry Williams, should have marched from
Port Antonio at the same time, but was delayed because
the ship bringing provisions was kept out at sea for over a
fortnight by contrary winds.

Captain Allen, with a party led by a famous black guide
called "Sambo", set out on May 13th, 1732, when the
weather turned fair. They pursued a rebel party for days in
the Plantain Garden River area, but only managed to capture one man. Henry Williams and his party coming from
Port Antonio reported goat tracks in the region of a place
called Cotterwood.

Both parties were repeatedly forced to return to base
because of violent rains and floods; but one party came
upon a new settlement started by rebels who had been
driven from their towns. They captured a woman and six
children. The woman who spoke good English, said she
had been born in a rebel settlement. She informed her captors that soon after the towns had been taken her people
found themselves desperately short of provisions. They
argued over whether to keep in one body or divide into
groups to make foraging easier. Eventually they broke up into
three groups each going its separate way.

Rebel gangs ousted from their towns, walked all the way

to St. Elizabeth in the south-west, and fell upon the plantations of Messrs Barclay and Woodstock, killing and carrying off slaves.

The war now reached a very bitter stage.

> Whole parishes such as St. James and St. George were
> virtually desolate no-man's land and travelling was not
> safe anywhere on the island.
>
> EDWARDS - *History of the West Indies.*

Any adult Maroon who was captured was tortured and
killed, and children who were caught were sold into slavery
in other Caribbean islands. The Maroons on their part
killed just about everybody who fell into their hands.
Neither side would give any quarter. The Maroons preferred death to capture or defeat.

In 1733 the Legislature noted that within a few years
the Maroons had greatly increased in number, notwithstanding all the measures that had been taken to suppress
them.

> ...they had grown very formidable in the North-west,
> and South-western districts of the island. In St.
> Elizabeth, Westmoreland, Hanover and St. James they
> were considerably multiplied and had large settlements
> among mountains and least accessible parts; whence
> they plundered all around them, and caused several
> plantations to be thrown up and abandoned, and pre-
> vented many valuable tracts of land from being culti-
> vated, to the great prejudice and diminution of His
> Majesty's revenue, as well as the trade, navigation and
> consumption of British Manufacturers; and to the man-
> ifest weakening and preventing the further increase of
> the strength and inhabitants in the island.
>
> EDWARDS - *History of the West Indies.*

A disheartened Governor Hunter wrote home to say
that:

"The danger we are in proceeds from our slaves in rebellion. We have for several years (been put to) an extra-ordinary and almost insupportable expense in endeavoring to suppress them... But our attempts... having been in vain, only convinced me of our weakness. Instead of being able to reduce them, we are not in a condition to defend ourselves.

The terror of them spreads itself everywhere, (and several planters have abandoned their settlements). Their success has had such influence on our other slaves, that they are continually deserting to them in great number; and the insolent behaviour of others gives us...much cause to fear a general defection."

CHAPTER 9

STORMING THE MOUNTAIN STRONGHOLDS
MORRISON AND ENGLISH

Captain Morrison and Sergeant Robert English headed one of the parties which marched out in the year 1732, to participate in the sustained assault on the rebel towns. Their targets were two towns known as the "Middle or Upper town", and the "Lower or Greater town". They drove the rebels from both towns. The Middle/Upper town was occupied by a detachment under English, and the Lower/Greater town by a detachment under Morrison.

The rebels returned in force and attacked Captain Morrison in the Lower/Greater town. Sergeant English had been given strict orders to hold his position in the Middle/Upper town, but when he heard the sounds of battle coming from the other town, he abandoned his position and marched to Morrison's assistance.

As English drew near to the Lower/Greater town he seemed to lose his nerve. Apparently there was a lull in the fighting and he got the impression that Morrison's men had either been destroyed or had fled. Even though he actually only saw two rebels, his past experiences made him suspect that others were probably hiding in ambush behind rocks and trees, of which there were a great many in and about the town.

English felt he was in the presence of a numerous enemy, whose "force and fury" could not be resisted by his small party. So instead of trying to enter the Lower/Greater town to see what had happened to Morrison, he retreated to Port Antonio. He was promptly thrown into jail for abandoning his post and for failing to attack the enemy and assist Morrison.

English was tried by court martial on February 23rd 1733, in Port Antonio. After going over the facts and hearing the evidence, the eight-man court acquitted him. It said that his abandonment of his post in order to assist Morrison was in conformance with the 'Rules and Discipline of War'; but that to have attacked a numerous and hidden enemy with his tiny force would have been "impracticable and desperate". One of the members of the court martial was Henry Williams, who, in less than two weeks after the trial, would again be leading a party against the rebels.

CHAPTER 10

THE INTREPID EBENEZER LAMB

Perhaps the most courageous and active of the commanders, appearing in the records of the time, was Ebenezer Lamb. He had come to Jamaica as an indentured servant and so was at the bottom of the island's white society.*

Indentured servants were in great demand in Jamaica in the eighteenth century, as a means of increasing the European work force and keeping a balance between Europeans and African. The Deficiency Laws of 1703 required any one who owned three hundred African slaves and one hundred and twenty head of stock, to keep a quota of seventeen indentured servants. In 1770 the quota was reduced to eleven.

Usually indentured servants were poor Britishers (English, Scots, Welsh and a great many Irish) who either sold themselves into service for a period of four to seven years, or were kidnapped by "man traders" and shipped out. After their term of service they were free to pursue their own fortunes.

The Legislature of Jamaica did a lot to encourage the trade in indentured servants. In 1703 a law was passed exempting masters of ships from paying port charges for voyages on which they brought in thirty "white men servants".

Lamb said he had once been a merchant. When he arrived in Jamaica as an indentured servant he was bought by a Mr. Williams for twenty-two pounds. He served Williams for about three years as schoolmaster to his children.

Consequently, hardly a ship arrived from Britain without indentured servants on board.

They were "shipped like so much merchandise, and bills of lading were given for them just as if they were barrels of pork instead of human beings". Great numbers constantly perished on the voyage. On arrival the survivors were lined up just like the incoming Africans, for inspection by the planters.

Indentured servants were often brutally treated by their masters and could be punished with years of extra service for certain offences. Nevertheless quite a number succeeded in lifting themselves up the social and economic ladder. By as early as 1680:

> Many a convict from Bridewell or a young plough man from the midlands, who had been sent out under seven or four years indentures, was in possession of a valuable plantation making his thousand pounds a year, and owning a coach and horses.

Ebenezer Lamb was one of those indentured servants who was determined to succeed, and because of the state of emergency which existed in the colony at the time, military service seemed a promising, if highly dangerous road to success. Lamb's opportunity to prove himself came in September 1732, when he was put in charge of a party operating in the north-west of the island.

On Saturday morning September 22nd, Lamb marched south-east for nearly four miles on the track of rebels. He lost the trail for over three hours but found it at about eleven o'clock between two steep cliffs that seemed impossible to climb. They got "through the cliffs" with much difficulty, marched south for about two miles and came to a large "cut path" over a very steep rocky hill.

They went for a mile along this path but when it started to rain very heavily, they stopped to take shelter. While they were sitting down they heard the voices of rebels

"playing" on top of a high hill above them. Lamb thought it
was a good opportunity to surprise them in their houses
and as there was plenty of daylight left, decided to attack
right away rather than wait for morning.

When the rain stopped the party started off for the foot
of the hill. On the way, the sergeant and some of the baggage carriers saw three rebels coming up behind. One had
a gun which he levelled at the sergeant. The gun misfired
and the sergeant shot and wounded the man.

The sound of the shot alerted the rebels in the town, and
Lamb called to his men to hurry as they had been discovered. The rebels on top of the hill dared them to come up,
for they were ready for them. According to Lamb, they
shouted three times: "You come here to fight us and run
away like a parcel of white-livered sons of bitches".

Lamb ordered his men to keep talking to the rebels
while he climbed the hill out of sight with some of his nim-
blest shots. The rebels did not see them until they were
within forty or fifty yards of their guard house which was
on the "pitch of the hill".

Several huge stones were tied up with wythes to the
posts of the guard house. The rebels cut the wythes and
the great stones hurtled down on Lamb and his squad of
Shots. The rebels hurtled down other large stones by hand,
threw smaller ones and fired at the climbing party. Lamb
and his men avoided most of the stones by ducking down in
the path, which was crooked at that point and somewhat
under the defenders. Shots and stones flew over their
heads. They had thirty or forty yards to go but the missiles
were coming down thick and fast and they dared not move.

Lamb shouted to the main body at the foot of the hill to
keep up a continuous fire at the rebels in the guard house.
Under cover of this he and his Shots scrambled up the
remaining distance. When they got close to the guard
house they found they could only go two abreast.

Lamb and one of his men leapt side by side into the

town and a rebel fired a pistol point-blank at them. Lamb said he believed there was no ball in the pistol otherwise one of them would have been hit. They fired at the rebel and he dropped his pistol and fled.

Another rebel blew his 'calabash' to warn everyone that the enemy had entered the town. Lamb's men fired at him and he dropped his gun, staff and calabash as he ran. While the fight was going on the women and children got away. The bushes were very wet from the recent heavy rain so after a short while Lamb called off the pursuit for fear of "spoiling" his munitions. He ordered all the Shots to stand sentry round the town, and to pay special attention to the two hills on either side. They saw a rebel climbing up one of the hills and several shots were fired at him; but he got away.

At about this time the sergeant arrived with the baggage carriers, four Black Shots and one white man who had hidden himself in the bushes. The Sergeant reported that he had shot a rebel who was not more than fifteen yards from him, and had seen him fall. The baggage carriers confirmed this. Lamb sent ten men with the Sergeant to find the wounded rebel. While they were gone he explored the town and discovered a great deal of blood in and about the guard house and all along the route which the retreating rebels had taken.

The Sergeant returned when it was almost dark and said he had found blood at the place where the shot rebel had fallen. He followed the trail of blood for almost a mile but did not find the wounded man.

Lamb and his men slept in the rebel houses and kept "strict watch" all night. The next day, Sunday, September 23rd, he sent six Shots and several baggage carriers to look for water. They found a spring a short distance away, at the foot of a steep hill.

Rebels on top of the hill threw down large stones and drove off the water party. Lamb set out after the rebels with eight Shots. He followed them closely for a considerable distance until it began to rain. The rebels dropped bowls, lances, and pieces of clothing as they retreated, and Lamb brought back all these articles to the town. Rain came so hard that they could not stir out of the houses until dark.

On Monday, September 24th, Lamb examined the town thoroughly. It was situated between two high hills to the east and west, that could not be climbed by the party. To the north and south were two steep downward slopes, one of which they had climbed to enter the town. At the top of each slope was a guard house, thirty-five feet in length.

The level on which the town was built was about one acre in size. It contained thirty-five houses each divided into several apartments. From these houses the men took between forty and fifty bags of corn, plantain flour, corn flour, dried plantains, jerk hog, dried hog meat, several bags of peas, cocos, cassava (all apparently brought from Montego Bay); plus wild yams, china roots, thatch cabbage, and mountain cabbage which must have come from the mountains as there were no cultivations within two miles.

The soldiers also found eight iron pots and a tin kettle, medicines "proper for green wounds", bags and blankets, several earthen pots and dishes, over one hundred cedar bowls, vast quantities of calabashes, bags of old irons from old guns (e.g. old cocks, locks, screw pins, broken gun barrels, etc.) three good guns, two pistols, several lances, pewter plates, dishes, basins, spoons, looking glasses, bills, hoes, axes, vast quantities of old clothes, tobacco, and a "curious color of their own staining". They took away most of the things that were of any value, and destroyed the rest along with the houses.

Laden with this odd assortment of the spoils of war, Ebenezer Lamb (Lamb by name, Lion by nature) marched back to base. As a result of the important services he had rendered, the Assembly agreed that he should be set free at once, and his master compensated.

Lamb was asked to attend the House of Assembly where he identified the settlement he had captured as Wiles' Town. He said it was in the vicinity of Mountain Spring, in or near the centre of the area occupied by the rebels, and about twenty-eight miles from Montego Bay. (Wiles' Town stood between today's Falmouth and Duncans.) Wiles' Town was well watered, contained provisions, and had good lands adjoining it which were capable of producing any quantity of provisions. It was an easy day's journey from a rebel town lately discovered by a man named Scarlett, and about the same distance from a rebel settlement in St. James. Because of the strategic position of Wiles' Town the Assembly felt that a barracks should be built there as an advance post against the rebels.

CHAPTER 11

LAMB, CROSSWELL AND WILLIAMS

Early in 1733, a decision was made to divide the force stationed at Port Antonio into two parties and to attack the Windward rebels from two directions. Ebenezer Lamb, fresh from his victory at Wiles' Town, shared the command of one party with Edward Crosswell. The other party was commanded by Henry Williams.

The party of Lamb and Crosswell consisted of one hundred and four men and thirty baggage carriers. It was to leave Port Antonio on February 27th, and take the long route to the rebel towns. Williams' party, consisting of one hundred and twenty-three men and thirty-four baggage carriers was to leave about six days later, on Sunday March 4th, and take the short route to the towns. Both parties were expected to be in position to attack the Windward rebels on March 8th.

Lamb's journal gives an account of the tiring march and the exciting events which followed. He and Crosswell left Port Antonio on February 27th as scheduled, and marched to the Rio Grande. The next day they met Black Shots from the parishes of St. George and St. Mary and provided them with ammunition, provisions and other necessaries.

On March 1st they marched to Stringor's Pen where some of the white soldiers, contrary to orders and without the knowledge of their commanders, slaughtered a cow. This detained the whole party at Stringor's for the night. On March 2nd they resumed the journey, reached Hobby's and packed up their provisions in preparation for the march into the woods.

At about ten o'clock on the morning of March 3rd Lamb and Crosswell reviewed their force and found that three White Shots, two Black Shots, and some of the baggage carriers had deserted. They left Hobby's without trying to find them, went about four miles south and south-east, and made camp at about three in the afternoon on top of a high ridge.

The following day they pushed on south and south-east, for five miles along the top of the ridge and then down a steep gully. When they halted at eleven o'clock, a baggage carrier named "Cuffee" threw down his load, took out a calabash of rum and ran off into the woods. Then it rained, from noon until midnight, and up to ten o'clock the next morning.

When the rain held up they marched in the gully for a mile and a half to Foxes river, and then three miles east south-east and south-west, down-river. At three in the afternoon they turned southward, about half a mile up a steep incline, and camped at 5 p.m. at Captain Peters' Hut.

The next day, March 6th, Crosswell's sergeant fell ill with a violent fever, and Robert Revett was found to be lame. A guard was left with them, with orders to follow as fast as possible. The party marched two miles south and south-west uphill and on to a ridge, where they came upon a rebel track and hunting hut at the site of an old rebel town that had been taken earlier by a man named "Soaper".

A mile further on to the east down a gut, brought them to the right arm of the Back River. From there they marched two miles more, south, south-east, up the river until four in the afternoon, when they made camp.

On March 7th they went one mile south and south-west,

up-river, then turned south-east for three miles, up to the top of the Blue Mountain and along the ridge. They camped on the top of the ridge.

March 8th was the day scheduled for the two-pronged attack on the Windward towns. Williams and his party were supposed to be at their designated position. Lamb and Crosswell left Thomas Whitby on the ridge with a guard of six Black Shots and two baggage carriers, and marched westward for a mile down the mountain. Then one of the Black Shots accidentally fired his gun.

Everyone was alarmed, wondering if the shot had alerted the rebels. The Black Shots refused to go any further. Lamb and Catchman, the overseer of the Pioneers, went out in front and encouraged them to resume the march.

They cut a path to the North-east River, and after going westwards for a mile, came to a newly-planted field. Walking through it they found themselves in what Lamb called "the Man's Town". The rebels were waiting there in ambush.

Lamb reported that his party fired a volley of sixty guns at the rebels who were just thirty yards away. They fell to the ground but did not return one shot. The party rushed forward into the town, confident of victory. When they reached the dancing place (or platform), the rebels let off a volley. They kept on, however, and entered a gully where the rebels fired "smartly" at them for half-an-hour, pinning them down.

Several of the Black Shots were wounded as they attempted to cross the gully. Lamb managed to get across with four White Shots and a Black Shot. They fought off the rebels for a considerable time during which one White Shot was killed and another wounded.

The other two made their escape when they saw that the rest of the party across the gully was beginning to retreat.

Rebels closed in on Lamb. One of them was beating a calabash drum. The badly-wounded White Shot advised him to make his escape, otherwise he would be taken alive. Shots were flying about them, and as Lamb hesitated, the wounded man looked around and said, "Rebels are just over your head".

Lamb jumped into the gully and crouched there quietly. When the rebels went up to the wounded man and were about to lay hold on him, Lamb fired and hit one, who fell into the gully. He tried to cross the gully but the firing was so heavy and the ground so uneven that he turned downwards instead and raced to the river. Five minutes later he heard firing at a great distance, and presently rebels began to cross the river, carrying baggage and provisions that belonged to his party.

Lamb loaded his gun, and when the rebels passed about seven or eight yards from his hiding place he shot one. The other two ran towards the town yelling that a white man was in the river course.

Lamb ran across the river, hid in some bushes and loaded his gun. Several rebels came in search of him and approached so close that he fired again and raced up the river course. They followed and cornered him on a high cliff. He jumped off, into the river. They fired at him as he thrashed about in the water, and ran back down the cliff to get at him; but by the time they reached the bank, Lamb had escaped up-river.

That night when the moon was down, he crept along the river past the rebel's town. He said he heard them burying their dead. He continued walking until seven o'clock the next morning, when he saw men from the parties ahead of him.

*   *   *

Meanwhile Henry Williams and the second party had left Port Antonio on March 4th as scheduled, on the first leg of the short route to the Rebel towns. The route was well marked with huts built at certain points in which troops could be accommodated. They spent the first night at the strong-point known as Breastwork. The next day they marched up the Annotto river until they reached the "open huts" which had been constructed earlier by Crosswell. They slept in the huts that night.

On March 6th, they climbed a very steep high ridge to Crosswell's "farthest huts", where they camped. On the 7th, they marched along the side of the ridge until they came upon the "Pointer" which marked the spot where Croswell had turned back on a previous expedition. From that spot they could see the Rebel town, a great distance away. They started the descent, and kept going until late afternoon, before making camp.

On March 8th, the day scheduled for the joint attack, they marched behind the place where de la Millière had been ambushed, and found a fresh track. While they were examining it, they heard a shot. Williams thought it was a rebel signal. He called a halt while he listened intently, expecting to hear battle sounds which would indicate that Crosswell and Lamb had launched the attack. He was unwilling to risk marching his men past the old de la Millière ambush, as they were only about a mile from the town; but he held them in readiness to rush to the assistance of Lamb and Crosswell. It was not until about four in the afternoon, however, that gunfire came from the direction of the town.

Williams immediately ordered his men to advance, but before they reached the open ground they met the other party coming towards them in the river course in great confusion, having been beaten back by the rebels. Lamb was not with them, but in the morning at about seven, they encountered him walking in the river course.

The two parties now advanced together and entered the Rebel town (the Man's town) at about nine. They were met by gunfire and a White Shot was killed. Williams sent a party above the ambush and they fired down and forced the rebels to retreat. The Black Shots led the advance into the town, and were just entering a gut that had been cleared of bushes, when the rebels fired a volley that wounded several of them.

The Black Shots broke through this second ambush but refused to go any further. The sun was too hot, they said, and they would rather fight in the cool, in their country (native) way. They refused to let the White Shots join them in the front.

Five or six rebels had been killed in the river course. Williams sent a squad to cut off their ears, which could be presented as proof and allow them to claim the reward offered for killing rebels. But men lying concealed nearby, fired at the squad and drove them off before they could achieve their objective. At four in the afternoon the Black Shots were asked if they were ready to move forward. They said they would spend the night where they were and attack in the cool of the morning.

In the morning (March 10th) the Officers and the scout named "Black Sambo" tried to get the Black Shots to attack, but they insisted that the commanders lead the advance.

Lamb and Williams went out in front. The rebels opened fire and Lamb was wounded. The men immediately began to run, and nothing the officers could say or do could get them to turn back. At this point, one of the rebels called out in his "country language." Neither Lamb nor Williams understood what he said, but some of the Africans in their parties knew the language and acted as interpreters. According to them, the rebel said that if they would not kill him he would come in and give himself up. This seemed like a good omen.

One of the Africans who spoke the language was instructed to encourage the rebel to come forward, and to assure him that he, and any others who came in, would be given liberty. The rebel advanced and continued talking to the interpreter until he got a clear sight of him. Then to every one's astonishment, he shot the interpreter, who died a short while after.

This startling demonstration of the defiant and determined spirit of the rebels made the Black Shots more uneasy. They refused to advance. The front ranks retreated to the Rebels' dancing platform, where they concealed themselves in rocks and bushes and fired off most of their ammunition.

Lamb and Williams went repeatedly among them but could not get them to advance. If the rebels were to launch an attack it seemed certain that they would throw away arms, ammunition and baggage and run for their lives.

The officers held a consultation and a decision was made to withdraw. At two in the afternoon, a front guard of sixty Shots was sent off with the wounded men and the baggage carriers. Shortly after, the rest of the combined parties followed. They set an ambush at an appropriate place in case the rebels decided to pursue them. When no one appeared they marched three miles from the town, and camped for the night. The next day, March 11th, they went down-river until they reached de la Millière's old huts, in which they slept that night. On March 12th, they marched into Port Antonio.

On March 15th, Governor Robert Hunter received the news of the defeat (or what he called the "shameful retreat of our parties") in an "express" from Colonel Jasper Ashworth, the commanding officer at Port Antonio. Writing to the Duke of Newcastle on March 27th Hunter said:

> "If this miscarriage is to be ascribed to the causes mentioned (you) will perceive where the blame is to be laid; for I could not obtain any other punishment for disobedience, mutiny or desertion... than such as the slaves

and (indentured) servants (of which the party is chiefly
made up) are inured to every day of their lives, and
value not."

Because of the conduct of the Black Shots, Hunter
ordered that those who could be reached should be dis-
armed and imprisoned.

CHAPTER 12

LAMB AND WILLIAMS STRIKE AGAIN

In spite of the "shameful retreat" of their parties, Lamb and Williams apparently were not disgraced. In June, 1733, they got an opportunity to avenge their defeat when they once more set out for the Rebel towns, with a strong party supported by regular soldiers and sailors. Before they reached the towns, however, they fell into the inevitable ambush. Taking thirty or forty men, Lamb marched around "aback of the ambush", and opened fire at the rebels, who retreated and set fire to all their houses. When the party advanced into the towns they found nothing but burning buildings. Apart from a few pots and crockery ware, the rebels had carried off everything.

The rebels took refuge on top of Carrion Crow hill, which, like other Rebel towns, was fortified with vast heaps of large stones placed on steep slopes and held in place by wooden props. On Friday morning, the day after they entered the towns, Lamb and Williams dispatched fifty-two men under a Lieutenant to dislodge the rebels from Carrion Crow Hill. They climbed up, firing briskly. When they neared the top where the going was steepest, the rebels knocked away the props that held the piles of stones in place, and these rolled down with great violence.

Lamb had been faced with a similar situation when he attacked Wiles' Town, but he was saved partly by uneven ground which deflected the plunging rocks. This time it was different. The rocks flew unhampered at the climbing men who were thrown into great confusion. Trying to escape they jumped down a "horrible precipice". Some were killed and several badly hurt. Others were shot as they fled. The rebels leapt down in the wake of the falling stones and completed the rout capturing three of the contingent.

The rebels now launched an attack on the towns from two directions. Once more Lamb and Williams found themselves in a desperate situation. They divided their force into three groups for "safety and defence" and wrote to Lieutenant Draper, commander of the post at Port Antonio, requesting reinforcements of White Shots, ammunition, provisions and spare guns, "because a great many of our arms are bursted and broke through casualties". They warned Draper that if they did not receive the supplies "with the utmost speed" it would be impossible to "maintain and keep the towns above five or six days longer, for our ammunition already is above the half expended". A sergeant was sent with the message, accompanied by five Black Shots and forty baggage carriers.

Apparently all the rebels had not been in the towns when Lamb and Williams launched their attack, but after the action at Carrion Crow Hill, those who had been absent returned. Lamb and Williams thought the number had been increased by several hundreds and that the Leeward Maroons (Cudjoe's people) might have sent in reinforcements.

The rebels taunted the party. "Do you want any powder and ball?" they asked. "If you do we will let you have some." Several called out to Williams giving rise to the feeling that they were former party members who had deserted. This feeling was strengthened when they began asking about their wives and acquaintances, requesting that their relatives and friends be told how well they were living, and that if they would come to them they would also live well.

One rebel requested the party to give his regards to several of Colonel Needham's slaves, and to other slaves of the "Kings" on Navy Island. He advised the Black Shots and baggage carriers to quit their "Slavish life". "Come and join us!" the rebels shouted to the Black Shots and baggage carriers. "Don't fight for the English."

Saturday and Sunday passed quietly, but on Monday at about eight in the morning the attack was renewed, when the rebels surrounded the towns and opened fire.

"We will starve you," they shouted. "We know a detachment has gone to Port Antonio for provisions and ammunition; but we have sent men to intercept them. Though you have occupied our towns, many of our people have come to help us. The longer you stay, the more our strength will increase."

The towns were under fire until about three in the afternoon. At that time Lamb and Williams decided to leave while they still had ammunition to fight their way out. Meanwhile, the Sergeant with his party had arrived at Breastwork with the message requesting reinforcements and supplies. Draper was jubilant when he learnt that the towns had been taken. He thought the Sergeant's detachment was too weak to protect the ammunition and provisions, and reinforced them with several men who had been sick or hurt when the party marched, and had been left behind. There was a great shortage of provisions, arms, powder, ball, cartridge paper, flints, etc, but Draper obtained these from Captain Knowles of the Navy, together with bags to carry them.

On June 26th, Draper went to Breastwork to dispatch the detachment, but at about four in the afternoon just as they were about to march, an advance party of five men arrived with the news that the rebels had re-taken the towns, and that Williams and Lamb were within five or six miles of Breastwork. They arrived at eight or nine o'clock on the morning of June 27th.

"How did you come to let the Wild Negroes drive you out of the towns?" Draper asked them. "We kept possession as long as we had ammunition," Williams and Lamb replied; but Draper was sceptical.

His fellow officer, Jasper Ashworth, remarked in a letter to Governor Hunter on June 27th, that it was a mystery to him that with so much ammunition (sixteen cartridges at least to each man and spare powder in their horns) they should be driven from the rebel towns with the loss of four White Shots taken alive and four killed (Draper thought it was five or six killed and as many wounded) and not the ear of a single rebel brought in to prove that even one had been slain. Draper ordered Williams and Lamb to remain at Breastwork until he could make proper arrangements to secure the place.

* * *

The many desertions by Black Shots and baggage carriers on the various expeditions caused great concern. To encourage loyalty, the Legislature resolved that instead of placing emphasis on the punishment of deserters, extra inducements should be offered. Therefore, in addition to awarding sums of money to the faithful, a store house was established at Manchioneal for the benefit of black soldiers, and they were allowed to share in the plunder.

Prominent among several loyal slave soldiers mentioned in the minutes of the House of Assembly in 1733, was one "Cuffie", belonging to Williams, who was said to have "killed Nanny, the rebels old obeah woman". Six years later, however, a British soldier encountered "the Old Obeah woman" in Quao's town, just prior to the signing of the peace treaty with the Windward Maroons.

Among others recognised in the Assembly's minutes was Black Sambo, set free with his wife and children as a reward for loyal service. Philip and several others were freed, on condition that they go out against rebels whenever called upon.

Apart from freedom, there were lesser rewards given to slaves for assisting the Colonial government, such as gifts of "a common silver-laced hat, a good blue baize coat with a red cross upon the left breast, and ten yards of osnaburg cloth".

CHAPTER 13

THE SWANTON BROTHERS

Ebenezer Lamb was not discouraged by his last defeat, and about two months later, he was prominently involved in yet another expedition against the Windward towns. The expedition, consisting of a strong body of sailors and soldiers, set out early in September, 1733, under the command of Lieutenant Thomas Swanton. His brother, Lieutenant Robert Swanton, was in charge of the advance guard, and the chief pilot (guide), who led the advance guard, was Ebenezer Lamb. Two other pilots, Weaver and Henry Hossip, were with the main body.

At about four in the afternoon the advance guard was near the "foot of the Blue mountain, within half a mile of the North-east river," and about two hundred yards from an ambush in which a captain Lee had been killed previously. The Rebel towns were not more than two miles away.

Lamb suddenly gave the word to halt. He turned and looked across a gully, and saw rebels in ambush, about nine yards away. Their guns were resting on crutches and were levelled at the advance guard. Lamb fired a warning shot, then threw himself down a steep precipice, and disappeared from sight.

Robert Swanton immediately gave the order to fire, and the advance guard poured several rounds into the rebel ambush. In the exchange of shots men were killed and wounded on both sides.

The commander, Thomas Swanton, rushed forward with the main body to support his brother Robert and the advance guard. As they came up, the advance guard broke past the ambush and took cover on either side of the river. The main body came under fire from the rebels and Thomas Swanton was shot in the right side of the chest. Weaver, one of the pilots, was killed.

The wounded Thomas Swanton fell opposite the ambush and the rebels took several shots at him, but missed. He shouted for Lieutenant Thompson to continue the advance. Thompson came forward and "cheered up his men with such a spirit as can scarce be imagined". They advanced resolutely but soon found themselves in need of a guide. Weaver was dead, and Lamb had disappeared, so the cry went up for another pilot to come forward to show the way.

Henry Hossip appeared. He ran down nervously to where the main body was engaged with the rebels, then ran back up. Then down again to the scene of the action, and up once more. This time he kept going, away from the battle. As he ran he shouted to the sailors around him. "Don't go down there, or you will be cut off. Leave the pass, the rebels are surrounding us. Get back up the hill or you will be cut off."

The men panicked and most of them ran up a ridge after the fleeing Hossip. Thomas Swanton and Lieutenant Thompson were in an open place, with about thirty-five or forty men. They were surrounded by rebels. Seeing their comrades flee in terror Thompson's men broke and ran. He raced after them, trying to rally them, but in vain.

Thomas Swanton, Lieutenants Shutten and Mitchell, and seven men, were left to the mercy of the rebels, who tried to take them alive. They took refuge under a large rock, however, and the rebels were not able to get at them without the risk of being shot.

In the meantime, Hossip and the front-runners in the fleeing mob of men, reached the soldiers in the rear and told them that the Commander, and most of the officers had been killed. Passing through bushes to the place where the baggage was being guarded by a detail of officers and soldiers, they repeated their terrifying tale. Night was coming on and the baggage carriers were ordered to lay down their loads and flee, which they did. The sailors and soldiers immediately began to plunder and destroy the baggage. They broke and threw away all the surgeon's instruments and medicines, pulled beef and bread out of bags and hurled them down a precipice; and, to prevent any attempt to rally them, tore open some of the ammunition boxes and threw away powder and ball. In addition they drank all the liquor they could and destroyed the rest. Some got so drunk they could hardly move, and one man was left dead drunk in the path.

Cut off from the advance guard and abandoned by the main body, Thomas Swanton crouched beneath the sheltering rock with his handful of officers and men. The area was surrounded by rebels except for one pass which was unguarded. As night fell, a heavy shower of rain came down. Under cover of the darkness and the rain, Swanton and his tiny band crept through the unguarded pass and escaped into the woods. They ran into Lieutenants Allam and Thompson, several other officers and a few men. A conference was held and it was agreed to make another attack in the morning. Orders were sent out for the men to assemble, but no one came.

At dawn it was discovered that Allam's men had deserted him, and that most of those who had stayed with Thomas Swanton were wounded. They climbed the hill to where the baggage had been left, hoping to find the guards and baggage carriers; but no one was there. Mr. Cox, the surgeon, discovered that some of his medicines had survived the destruction, and he was able to dress the wounded men, who numbered fourteen. Ten men had been killed outright in the rebel ambush. Thomas Swanton felt that, under the circumstances, he had better return to Breastwork.

Young Robert Swanton and the survivors of the advance guard, lay in concealment on either side of the river all night, hoping to ambush rebels. They saw thirty go by, each carrying two or three muskets; too many to attack with their small number. When five rebels came straggling behind, however, they fired and killed them, then cut off their ears in order to be able to substantiate the killings when they returned to base.

Ebenezer Lamb, crouching at the bottom of the precipice down which he had jumped, counted ninety-six rebels go by his hiding place. Each had two or three muskets. Afterwards, he joined Robert Swanton's group. In the morning they all went up the hill and found the commander, Thomas Swanton.

The shattered Swanton contingent arrived at Breastwork on September 2nd, at about four in the afternoon. Thomas Swanton still with the bullet in his chest, was depressed by the humiliating defeat. In his report, written at Port Antonio on September 4th, he said that Henry Hossip "whose cowardly behaviour and exaggerated statements had confused and demolished the men and caused the rout," had been arrested, along with other deserters.

He praised Ebenezer Lamb, saying:

> "I must beg leave to recommend Lamb to your Excellency; his behaviour deserving your notice."

Draper tried to persuade Thomas Swanton to make another attempt on the Rebel towns, but Thomas was so upset by the bad behaviour of the soldiers and sailors, particularly their drunkenness and looting, that he made no reply. Instead, he ordered his men to march early in the morning and get on board the ship, *Deal Castle*. Then, faint from his wound, he was hurried aboard a hulk to have the bullet removed from his chest. As a result of the Swanton defeat, settlers living in exposed areas moved into Port Antonio and many felt that the rebels would attack the town. A night watch was placed on the hills, overlooking the isthmus.

Writing from Titchfield on September 4th, Captain Jasper Ashworth proposed that a guard be posted day and night near the pass at the foot of the hill, and that a guard house be built and a defensive stone wall erected across the isthmus. He also requested that the Commodore station a ship in the East Harbour.

> "If the Gentlemen of this island will seriously consider these misfortunes they must admit that unhappy Jamaica is in a tottering state, and requires nothing less than the most vigorous and speediest means to save it from the impending danger which now seems to be ripe; for everybody believes that (the rebels') numbers are greatly increased".

Ashworth reported that horses had been sent to Breastwork to bring in Lieutenant Allam, young Robert Swanton and others who, through fatigue or wounds, were unable to travel. He deplored the loss of clothes, bagging, hammocks, provisions, powder and shot which would now fall into the hands of the rebels.

The two hundred and two sailors who had participated in the Swanton failure sailed back to Port Royal; but the Independent Companies were kept busy. A detachment marched from Breastwork with eight days' provisions, and destroyed a great "plantain walk" belonging to the rebels. They returned without loss. Another party marched to Hobby's in pursuit of rebels, who fled to the woods on their approach and escaped. A strong barracks was built at Breastwork to secure the isthmus at Titchfield against sudden attack, and Henry Hossip, the guide, was tried, sentenced to death and executed.

On January 11th, 1734, the rebels, numbering about two hundred, attacked Breastwork. They were repulsed by the party guarding the workers who were completing the barracks. More slaves in the area deserted their masters to join the rebels.

The harassed Governor, Major General Robert Hunter, died on March 31st, 1734. Apparently, he never managed to take his six months' leave, nor did he have the satisfaction of achieving a major victory against the Maroons during his administration. Ironically, this was to come only two months after his death, when Nanny Town was stormed, taken and occupied.

Hunter was succeeded by John Aysegough, President of the Council. Writing to the Secretary of State on April 4th, 1734, Aysegough said:

> His Majesty will be in a great measure informed of the weak state and condition the island lies under by the humble address of the Governing Council and Assembly, that hath been already sent home to his Majesty in relation to the strength of the Rebellious Negroes, who have infested some settlements towards the North-east part thereof, which are situated nearest to them I hope the measures already taken will for the present put a stop to their incursions".

Aysegough died on September 21st, 1735. He was succeeded by John Gregory who sent the following report to England:

> "We will continue in possession of the Negro Town (Nanny Town, captured in 1734) which formerly gave us so much trouble
>
> Through Martial Law the rebels were dislodged from their fastnesses and the Plantation slaves discouraged from joining them. But the rebels lost very few of their number. They divided into two bodies for the better convenience of subsistence. One, of about three hundred°

men, women and children (the Negroes don't know how to explain themselves by numbers) marched from the East to the West, near one hundred and fifty miles, without receiving much damage, though they were attacked twice or thrice on the march. But they marched through vast mountains and thick woods, and it was almost impossible to pursue them with any success. Recently they have been pretty quiet but reports from one or two who were captured (indicate) that they have joined with another large town in the West (probably Cudjoe's town), where they are fixing themselves and planting provisions for the increase. I am confident we shall soon hear of some sudden and dangerous eruption.

The soldiers have not had much success against them. Many soldiers are dead, not one half remaining, having received no recruits since their arrival. Three out of the five Captains that came with them are dead and several lieutenants. In two of the companies only one officer commissioned by the King is alive, and he incapable of acting (because) of some disorders in his head.

To keep the companies from falling into confusion Warrant Officers have been made here. We are trying to preserve their health by keeping them from strong liquor.

An Act has been passed for the building of twelve barracks in the places most infested by rebels, and roads directed to be cut across the island to open a better communication. It will take time and much money, and it will be difficult to garrison the barracks unless the companies are completed.

If two companies of (Scottish) Highlanders were added, it would effectually secure us against intestine enemies".

CHAPTER 14

INTO THE COCKPITS

According to the records Cudjoe was not a tall man, but he was physically impressive because of his massive shoulders and thick limbs, which made him seem shorter than he was. A British observer thought he had a lump on his shoulders.

Cudjoe was a born leader, a man of great courage and high morale, with the ability to organize and inspire. At the worst of times he held his people together with his indomitable spirit; but in spite of this, it is said that his followers were shaken in 1734, when they heard of the destruction of Nanny Town.

Why the fall of Nanny Town should have so deeply affected them is not clear. Rebel towns had fallen before and been burnt, re-taken and re-built. Nanny Town itself was apparently attacked more than once and temporarily occupied.

But where exactly was Nanny Town? Was it located next to Carrion Crow hill? Was it the main town that numerous parties had set out from Breastwork to conquer? If it was, then it was not always called Nanny Town.

John Gregory, who succeeded John Aysegough as governor when the latter died on September 29th, 1735, had written about the three hundred men, and women and children of the Windward rebels who had marched to the west after being driven from their town. They were called Cotterwoods and they had joined Cudjoe's people. The presence of this large body of fugitives in Cudjoe's settlement must have brought home to the Leeward rebels the desperate heights that the struggle in the west had reached.

Apart from the Cotterwoods, a group called Madagascars, who escaped from settlements around Lacovia in St. Elizabeth shortly after being brought to Jamaica, also sought out Cudjoe.

The newcomers placed an extra burden on Cudjoe's resources, and in addition new forces were being brought into the field against him.

The first body of Mosquito Indians had been unable to cope with the rugged Jamaican countryside and had either been killed or forced to join the rebel gangs. But now, in 1737, the Assembly resolved to bring in 200 more. Sloops were sent to the Mosquito coast to get them and their hunting dogs. They were formed into companies under their own officers, and each man was given 40 shillings per month together with shoes and other articles.

White guides were assigned to conduct the Indian companies against the rebels and apparently they did better than their predecessors. While they were on the march they kept a profound silence and it was said that once they hit on a Maroon track they were sure to discover the haunt to which it led.

In addition to the Indian reinforcements the Government built fortified advance posts near the rebel settlements, so as to cut down on the long marches that were previously necessary. The plan of action was for the garrisons of these posts to find and destroy the provision grounds and camps of the rebels. Search parties were required to take provisions to last for twenty days, and every post was provided with a pack of dogs by the church-wardens of the parish in which it was situated. The dogs

79

were used to guard against surprise attacks at night and to track down rebels. The posts were linked by footpaths chopped through the bush.

A big post was placed in about the centre of the island by the Cave River where it was thought that Cudjoe had his main camp. It stood on the western edge of a flat piece of land, seven miles long and three miles wide, and was surrounded by very high mountains. It was strongly garrisoned and well stocked with supplies.

Garrisoning these posts was not always easy. Regular troops could not be used as they were busy with their normal duties. It was not practical to use the Militia as it was made up of civilians who had jobs to do, especially on the sugar estates. The Government was therefore forced to organize independent companies and ranger squads to man the posts and only when things got particularly difficult was the Militia called upon to help.

The Mosquito Indians and Black Shots were attached to the Rangers. The Black Shots were invaluable in discovering the rebels' vital provision grounds, which were destroyed one by one. Their loss exposed Cudjoe's people to the danger of slow starvation. It was particularly hard on the women and children. One indication of how the pressure from the colonial government's offensive was affecting Cudjoe's people was recorded in a letter written by Colonel Blake on January 29th, 1737.

Blake gave an account of a young black woman who had been taken from Barbados Valley estate some years before, "and had been wife to one Cudjoe, a rebel Captain". She had deserted and come in to the military authorities, giving information on the number of rebels and the locations of their settlements. She offered to act as a guide to any party sent out against the rebels. It was resolved in the House of Assembly that a claim be inserted in "some Bill", to make the woman free, and for a payment of forty pounds to be made to her owners to secure her freedom.

But the pressure of rebel resistance and counter-attacks was also severely affecting the colonial establishment.

Colonel Tobias Fitch, while in Debtors' Prison in Spanish Town, wrote the Government recommending that Chickesaw or Creek Indians be brought from South Carolina or Georgia to help fight the rebels. There was also a suggestion that Scottish Highlanders, accustomed to a hilly environment, be imported to assist. John Gregory, the Acting Governor, hinted that peace might have to be made when he wrote in 1737:

> "I know but two ways of dealing with an enemy: either by FORCE or TREATY. The first we have often unsuccessfully tried".

Rangers, Indians and Black Shots penetrated the rugged interior and kept Cudjoe harassed and on the move. There were frequent clashes during which the Maroon tactics of ambush and withdrawal always resulted in heavier losses for the Rangers and their allies. But even though he punished his enemy and skillfully avoided defeat, Cudjoe could not replace his casualties or easily replenish the expenditure of gunpowder and shot.

His situation was now quite precarious. The old haunts, once secret and secure, were being revealed by the Black Shots. Provision grounds were being destroyed, and Ranger patrols were making it difficult for foraging parties to maintain contact with old friends who would sometimes supply him with food. Cudjoe therefore decided to withdraw into the Cockpit Country in the West-central part of the island, now part of the parishes of Trelawny and St. James.

Over half of Jamaica consists of hills and plateaux of a rock formation known as white limestone. In the high regions of this area, the intense action of rain-water, dissolving the extremely soluble limestone, makes sink-holes and underground caverns and creates a characteristic honeycomb appearance. Rain-water settles rapidly through the joints and fissures and either runs by underground tunnels and by seepage to the sea, or is trapped in great subterranean reservoirs lined with impervious clay or hard limestone. Consequently there are few surface streams.

In certain areas deep depressions or glens are formed which are called Cockpits. These Cockpits are separated from each other by precipitous towers of rock covered with dense bush. The Cockpits are found mostly in the parishes of St. Elizabeth and Trelawny.

Seen from the air, the Cockpit Country appears to be a bewildering jumble of hummocky hills and intervening depressions. Some of the Cockpits have fertile soil and along the northern slopes of the area there are springs which have water even during drought periods. Today the 500 square mile block of Cockpit Country is almost uninhabited, because the absence of surface water and communications make cultivation uneconomic.

Cudjoe set up headquarters near the entrance of the Cockpits to the north-west, where goats, wild hogs and plenty of pigeons were to be found. It was in the first of these great Cockpits called Petty (Petit) River Bottom, that his main camp lay.

By comparison with the other Cockpits, Petty River Bottom was very large, containing seven acres of land and a spring of water. The only entrance was through a long, narrow pass, so narrow that a party of men had to move in single file. From Petty River Bottom led a series of Cockpits from east to west each joined by a difficult pass. Some of the Cockpits in this area also ran parallel to each other but their sides were from fifty feet to eighty feet high and so steep that it was almost impossible to climb from one cockpit into a parallel one, although the agile Maroons could manage it.

Cudjoe began operating in the region about Mouth

River, Hector's River, the Black Grounds and areas to the
east of the greater Cockpits. Petty River Bottom was so
placed that Cudjoe could easily attack the parishes of St.
James, Hanover, Westmoreland and St. Elizabeth. The
borders of these parishes were open and difficult to defend
and he could send small raiding parties into them at any
time to gather food.

The narrow passage into Petty River Bottom could easily
be defended. The narrowest part of it alone ran for nearly
half a mile. Whenever the lookouts sounded their abengs,
warning that an enemy force was approaching, the
Maroons would climb onto the ledges on either side of the
passage and conceal themselves behind large rocks. From
there they could bottle up an attacking force by rolling
down large boulders at either end, and even without using
their guns they could destroy such a force with rocks alone.

Usually, however, when a hostile force approached,
Cudjoe would intercept it long before it reached Petty River
Bottom. He would send out advance parties to set ambushes in the bush and rocks that bordered either side of the
winding, half-obscured trail. The troops, all wearied by the
long march, by the fear of imminent attack and by the tension caused by constant vigilance, would suddenly find
themselves fired upon from two or three sides. They would
return the fire but the Maroons would simply disappear.
Very often the troops returned to their posts without inflicting a single casualty upon the Maroons while invariably
they themselves would lose a good number of their own
men and much of their morale.

Cudjoe's raiding parties, in addition to operating in St.
James, Hanover, Westmoreland and St. Elizabeth, ven-
tured south as well, into his old haunts in the Clarendon
hills. His men seemed to turn up everywhere and this
greatly confused the soldiers as to where he really was. He
had earlier placed a strong detachment under the command of his brother Accompong, and he now increased the

size of this group and sent it into northern St. Elizabeth to establish a camp. Accompong chose a place above the Nassau Mountains. There he built a camp which later grew into a town and which was named Accompong after him. Accompong Town still stands today on the site chosen by its founder.

There were many English settlers and a great number of cattle in the vicinity of Accompong. The Maroon raids from this new camp were frequent and devastating but the settlers, being sturdy folk, fought back with great vigour.

The struggle between the Maroons and the English settlers and soldiers dragged on. Both sides suffered greatly but the English never realized how hard-pressed the Maroons were. All that was painfully obvious to them was the absolute failure of all their forces to defeat the Maroons. The Government finally decided to put everything it had into a massive assault on Cudjoe with the object of destroying him completely.

The House of Assembly voted funds for a large-scale offensive. Many of the colonists who could carry a gun volunteered to go; more Mosquito Indians were recruited and companies of freed slaves were formed. A large force was assembled under Colonel John Guthrie of the militia and Captain Sadler of the regular army.

But Cudjoe and his colleagues had done their work well, and the years of warfare had completely undermined the morale of the colony. As the first heat of righteous enthusiasm cooled, the feeling spread throughout the colony that if this latest offensive should fail as all others had, the Maroons would be encouraged to consider themselves invincible and the slaves might lose complete respect for their masters.

Several of the influential and experienced colonists urged Edward Trelawny, now the Governor, to make a peace treaty with the Maroons. The Governor agreed that this should be attempted and ordered Colonel Guthrie and

Captain Sadler to get in touch with Cudjoe as soon as possible.

Cudjoe, meanwhile, was desperately short of food despite his far-ranging patrols. Indeed, the difficulty of finding food for all his people may have been one of the reasons why he detached Accompong's command and sent it into the well-stocked northern St. Elizabeth region. The constant need to fight had probably reduced his scanty store of gunpowder and bullets to almost nothing and, added to this, his warriors were weary from the years of almost ceaseless endeavour. Where the regular troops, militia and rangers could get some relief from their duties, Cudjoe had no replacement for his men and the strain on them was constant.

Apart from this, Cudjoe was now probably more than sixty years old. After forty-eight years of strenuous living, the last eighteen of which had been marked by increasing responsibility; he was about ready for peace. Nevertheless, when he heard that Guthrie and Sadler were seeking him out to offer peace, he called in all his patrols and got ready to defend his stronghold. The wily old warrior who had outclassed and outwitted his opponents ever since he first put his mind to it, had no intention of being caught with his guard down simply because there was talk of peace.

He gathered his men at Petty River Bottom. On the rock ledges which rose perpendicularly on either side of the entrance passage he placed in hiding a crowd of sharp-shooters. He sent out small advance parties for a mile or two beyond the entrance to the great Cockpit with orders to guard every approach to the place. These men stationed themselves at the most difficult places along the route and Cudjoe instructed them to keep a wary eye on the soldiers but not to fire a shot. The lookouts with their abengs were perched in the usual places to give warning of Guthrie's approach.

Cudjoe had no need to worry about his rear which was

naturally guarded by the line of almost inaccessible Cockpits. His flanks likewise were protected by the high Cockpit walls. In the heart of Petty River Bottom itself the women and children and valuables were placed. On the open ground before the entrance passage where the huts of the settlement stood, the rest of the warriors gathered fully armed, ready to fall back upon their natural rock fortifications if need be. Having thus arranged his forces, Cudjoe settled down to await Governor Trelawny's peace party.

CHAPTER 15

JOHN GUTHRIE'S MISSION OF PEACE

There are two versions of the signing of the peace treaty. One said that John Guthrie and his men came along the Maroon path, passing safely through places where they would easily have been ambushed had this been a fighting mission. Every now and then as they marched, the far-reaching notes of Maroon abengs rose around them; behind, to the sides and in front; but they saw no one.

Presently, before them there arose the smoke from the cluster of huts in front of the entrance to Petty River Bottom. They halted a few hundred yards away from the huts. No one appeared and after a period of anxious waiting Colonel Guthrie said in a loud voice that he had come by order of the Governor and at the sincere wishes of the colonists to treat for peace and to make an offer of terms.

Out of the rocks and bushes a voice arose saying that the Maroons also wanted peace but that the troops should remain where they were. Realizing that the Maroons would not come up and talk with him in the presence of all his men, Guthrie raised his voice again and said he would show that he had confidence in the Maroons by sending forward a single man to assure them of the Governor's sincerity. This man would state the terms of peace which he had been authorised to propose.

Guthrie selected one Dr. Russell for the task. Russell strode confidently towards the huts and as he neared them two Maroon warriors appeared. He told them he had come with the peace terms and asked if either of them was Cudjoe. They replied that neither one of them was Cudjoe, but that if he would wait a while and if none of his party attempted to join him, he would see Cudjoe.

The two guards shouted towards the cliffs of the Cockpit in what Russell described as the Coromantee language, and several Maroons rose out of the rocks high above Russell's head. He called out to them, praised Cudjoe in high terms and begged to be allowed to speak to him.

Cudjoe, crouched in his rocky fortress, looked down upon this scene and heard Russell describe him as a brave and good man. He weighed in his mind the possibility of treachery and finally decided that for the present the advantage lay with him. So he arose and descended from the heights with a bodyguard of his men. Russell looked at the group of men advancing towards him and said afterwards that he had no difficulty making up his mind which was the notorious Captain Cudjoe. Dominating the others and holding his eyes from the beginning was a fierce-looking man below middle height but so broad and husky in build that he looked shorter than he was. He wore an old blue coat and a pair of loose fitting pants that came to about his knees. A short piece of white cloth was tied around his head, and on it rested a small close-fitting round hat with the rim cut off so near to the crown that it looked like a calabash.

He was armed with a gun and a cutlass with a blade three inches wide. The cutlass was carried in a leather sheath suspended under his left arm by a narrow strap that went round his shoulder. On his right side hung a cow horn filled with gunpowder and a bag of large-cut bullets.

Cudjoe's garments were ragged and deeply stained with the red dirt of the Cockpits. His men, who were as heavily armed as himself, were equally tattered and soiled. They all showed the effects of the long months of intense guerilla warfare through which they had just passed.

Cudjoe and his men halted some distance away from Russell. Still suspicious, the Maroon Chief asked the doctor several questions, all the while casting quick looks towards the place where Guthrie and his men stood waiting. Finally Cudjoe walked up to Russell who with quick inspiration, offered to exchange hats with him as a token of friendship. Cudjoe took the doctor's ornate cocked hat. There is an old print of the scene which shows him with the hat on his head. In the print Dr. Russell holds Cudjoe's calabash-shaped head-piece in his hand but it is not known whether he put it on his head.

The two men began to speak quite freely and at this point Colonel Guthrie, seeing that all appeared to be going well and anxious to talk to Cudjoe, shouted to the Maroon Chief and asked to be allowed to join them and to bring a few of his officers to act as witnesses to any terms that they might agree on. Guthrie promised to come unarmed and Cudjoe, while consenting to this request, called down a few more of his armed warriors from the rocks, just in case Guthrie should attempt to trick him. Up to the very end Cudjoe refused to trust his enemies. He seemed to have no confidence in their word.

As Guthrie and his officers approached, Cudjoe became greatly disturbed. The moment was coming when he would have to decide to make peace or continue to fight. It was a decision that he would finally have to make alone. As the most famous chief, and as leader of the largest Maroon community, his decision would have far-reaching effects. Two-thirds of the settled areas of the island had felt the sting of his relentless raids and his example had encouraged the Windward Maroons who kept the other third of the island constantly on the alert.

Failing food supplies, dwindling munitions and the feverish attempts to subdue him had taxed his resources to the utmost. Only his brilliant and suspicious mind, coupled with the ruggedness of the Cockpit terrain, had saved his people. He was by no means beaten but he needed a breathing space.

In the Cockpit of Petty River Bottom the women and children with their few valuable possessions awaited his decision. The men gathered about him or crouched in the high rocks also awaited his move; and in the balance, the old, free way of life hung against an uncertain future. Cudjoe stood alone in his thoughts as he watched John Guthrie walking up to him with his hand held out in friendship, and Dr. Russell observed the great emotional stress which was now visible on Cudjoe's face.

The report of Cudjoe's falling at Guthrie's feet and kissing his hands makes no sense. However, another version of the meeting, by an eyewitness, gives a more plausible account of what happened.

This second version, written by an officer under Guthrie's command, who kept a diary of the events leading up to the signing of the peace treaty with Cudjoe, was introduced as the:

> "Exact journal of the Proceedings of the Party commanded
> by the Hon. John Guthrie, Esq, joined by Lieutenant
> Francis Sadler, Commander of the Independents."

The document gives a vivid and sometimes amusing description of the meeting of the two forces.

Guthrie's force left Montego Bay at three o'clock on the afternoon of Tuesday, February 13th, 1739. It included "178 of the Militia, Black and White shot, 45 independents and 112 baggage carriers." They marched east and south-east for three and a half miles to Sandy Gut (between Irwin and Orange Estates) where they made camp. The weather was fair all day.

The next day, Wednesday February 14th, was also fair. They marched south-east and east-north-east for about five and a half miles, to the vicinity of "the line of Williamsfield and Flamstead estates," which the writer described as "the rebels old hunting" place. The contingent arrived at one o'clock and their guide informed them that if they went any further they would find it difficult to obtain water. They therefore made camp.

Rain fell as they resumed the march on Thursday the 15th. They went south and by east and south until they came to Guthrie's Horse Stable at Crooked Spring, Orange River, where a halt was called to allow the rear to catch up.

The horses were left at Guthrie's stable and the column pushed on until they came upon "the rebels old hunting path" which they followed.

The path led to several old hunting huts on Sunderland estate which had apparently been used by a couple of Maroons about two days before. The path became plainer as they went, and presently they entered the Cockpit Country, the haunt of Cudjoe and his followers.

The guide informed Guthrie that there was a small river beyond one of the Cockpits where they could camp for the night. They marched very quickly through the wet country-side and between five and six o'clock came to the river near a place called Summer Hill. They camped there for the night having covered nine miles that day, some of it in rain.

On Friday the 16th, rain fell as they marched out, heading south and by west and south. After about four miles, the advance guard came in sight of the Maroons' plantations in the vicinity of Drayton, where the New Maroon town would later be built. They could hear people talking and working in the fields. Word was passed back along the column for absolute silence to be maintained. They were now on the verge of the lion's den.

Several officers together with some of the most active men went up to the front of the line. The guide was asked if he could lead the contingent in another direction so they could come upon the Maroons without being detected. He said the route they were following was the best one. So they started out, going very quietly, walking to one side of the open ground.

They entered the Maroon plantation which was large and not well cleared. A man was standing there, with a gun. They thought it was Cudjoe. He fired a shot and ran off.

Maroon women and children were in the field, some distance away. They ran towards the woods and the contingent pursued, firing as they ran. A child was hit and fell. A girl, perhaps hanging back to help the child, was captured. The rest got safely into the woods.

The firing alerted some Maroon men who were in their town repairing houses which had recently been burnt because of their own negligence. They hurriedly got their weapons and took up positions in ambush between two Cockpits where Guthrie's contingent would have to pass in order to get to the provision ground at Old Ginger Town (sometimes called Old Cudjoe Town).

Guthrie halted and waited for the baggage to catch up. Then he advanced into the trail between the two Cockpits. The Independents under Lieutenant Sadler marched in front with the militia close behind. They were well into the path when shots were fired from ambush. Guthrie's men returned the fire, shooting at every shadow that moved and every bush that shook. When they emerged from the passage they gave a loud cheer and pressed on in the direction of the Ginger Town provision grounds. They looked for the guide who had been leading them but he was nowhere to be found. Frightened by the shooting he had run back to the baggage. Nobody else knew the way, so they had to stop.

Twenty Black Shots were sent back to find the guide and reinforce the baggage. When the baggage and guide finally arrived however, it was too late to go any further, especially as it had begun to rain. They made camp for the night. One Independent had been killed and two wounded. There was no report of any Maroon casualties.

Maroons on top of a Cockpit fired four shots at them through the haze and an abeng horn was blown. More shots flew down in the evening but no damage was done. Guthrie placed guards on Cockpits overlooking the camp to prevent them from being used by Maroon snipers.

Saturday, February 17th, was the crucial day. At dawn the drums "beat to arms". Guthrie left eighty Shots behind in the camp to guard the baggage and set off for Petty River Bottom, which was south-west by south and about a mile from Ginger Town. They marched through provision grounds in a glade and started up an incline between two Cockpits. The area was later to be known as Guthrie's Defile.

The passage through the defile was blocked by plantain trees which the Maroons had cut down and laid across the path. As on the previous day, the Independents were in the lead, with the militia close behind. When they started to penetrate the plantain tree barrier, shots were fired from both sides of the trail. The contingent replied with volleys to right and left. More shots appeared to be coming from the right so they swerved in that direction, breaking into the bushes to clear away the assailants. Apparently they encountered no one.

About one hundred and ten yards ahead (half a furlong) stood Cudjoe's Town. They advanced into the town and a few shots were fired as they entered it. The town was situated "at the north-east corner of the Maroon lands near a stream called the Pettie River." It would later be known as "Trelawny Town". Guthrie placed guards on all the heights overlooking the place, to protect his men from snipers.

Maroons on a hill some distance away blew their horns and started to sing. Guthrie's men raised their voices and appealed to them to come forward and talk. They were on a friendly mission, they said, and would not burn the town. The Maroons shouted words which they could not understand.

Communication seemed impossible. Guthrie finally gave up. He burnt a few houses, then called in his guards and returned to where he had left his baggage. Three more of his Independents had been wounded and a shot had struck his cane as he had entered the defile. It rained heavily just before nightfall and the camp was very uncomfortable.

On Sunday, February 18th, Guthrie ordered thirty Shots and sixty "baggage Negroes" to return to Montego Bay for provisions. As the men were lining up, Maroons on top of a Cockpit that Guthrie had neglected to secure, fired a volley. No one was hit. The Maroons appeared to be in three groups. They blew their horns and started to sing. Their purpose seemed to be to attract Guthrie's attention rather than to attack him.

Guthrie cancelled the mission to Montego Bay and ordered the contingent to stand to arms. They waited, listening to the horns and the Maroons' songs. Then a single voice, loud and clear, called out to them. Guthrie and his spokesmen, eager to communicate, began once more appealing to the Maroons to come forward and talk.

"Come down and talk with us!" they shouted. "We want to make peace. We will not destroy your provision grounds. You will live as free people. All we ask is that you agree to destroy all rebels and bring in runaways."

After much entreating and arguing, a Maroon called "Prince" climbed down from one of the heights, and stood some distance away from the contingent. One of Guthrie's men took a hat to him, saying it was a gift for Cudjoe. Prince climbed back up with the hat and returned soon after, coming much closer this time. As a further show of friendship, some of Guthrie's men took a bag of beef and a bag of bread out to him.

At that moment Cudjoe appeared on the side of a hill at the edge of the open ground. He was surrounded by a group of his men. He stood looking down for a while, and then descended with one of his officers (Captain Cuffee) to a gut (a narrow channel) about a hundred yards from Guthrie's contingent. There he waited.

Guthrie and Captain Sadler walked out to him. They began to talk, while the forces on both sides looked on. After a long discussion in which Guthrie made his case for peace, Cudjoe asked that he be given three cartridges as a token of friendship. Guthrie readily agreed, and the tension was broken.

The Maroons came down from their heights. Guthrie's men came forward. They mingled, shaking hands and smiling. Guthrie's military band began to play. The Maroons were delighted with the music and several began to dance. The occasion ended on this happy, relaxed note, with Cudjoe's people and Guthrie's men parting as good friends. No longer fearing attack, Guthrie sent the baggage with an escort to Montego Bay in the afternoon to get provisions, and to deliver a report to Governor Trelawny. It had been a day of fair weather.

Early on Monday morning, February 19th, Cudjoe, Cuffee and about fifty or sixty Maroons, came into the plantain walk in front of Guthrie's camp and called out. Guthrie's men went to them, and some of the Maroons entered the camp. It was a very friendly scene. Once again Guthrie gave assurance that the provision grounds would not be destroyed. To show that he was sincere, he offered to move his camp to the far side of the field through which he had marched on the day he had entered the settlement. He also said he would return the Maroon girl he had captured if Cudjoe would give back a little girl he had taken from a settler named Welch, and another from a Mrs. Chambers.

Cudjoe agreed. The exchange of captives took place, and Guthrie marched his men to the new camp-site further away from the town. Several Maroons accompanied them, bearing presents of cocoa, plantain, and other produce.

Tuesday, February 20th, was spent by the contingent in

sorting things out in the new camp. Captain Downer who had fallen ill, and John Rusea who had a sore leg, were allowed to go home. Maroons paid several visits with more gifts of food, including cured wild hog. The writer of the report of the expedition thought that the meat was indifferently prepared.

Trade between the two sides began to increase, and this worried Guthrie. As a precautionary measure, the Black Shots were relieved of their ammunition and a strict guard placed over them, to prevent any trafficking in gunpowder and bullets with the Maroons.

On Wednesday morning, February 21st, two Maroons came to the camp to say that Cudjoe was in the open ground with some of his people and was requesting Colonel Guthrie to meet him there with his musicians. The Maroon messengers said that the reason Cudjoe had not come to the camp was that it was located in the woods bordering the fields, and there was no room to dance. If Guthrie wanted he could bring guns with him, but they must be carried with "the butts foremost".

Having agreed to this strange request, Colonel Guthrie, Captain Sadler and ten other gentlemen, went to meet Cudjoe in the open ground, carrying guns with the butts foremost. The military musicians accompanied them, bearing drum, French horn and bagpipes. Twelve or fourteen of Cudjoe's Maroons carried guns, "butts foremost." The military musicians were given a joyful welcome by the music-loving Maroons. They began to play: drums, horn and bagpipes, to the enormous delight of the audience.

The high point however, was when Cudjoe began to dance. He displayed a great many intricate and spectacular movements and fell several times at Guthrie's feet. Suddenly, as he whirled about, he hugged the amazed Guthrie. Rising to the occasion, Guthrie drew his sword and laid it on Cudjoe's head, apparently in a mock ceremony of knighthood. At the end of the performance

Cudjoe and Guthrie had another long conference. They had quickly developed a warm and harmonious rapport which infected their followers. In a spirit of candour Cudjoe revealed that he had seventy-one fighting men in camp, and forty more outside in several parties. He said that his brother, Captain Accompong (who was not present), had one hundred and three men in his camp, and an unknown number out in parties. And so another day of peaceful and harmonious interchange came to an end.

Five or six Maroons entered the camp on Thursday, February 22nd. Among them was one of Accompong's senior officers. He informed Guthrie that Accompong was participating with Cudjoe in the peace negotiations. The only reason he was not present was that he had to deal with a military party. As a token of friendly intentions he sent an iron ring to put on Guthrie's wrist. In return he requested that Guthrie send him a paper signifying that peace was being made, so as to stop hostile troops from molesting him. Guthrie complied with Accompong's request, and in the evening, five Maroons came in with more gifts of food. Two days later, on Saturday, February 24th, Guthrie received an order from Governor Edward Trelawny, officially empowering him to make a treaty of peace.

There are significant differences in the two accounts of the signing of the peace treaty with Cudjoe. In the first account Guthrie enters Cudjoe's territory and speaks to him without incident. However the air is full of uncertainty and tension, the details of the journey are not set forth, and the sequence of events are compressed, ending with an incredible situation.

In the second account, Guthrie's progress is accompanied by quite a bit of shooting, a chase and a little burning; not at all in keeping with a peace mission. The troops suffer a few casualties but the Maroon fighters appear to be unscathed, and are never seen close-up by the troops. It is almost as if Cudjoe is toying with them and keeping them off balance, even though disposed to talk peace. The dispersal of suspicion and the fairly rapid drawing together of the two groups, with generous gifts of scarce food and a concert of music and dance, are well described. The change from hostility to appreciation is dramatic, once Cudjoe has been persuaded to come down from his rocky fortress. The second account also reveals the love of music, song and dance which lay beneath the tough exterior of the Maroon warrior; and also the capacity for goodwill and generosity.

The success of the mission was probably due in large part to the rapport which quickly developed between Cudjoe and Guthrie. Friendly discussion, mutual respect, and a sincere desire for peace had brought about the desired results.

The treaty was concluded with Cudjoe by Colonel Guthrie and Captain Sadler. The formalities were carried out on March 1st, 1739, under a large cotton tree growing in the centre of the cluster of Maroon huts at the entrance to the long passage which led into Petty River Bottom Cockpit.

The treaty called for the cessation of hostilities between both parties forever. It guaranteed full freedom and liberty to Cudjoe and his people and gave them ownership of one thousand five hundred acres of land. One hundred acres were also assigned to the Accompong Maroons around the site of their town. They were at liberty to plant this land with such crops as coffee, cocoa, ginger, tobacco and cotton, and to breed cattle, hogs, goats, or any other flock. They could sell their produce and livestock anywhere, but if they wanted to sell in the market they would first have to get a licence from the Custos or any other magistrate of the parish in which the market lay.

There were many other detailed terms, such as the one which permitted the Maroons to hunt wherever they chose except within three miles of any settlement, crawl or pen;

A Maroon warrior

A Mosquito Indian

Governor Robert Hunter (1729-34)

Cudjoe of the Maroons

Philip Thicknesse

An artist's impression of Trelawny Town

and another which said that if a European did any manner of injury to the Maroons, they should apply to the commanding officer or magistrate in the neighbourhood for justice. The Maroons were to cut, clear and maintain roads from Trelawny Town (the name given to Cudjoe's town) to Westmoreland, St. James and, if possible, St. Elizabeth. Two Europeans nominated by the Governor were to reside with them in order to "maintain a friendly correspondence with the island."

But the most important of these articles were the ones which required Cudjoe and his successors:

> " to use their best endeavors to take, kill, suppress or destroy, either by themselves or jointly with any other number of men... all rebels wheresoever they may be throughout the island, unless they submit to the same terms of accommodation granted to Captain Cudjoe and his successors;

> If any negroes shall hereafter run from their masters or owners and fall into Captain Cudjoe's hands, they shall immediately be sent back to the Chief Magistrate of the next parish where they are taken; and those that bring them are to be satisfied for their trouble as the legislature shall appoint."
>
> DALLAS — *History of the West Indies*

These were the articles which were to change the relationship between the Maroons and the rest of the African population.

Cudjoe was made Chief of his community for life, but he, and his successors, were required to wait on the Governor or Commander-in-Chief every year if necessary. He was also given power to inflict punishment for crimes committed by his men, all except the death penalty. Those Maroons thought to be deserving of death were to be brought before any Justice of the Peace who would try them.

Except for peace, the treaty gave the Maroons little that

they did not already have, but it placed them under the jurisdiction of their late enemies who, while giving them the appearance of autonomy, really had final authority over their affairs. It also provided the colonists with a ready-made and well-trained mercenary force to help maintain the iron control necessary in a slave society. It was the triumph of a literate, sophisticated, cynical society motivated by expediency and gain, over an illiterate, vigorous but simple community skilled only in warfare and physical survival.

To the last, old Cudjoe was suspicious and uneasy. Perhaps he sensed that what he had to fear most was not the guns of his enemies, but their devious pens, wielded by minds well schooled in treaty-making, and in the art of dividing people so as to rule them more effectively. For the moment however he had preserved his people: first in war, and now in peace. The reckoning would come later.

We do not know when Cudjoe died, but the historian Long says that when Governor Lyttleton visited St. James in 1764, the Trelawny Maroons went down to Montego Bay to greet him. They were led by Cudjoe who made a speech on the occasion. He must have been well over eighty years old at the time.

On April 6th, 1739, the House of Assembly voted one thousand five hundred pounds to Colonel Guthrie and six hundred pounds to Lieutenant Francis Sadler for their services. Colonel Guthrie (who was Custos of Westmoreland) died that same year on June 13th, 1739 at the age of fifty-two, while on an expedition against the Windward Maroons.

CHAPTER 16

NANNY TOWN

Some of the wildest stories in Maroon history revolve around Nanny Town, the great stronghold of the Windward Maroons which lay in the heart of the vast and seemingly impenetrable fastnesses of the Blue Mountains.

The story of Nanny Town is shrouded in legends and kept alive by controversy. One of the legends says that it was named after a mysterious woman called Nanny who was the wife or sister of Cudjoe. It is said that she was a most bloodthirsty person, who was possessed of supernatural powers and spirited away the finest slaves from the estates which lay around. In battle she caught all the bullets of the enemy and returned them in an obscene manner with deadly effect.

Some accounts say that the town probably stood on the brink of an awesome, nine-hundred foot precipice. At the foot of this precipice, close to the confluence of the Nanny (or Macungo) and Stony Rivers, Nanny was supposed to keep a huge cauldron which boiled continuously without the aid of fire. Enemy troops, coming near to inspect the cauldron would fall in and suffocate. The cauldron was actually a circular basin hollowed out in the rock by the waters of the Nanny River which fall from the heights above, and are joined by the plunging waters of the Stony River. The continuously falling water keeps the pool in a constant froth and turmoil and gives it the look of a boiling cauldron.

In the military and official reports of the many battles and skirmishes between the British forces and the Maroons, Nanny does not emerge as a field commander like Cudjoe and Quao, or like Johnson, Smith, Parkinson and Palmer in the Second Maroon War. But today's Windward Maroons believe she was a major military influence in the long, ferocious struggle.

Nanny's mysteriousness enhanced her image as a superhuman being. Leaders such as Cudjoe, Quao, Johnson, Smith, Parkinson and Palmer were identified and described by the soldiers and officials who had to deal with them. Eyewitnesses have recorded for posterity the commanding figure of Cudjoe, the balanced personality of Quao and his mischievous children poking their fingers at the chest of a hostage, the magnificent physiques of Smith and Parkinson and the strenuous figure of Johnson. Nanny remained an enigma until the time of the treaty with the Windwards, when two documents dealing with that event penetrate the shroud of mystery and bring us closer to her.

Despite stories of Nanny catching bullets and hurling them back at the soldiers, or luring the enemy to death in her boiling cauldron, it seems she was more a motivator and a shining inspiration, like the Tudor Queen of England, Elizabeth the First, rather than a Joan of Arc with sword in hand. Her champion and Field Marshal was the intrepid Quao, the Invisible Hunter of the eastern highlands. But overall Nanny looms tremendously, a towering figure. High Priestess of the Windward Maroons, inspiring them to feats of heroism and endurance.

The site of Nanny Town had been raided before but, in 1734, a major attack was led by Captain Stoddart who took along some portable swivel guns. According to the report, Stoddart, moving silently and with great care, approached near to the town without being discovered. After a short rest he ordered his men to climb up the steep path which was the only way to get at the town itself. The path was so narrow that they had to go in single file. With much labour they dragged up the swivel guns and finally came out upon a height which overlooked the town. Stoddart mounted his guns and opened fire.

The attack may have taken place at night for Stoddart claimed that the Maroons were asleep in their huts. The swivels were worked very rapidly by the gunners and the shots plunged and ricocheted into the gorge at a great rate. The town was smashed. Many of the Maroons were killed in their huts and many more, terrified by the sudden attack or preferring death to surrender, threw themselves over the precipice. According to the military account, Stoddart followed up this initial advantage and killed or captured a great number of the surviving Maroons. Then he put Nanny Town to the torch and completely destroyed it.

The Maroons have their own version of the fight. They say that their lookouts spotted Stoddart's soldiers and gave a warning. The inhabitants evacuated the town, camouflaged themselves and waited. The soldiers passed very close without seeing them and entered the village. Finding it deserted and being very tired, they settled down to sleep in the huts.

During the night the Maroons threw burning slips of candlestick down on to the huts and, when they were all afire, launched an attack. The surprised and terrified soldiers jumped over the precipice. One survivor was found the next day and he wrote a note which the Maroons stuck up at the fording of the Rio Grande.

There may be some truth in the Maroon story, for it is difficult to believe that Stoddart could have made that herculean march without being spotted somewhere along the way. If he had been seen then it is likely that the town which he bombarded with his swivel guns was indeed empty; in which case the clash between the Maroons and the soldiers must have occurred when Stoddart descended into the town.

There are some who say that Stoddart was not the main architect of the destruction of Nanny Town. They give the credit for planning the expedition to Stoddart's superior, Colonel Brooks. This seems to be borne out by the fact that when the Nanny Town expedition was considered in the House of Assembly on July 13th, 1738, Colonel Brooks received a reward of £600 while Stoddart got only £300.

Another version claims that the attack on Nanny Town was led by Captain John Swarton in May 1734. Trying a new route, he dragged small field pieces to the heights above the town and surprised the Maroons. The battle lasted five days during which the Maroons suffered great losses and were only saved from disaster by flood rains which prevented reinforcements from reaching Swarton, who had to retire when his ammunition ran low.

After its destruction, Nanny Town was never re-settled and legends grew up about the ghosts which were supposed to haunt the site. Some say that at night the spirits of those who fell in the fight squeak and gibber about the place. Others put the noises down to rolling stones loosened by rooting hogs, and to the flapping wings of sea-going birds who roost among the heights and fly away to the ocean at dawn.

There are documents, however, which give some concrete facts about Nanny Town. On October 3rd, 1733, a man named Ned, while being interrogated, gave a graphic description of the way of life of the Nanny Town Maroons. He said that while he was there, there were three hundred men armed with guns or lances. They had more firearms than they could use. The women and children far outnumbered the men. There was one head man who directed everything.

If a man committed a crime he was instantly shot, but there were very few things that were regarded as a crime. Perhaps the most serious crime was lying with another man's wife.

Women were whipped for most of the crimes they committed. They, and those of the men who were least noted for their courage, did all the work necessary for the raising of crops. The practice was to work one day and play the next.

If the head man was found guilty of any great crime, his soldiers (as they were called) would shoot him, and appoint another in his place.

While Ned was at Nanny Town the head man was named "Cuffee". He was distinguished by wearing a silver-laced hat and a small sword. No one else dared to wear anything similar.

The Maroons had another town at the back, or rather, on top of Carrion Crow Hill. It was called Guy's (or Gay's) Town, from the name of the head man. There was a great deal of open ground around that town with plenty of coco, sugarcane, plantains, yams, corn, hogs and poultry.

There were about two hundred men in Guy's Town, and a greater number of women. The men were armed with lances and cutlasses, rather than with guns. They never went out to meet the (military) parties unless it was to defend the paths leading to their town. At such times they were joined by the best fighting men of Nanny Town.

When the Nanny Town Maroons were first beaten from their homes, they took refuge in Guy's Town; but as food began to grow scarce they returned to Nanny Town and made themselves masters of it again.

On hearing that strong parties were being sent against them, the Nanny Town Maroons searched the woods for seven to eight miles around for other settlements with which they could unite, in order to increase their strength; but they found none.

They encouraged all sorts of Africans to join them, and required the men to be true to them by taking an oath which they held very sacred. Those who refused to take the oath, whether they had come to them of their own free will

105

or had been made prisoners, were instantly put to death.

A guard was placed night and day over the women, who, for their defence, carried two or three knives. They got their salt from Long Bay and established a convenient place for boiling it. Sometimes they bought gunpowder in Kingston from a Jew who lived in the town.

Discipline at Nanny Town was strict; loyalty and reliability were essential, courage and initiative were highly esteemed; self-sufficiency was a desired goal, and the fidelity of women had to be ensured to prevent internal disruption. Surrender was out of the question. One withdrew or retreated only in order to re-group, recuperate, and counter-attack. The spirit of these people was unquenchable. They could not be subordinated or subjugated.

On October 9th, 1735, John Gregory reported that the military were still in possession of "the Negro town (Nanny Town):

> "it is a place very uncomfortable, though healthy, and the expense and difficulty of supplying it with provisions is very great. The soldiers who first possessed it quitted it on the pretence of wanting provisions.
>
> The Militia were afterwards sent (there) and remained over 6 months while Martial Law lasted. When that ceased there was no power to detain them longer, and no money to engage them voluntarily. So a party of soldiers have again been sent to relieve them. If they desert, the Negroes who are not far away, will be in again, and we shall have (to start all over)".

CHAPTER 17

QUAO, THE INVISIBLE HUNTER

The Windward Maroons who survived the destruction of Nanny Town in 1734 withdrew into the trackless wastes of the mountains. Among them was a man called Quao.

Quao appeared to be a fairly recent runaway. At the time of the fall of Nanny Town he may already have become a person of consequence among the Windward Maroons. Certainly in the next few years he rose to become their foremost military captain.

Soldiers and militia told tales about a refuge which the Windwards had in the Blue Mountains. According to the stories, the Maroons would be pursued into what appeared to be a dead-end gorge, blocked at the blind end by a waterfall. The sides of the gorge were high and precipitous and the waterfall was a thundering cataract against the far cliff. It would seem that the Maroons entering this place were bound to be trapped, but time after time, hunted Maroons, running into the gorge a dozen minutes before their pursuers, would vanish completely. It wasn't until many years afterwards, during times of peace, that it was discovered that there was a cave at a certain spot behind the waterfall and that the water itself was not quite the solid mass that it seemed. Fleeing Maroons would duck through the falls, enter the cave, then slip through a side passage into an adjoining valley where reserve supplies of food and powder were kept.

About the time of the last big effort against Cudjoe, which ended in the peace treaty, a force was assembled to seek the new town of the Windward Maroons. This force was commanded by Lieutenant George Concannon, who had lived in the island for some time and was the brother of Matthew Concannon, Attorney General of Jamaica. The second in command was Lieutenant Philip Thicknesse who had come to Jamaica to join an Independent Company, after failing to get a commission in a regiment being raised to serve in the Colony of Georgia in America.

When he first arrived, Thicknesse was stationed at a place called "Bagnell's Thickets" on the north side of the island. While there he was frequently sent out with about twenty-five men to search for "wild negroes". The Government awarded seventy pounds for every pair of wild negroes' ears that was brought in, but Thicknesse never managed to get a single pair. For this he was most grateful, for such a system of bounty-hunting appalled him.

After a year at Bagnell's Thickets, Philip Thicknesse was sent to a post at Port Maria in the parish of St. Mary. He was subsequently transferred to Hobby which was five miles from the sea in the parish of St. George, and was under the command of Lieutenant George Concannon.

The parish of St. George was one of the finest and most fertile in Jamaica. It had once abounded in sugar estates but had been "laid desolate by the Wild Negroes". Thicknesse found that the Hobby garrison had to send thirty miles to get rum and other necessaries.

At night they could not go outside the walls of the post as the rebels would be all around. Often when the sentries called out: "All's well", derisive rebel voices would reply from the darkness: "Ki! Ki! Buckra call 'All's well,' while we thief them corn."

Not long after Thicknesse arrived, Concannon was reinforced with fifty militiamen and seventy baggage carriers, and was ordered to locate a town of the Windward Maroons which was believed to lie at the head of the Spanish River, on or near its banks.

After three days of marching they came to a place where the recent footprints of many men and dogs were clearly visible. This was a sure sign that a Maroon settlement was not far away. It was getting dark, however, so Concannon and Thicknesse made camp for the night with the intention of launching a swift attack early the next morning.

At dawn they moved out and almost immediately sighted smoke rising in the distance. A little farther and they saw that it was coming from a cluster of houses just ahead. Forming up quickly they charged the settlement, confident of taking its inhabitants completely by surprise.

With guns at the ready, they went through the seventy-four huts which stood in the clearing. In each one a fire was burning but there was not a living soul in sight.

Quao's lookouts had long ago spotted the advancing force, and during the night the occupants of the huts had gathered up their belongings and fled, leaving fires burning in their huts to make it appear that they were still occupied. Fires were usually kept burning at night to drive off mosquitoes.

This settlement was not, in fact, the new town of the Windwards, but only a temporary resort built in the area because of the good hunting and fishing which it provided. Concannon conferred with Thicknesse and the young Scottish Surgeon. In their exuberance they advised him to burn the town and follow the Maroons. Concannon agreed.

The troops set fire to the huts and immediately set out in pursuit. It was easy to follow the trail of the Maroons, for they broke and cut away the bushes as they went, dropping a yam or cocoa here and a plantain there; fleeing as though in panic.

Marching at the double, the men came suddenly upon a cooking fire over which a piece of jerk hog was broiling. They were jubilant for it now seemed that they were so close to the Windwards that their cooks did not even have time to take the food off the fire. They pushed on at even greater speed; but this was rough, broken country, and presently their steps began to slow and the weaker men began to fall behind. They marched until they were utterly weary but they never caught sight of one Maroon; although they heard dogs barking in the distance. Presently they stopped and turned back.

But now they were in trouble for they seemed to be lost. No one was sure how to get back to the base in the lowlands, so they headed for the Spanish river. They planned to rest on the river bank and then follow the stream on its downward course to the sea. In this way they hoped to get back to country with which they were more familiar. According to Thicknesse:

> "The rivers in Jamaica are the best passes for foot passengers, except in heavy rains, and then they carry all before them".

Because Thicknesse was second in command he was at the rear of the column, behind baggage carriers and all. They marched "Hedge fashion", one after another in single file. Concannon was up front, just behind the advance guard. Thicknesse was about a mile away from him. He wanted to talk with Concannon so he asked that the militia Lieutenant take his place, so he could join Concannon at the head of the column. This was done.

On their way to the river they were overtaken by a heavy rainstorm. The trail turned to slippery mud under their feet and their misery was increased by wet, heavy, uncomfortable clothing. After a while they could see the river and their spirits rose.

All this time however, quite unknown to them, Quao's scouts had hung on to their flanks and rear. They had been under the observation of silent, fleet-footed scouts every step of the way; from the deserted village to the point where they turned back, and now on their present course to the river. The scouts had kept pace with them tirelessly and always out of sight. Concannon and Thicknesse had been hunting Quao and his people, but now they were themselves being hunted.

As soon as the scouts were certain which way the column was going they returned to the main body of warriors. Quao was informed of the number and composition of the enemy and was told that they were heading for the river. Travelling rapidly, the Maroons got ahead of the stumbling column and prepared an ambush for them not far from the river.

The men approached the river, thankful that they would now be able to find their way out of these terrible, unknown mountains. Quao, watching from ambush, allowed the advance guard to pass through the trap, and then fell furiously on the column.

The surprise was complete. Terror and panic exploded amid the ranks. The militia broke and ran. The slaves who were carrying the baggage threw down their loads and scampered after the militia. The regular troops plunged into the river with Concannon and Thicknesse and quickly waded for cover behind large sections of hillside which had fallen down and lay in the middle of the water.

Crouched behind this barrier they could hear the Maroons talking and shouting all around, but could see no one. Filled with alarm at the unexpected turn of events and fearful of being captured and perhaps tortured, they began firing wildly at every puff of smoke which indicated the presence of Maroon sharpshooters.

The rain clouds drifted away and the sun came out. Its rays bore down oppressively upon them. For four and a half uncomfortable hours they stood, up to their waists in water, loading and firing rapidly but with little effect, until their ammunition was almost finished.

Suddenly a shot rang out from the other side of the river

111

and a bullet went through a man's knee. It seemed that
some of the Windwards had crossed over and were preparing to attack on their exposed side. Once more panic rose
among the men. They abandoned their position and
splashing madly across the river in a hail of Maroon bullets, raced into the woods leaving their dead and wounded
behind.

Men who seemed mortally wounded, "defied their
wounds, agonies and miseries, and jumping up" followed
their fleeing commander and his deputy. One in particular,
had been shot through the body, and as he ran, received
another bullet which entered in the back, and came out
through his belly. Yet, he not only made it out of the river,
but clambered up a steep mountain before he collapsed and
begged his comrades to finish him off.

At the time of the Spanish River fight, Thicknesse was a
raw and inexperienced youth, perhaps not yet twenty years
old, and never before exposed to the fire of an enemy. He
admitted that they all ran in panic, and ascended the
steepest hills as fast as crippled, fatigued and frightened
men could. Behind them they heard "the horrid shouts,
drums and rejoicing of (the) victorious enemy in the river
below", as they took possession of the salt beef, bread,
hams, etc. from the discarded baggage.

The militia, who had fled nearly five hours before, managed to reach the safety of outlying settlements that same
evening; but night began to overtake Concannon and his
men as they clambered up the heights.

Concannon was seized with a violent fever before they
had gone up the first steep hill. Thicknesse thought it was
caused by standing so many hours in the water, with a per-
pendicular sun burning down on his head and a mind
deeply suffering from the shattering blow which Quao had
dealt him.

In spite of Concannon's condition they thought it prudent
to climb to the highest hill. There Concannon collapsed. He

lay down and told Thicknesse to go on with those of the men who were able to follow him. The drummer who had been shot through the wrist and through both thighs cried loudly for water. Concannon was also suffering from extreme thirst. They were all thirsty; but there was not a drop of water to be had.

One of the soldiers had a little hammock made from a barrack sheet. They slung it between two trees and with great difficulty, got Concannon into it; for he was a tall, bulky man. Concannon "made water" in his hat and moistened his lips with it from time to time.

Night fell. Because of their precarious situation it was necessary to maintain a profound silence. "Every man bore his wretched condition without a groan". Thicknesse lay on his back with his tongue out, praying to God to let the dew fall, even though it was considered fatal to those who exposed themselves to it.

Next morning, as the miserable group staggered along, they came upon an enormous cotton tree. Its spurs (exposed roots) had grown so fantastically, that they formed a great reservoir in which rain water had collected. It was black as coffee, but more desirable to them than a treasure of gold. On the evening of that day they arrived at the sea where they found people who ministered to them.

Quao's defeat of Concannon was a masterpiece from beginning to end; a brilliant exhibition of the art of guerilla warfare. It completely destroyed the confidence of the colonists and was the last major engagement in the First Maroon War.

Three months later a party of three hundred soldiers commanded by Captain Adair set out to find Quao to make peace. Along with them went Lieutenant Philip Thicknesse.

By this time Cudjoe had signed his treaty with Guthrie and Sadler, and Captain Adair was authorised to offer similar terms to Quao. Some time before Adair reached the

Windwards' town, however, Quao captured a soldier who told him that Cudjoe had made peace, and informed him of the terms of the treaty.

The captured soldier called himself the Laird of Leharret. He pleaded the case for peace so eloquently that Quao was persuaded. He put bracelets on the wrists of Leharret as a gift, and made up his mind to send him to Governor Trelawny offering similar terms to those which he was told Cudjoe had accepted. Before he could take such a momentous step however, he felt it necessary to inform the old woman who lived in his camp, who was a high priestess of Obi; and to get her consent. Philip Thicknesse, who came across her shortly after, was greatly impressed by her. She terrified him. He called her "the Old Hag" and "the Old Obeah Woman", and said she wore a girdle around her waist, which had "nine or ten different knives in sheaths" hanging from it. He had no doubt that some of those knives had been "plunged in human flesh and blood".

This old woman of tremendous presence and power was undoubtedly Nanny. When Quao told her what he wanted to do she opposed the idea. She felt that to make a proposal for peace would be interpreted as a sign of weakness. If the British wanted peace let them come and ask for it, as they had gone to Cudjoe.

The impression is given that Nanny would have preferred not to make peace; not to make any accommodation with the British. It is said that she decreed that Leharret should be put to death since he had led a party to their camp, presumably to attack it. Quao was disappointed but, at that moment, he dared not oppose the old woman.

Coromantees believed that practitioners of Obi had access to powerful spiritual forces, and that they made charms which could influence spirits and cause them to act for or against a person. The magical powers which old Maroon legends attribute to Nanny, were the powers that the old lady in Quao's camp was thought to possess, and Quao felt compelled to obey her. So, Leharret was executed, and Quao and his people waited to see what Governor Trelawny would do.

Captain Adair and his party, accompanied by Lieutenant Philip Thicknesse, made their way along the very difficult route towards Quao's town. Describing the terrain Thicknesse said:

> "The mountains are exceedingly steep and high, much broken, and split or divided by earthquakes, and many parts inaccessible, but by men who always go barefoot, and who can hold by withes with their toes, almost as firmly as we can with our fingers.

> Nothing but ocular demonstration can convey an idea of the steep and dangerous precipices we passed, and which men wearing shoes could not be so secure as Negroes barefooted, (who have) toe fingers as well as hands to secure them from falling."

Adair's party was guided by one of Quao's abeng men who had recently been captured. This man had learned that Cudjoe had made peace and was most anxious (or had been strongly persuaded) that his own people, the Windward Maroons, should do the same. However, he was not quite sure that Adair's intentions were really peaceful, so he warned him not to try to take the Windward Town by force as it was situated in a very strong position. He said that the lookouts, of which he himself had been one, could give warning of the approach of a body of men, or even of a single person, five or six hours before such a force or person could hope to reach the place.

After two days of marching through thickly-wooded country and on the edge of dangerous precipices; Quao's captured lookout led Captain Adair's men to the foot of a high and steep mountain where the Maroons had some of their provision grounds. Here they halted and the lookout

115

blew his abeng, giving a certain call whereby the Maroon guards would know it was their missing companion. One of the guards returned an answer on his abeng but no man showed himself.

After waiting a little, Adair shouted through a speaking trumpet that he had come to make peace. He said that Cudjoe himself had made peace and had been granted freedom, and that he had come to offer the Windwards the same terms.

Quao held a brief consultation with his principal warriors and then, with characteristic Maroon caution, agreed to exchange hostages to ensure good faith while Adair and himself discussed the preliminaries. A Maroon Captain was sent down the hill and Lieutenant Thicknesse went up in exchange.

As soon as this was done Quao gave an order and scores of Maroons, armed with cutlasses, quickly cleared away an acre of brushwood on the side of the hill. Quao's fighting force then drew up in formation on the cleared acre, exposed to the full view of the troops.

Quao heard the terms proposed by Captain Adair and agreed to them. He does not appear to have spent much time in weighing them for he had already got their substance from Leharret and was in favour of them, especially since Cudjoe had accepted similar terms. Nanny apparently raised no strong objection, for the British had been obliged to come to them. Nevertheless, a fundamental disagreement may have developed between Nanny and Quao which, later, may have caused a split in the ranks of the Windwards. Having made his decision Quao allowed a part of the troops to march to his town. It was only then that the soldiers began to appreciate the strength of the place, and how lucky they were that they had not been called upon to storm it. They climbed up a narrow path in single file and observed on every hand holes dug into the mountainside to provide cover for the Maroons. There were also sticks planted in the earth and slanted across each other so that guns could be rested on them. These were skilfully placed so that every angle and turn in the steep ascent could be raked with shot in the event of an attack.

The troops marched to the top of the hill and then found that they had to march down another narrow path into the valley before they could reach the town. Nearing the bottom the path widened and they were able to go two abreast.

They marched into the town in fine style, with drums beating and much ceremony. They came on so impressively that the women and children of the Maroons, still unable to believe that the English soldiers could enter their town on a peaceful mission, fled into the adjoining woods. However, when they saw their men stand fast and it became obvious that a battle was not about to begin, they returned.

An atmosphere of calm fell on the town, which was soon broken rather dramatically when a large party of militia under Colonel Robert Bennett came marching over the hill. Bennett had been ranging the countryside with his men also seeking the Windwards. When word reached him that Adair had been successful in getting Quao to agree to make peace, he hurried up determined to seize the glory for himself.

Being of superior rank to Adair, Bennett insisted that the treaty be signed in his name. Immediately a quarrel broke out between the regular officers of Adair's command and Bennett's militia officers. Adair ordered his men to stand to arms. The Maroons, watching the quarrel develop and not knowing how it might affect them, took up their weapons. But Quao, understanding the struggle for power and prestige that was taking place, quieted his men and watchfully awaited the outcome. Thicknesse, who witnessed the scene, thought that "if Quao had not (once) been a plantation slave, who knew something of the customs and manners of White people, all (would have) been lost".

Under the menace of the guns of the regular troops

Colonel Bennett backed down and the peace was concluded by Captain Adair who, in fact, had done all the work. Nevertheless, Bennett apparently pursued the matter under conditions where his rank stood him in better stead. The treaty with the Windward Maroons which appeared in the journals of the House of Assembly as being made with Captain Quao, was signed with Bennett's name. The document stated that the successors to Quao were to be "Thomboy, Apong, Blackwell and Clash".

Thicknesse wrote about his experiences when he was a hostage in Quao's town. He was a bright, curious fellow, eagerly observing things and not afraid to ask questions. He stayed in Quao's house, had friendly conversations with him and asked sharp questions about the fate of captured soldiers, which Quao evaded. He claimed to have seen "the poor Laird of Leharret's underjaw, fixed as an ornament" to the abeng of one of the hornmen; and also the upper teeth of men slain at the Spanish River fight, drilled through and worn as anklets and wrist bracelets "by women". He noted that even though Quao's children saw him in "civil conversation" with their father "they could not refrain from striking their pointed fingers (as they would knives) against his breast, saying in derision: "buckra, buckra (white man)".

Thicknesse said that Quao spoke tolerably good English and seemed a reasonable man. When he asked him if Concannon's contingent had done any damage to his men at the Spanish River fight Quao pointed to his face.

"You see this hole in my cheek?" he said. "One of your shot bounce against my gun, fly up, and make this."

Quao said he was the only one of the Windward force who had "lost a drop of blood".

It was in Quao's town at this time that Thicknesse saw the "Old Obeah Woman". He feared she might pass the "sentence of death" on him, as he had been told she had done to Leharret.

Quao's treaty was signed on June 23rd, 1739, nearly

four months after Cudjoe's treaty. It brought to an end the long drawn-out war with "rebellious slaves" which had started at the time of the British conquest of Jamaica; but it did not end the fight for freedom.

After Quao's peace, the question of where the Windwards should settle became a burning issue. It was at this time that the fundamental disagreement which seemed to have developed between Nanny and Quao, came out into the open. The Windwards split into two main groups. One group went with Quao and settled in a place called Crawford Town. The other group went with Nanny to live on land patented to them by Governor Edward Trelawny. The land was surveyed by Thomas Newland and the patent was entered on April 20th, 1741. The place is now called Moore Town.

Quao's group only remained at Crawford Town for about fourteen years. In 1754 there was a serious outbreak of violence in the town and, as a result, the Governor, Admiral Charles Knowles, removed them to a place three miles to the south where a new town was built. It was called Charles Town after Admiral Knowles. The site contained two hundred and six and a half acres and was purchased from one Colin McKenzie. It was not paid for until 1770 when John Henderson, then in possession of the title, received four hundred and twelve pounds.

When he was in his seventieth year, Philip Thicknesse looked back on those exciting days in Jamaica and said:

> "All the regular troops in Europe could not have conquered the Wild Negroes by force of arms; and if Mr. Trelawny (the Governor) had not wisely given them what they contended for LIBERTY, they would, in all probability have been, at this day, masters of the whole country".

CHAPTER 18

THE DEATH OF AN IDEA

The Maroon movement had grown out of an extreme crisis when the inhabitants of Spanish Jamaica were uprooted from their homes and driven out of the island by a superior British force. The Africans who held on and laid the foundations of the Maroon movement risked their lives and concentrated all their energies to maintain the freedom they had seized during the five-year struggle for the possession of Jamaica.

The rugged mountains and forests provided the physical environment for survival, but success depended on the extraordinary determination of the rebel/runaways and their ability to overcome every hardship. Of necessity they produced a warrior community whose virtues were strength, courage, endurance, skill in the use of weapons and in the practice of an unorthodox form of warfare.

The people who initiated the movement, and the rebels and runaways who later dominated it, were the toughest and most resolute of their kind; the best and bravest. Their proud spirit enabled them to prevail against the might of the British Colony and compel it eventually to sue for peace.

When the time came to negotiate the peace however, the Maroon society, based primarily on warlike pursuits, was at a distinct disadvantage. It lacked the required experience and the language and literate skills to counter the British, who were becoming more and more proficient in the subtle arts of diplomacy. The moment the Maroons ceased to oppose Imperial Britain, the noble purpose which had governed their existence started to decay, and the Colonial net which they had so heroically avoided began to entangle them.

One apparently harmless symptom of this was that Maroons began to adopt "the names of the gentlemen of the island". African names such as Cudjoe, Quao, Cuffee, Acompong, etc., began to disappear. According to the historian Bryan Edwards:

> "Of late years, a practice has universally obtained among the Maroons (in imitation of the other free blacks) of attaching themselves to different families among the English, and desiring gentlemen of consideration to allow the Maroon children to bear their names. Montague James, John Palmer, Tharp, Jarrett, Parkinson, Shirley, White, and many others, are names adopted in this way".

This was a kind of image superimposition, and putting up of oneself for adoption, a client's acknowledgement of the patron. It was in direct opposition to the old spirit of defiance which had seen the rebel/runaways through every kind of trouble, and it was the sort of guileless subordination which Nanny had feared. However, there were some who saw this 'name adoption process' as a mere ploy; an attempt to flatter prominent colonists into supporting the Maroons and becoming their advocates. The British were only too eager to enter into this client/patron relationship, and the increasing posture of superiority which it tempted them to assume, was to lead to an explosion in 1795.

Maroon chiefs were obliged by the treaties to wait on the Governor every year, if necessary. No office of chief which requires the holder to be at the beck and call of another power can retain its authority for long. Cudjoe and his immediate successors managed to maintain the prestige of their office for about thirty years, but they did it by the sheer force of personality, by a despotic exercise of power and by a tradition of respect founded on the memory of great deeds.

The last of the chiefs to wield this kind of strong influence and authority was a man named "Furry", who through some disagreement, left Trelawny Town with his supporters. He simply squatted (or captured) a section of Dr. Mark Hardyman's three-hundred-acre property in St. James, which was three miles beyond the limits of the one thousand five hundred acres allotted to the Trelawny Maroons by the treaty.

Hardyman got a patent for the property in 1755, and bought seventy slaves and the necessary mules and steers to begin sugar cultivation. But when he re-surveyed the land he found that Furry had built houses and planted provisions on a part of it.

Hardyman made a petition to the Government asking for an order to command Furry and his followers to get off his land and return to their town. He said he was willing to give Furry fifty pounds for any improvements he had made on the land. A committee of the whole House of Assembly in 1758, recommended that the Trelawny Maroons be required to clear, settle and plant "thirty acres of provisions", and assist Furry and his followers to build houses to accommodate them, on some part of the one thousand five hundred acres of the treaty land, at public expense. The new town to be built for Furry should be as good as that which he was being asked to give up on Hardyman's land. Furry's New Town was about half a mile from Cudjoe's Old Town (Trelawny Town) and was to play a big part in the coming explosion of 1795.

Throughout much of the period following the treaties, the Maroon chiefs or "Colonels", as they came to be called, paid regular visits to King's House, the residence of the

Governor. King's House stood in the square at Spanish Town, which at the time was the capital of Jamaica. The chiefs were accompanied by their principal officers and were received with ceremony by the Governor, who gave them old swords, pistols, finely-laced coats, ruffled shirts and waist-coats as presents. They also wore a silver chain with a medal on which their names were inscribed. It is said that the chiefs placed a high value on these gifts and that they wore them on special occasions, such as when they were visited by European gentlemen curious to see how the Maroons lived.

The inhabitants of Spanish Town would gape when the Maroons arrived in the capital dressed in their finery. The Europeans thought they looked very picturesque, but it was all a comic-opera kind of buffoonery which easily led to ridicule.

The European Superintendent, nominated by the Governor to live among the Maroons according to the terms of the treaties, was supposed to maintain friendly relations; preserve peace and prevent slaves from congregating in the town in which he resided. He also took an active part in adjusting disputes which arose chiefly from gambling and drunkenness, and sent patrols out on duty. He had power to hold a court with the assistance of four Maroons to try those who disobeyed orders, who provoked or participated in tumults, who departed from the town without leave or stayed out longer than was permitted. He could inflict any punishment, except those pertaining to loss of life or limb, or banishment to another country.

Every three months the Superintendent had to make a report to the Governor on the number of people living in his town, how many could bear arms and how many were unfit for duty. He also had to report on the number or women and children, the state of the roads, etc. The Superintendent, in fact, had the power of a chief, and although it was said that all the disputes of the Maroons were settled by their chiefs, and that they had implicit confidence in these chiefs and usually obeyed them without argument, yet the presence of the superintendent with all his powers helped to weaken the chief's authority. Indeed, after the death of Furry, the respect attached to the office of Chief Maroon Captain declined sharply until it became no more than a vehicle for the observance of a few ceremonies and courtesies.

From 1655 to the signing of Quao's treaty in 1739, about five generations of rebel Africans had participated in the struggle with the English colonists. Those eighty-four years of almost continuous hostility had seen many heroic deeds and had thrown up several great leaders. But now new generations were taking over who had not had to fight for freedom or been a witness to the great deeds of the past. The growing impotence of their leaders in the face of the representatives of the British King was especially obvious to these generations.

Shortly after the peace treaties and the installation of superintendents as watchdogs over the Maroons, colonial authorities began to curtail the freedom of the Maroons and undermine the authority of their communities with successive laws.

One of these laws prevented the Maroons from leaving their towns at will and from staying out as long as they pleased. They had to get permission to leave and if they stayed seven days beyond the time allowed they could be seized and sent home for trial. Another law which could be looked upon as an amendment to the one just mentioned, recognised the problem of the increasing Maroon population in relation to the restricted size of the treaty lands. It allowed them to give up their rights as Maroons and to live as free people in any part of the island except in other Maroon towns. In such circumstances they were no longer required to live under the supervision of superintendents but were obliged to join the militia and so be available for service whenever the need arose.

Many of the Maroons ignored both laws. They wandered all about the island and whole families sometimes left their towns without permission or without giving up their rights as Maroons, and settled on the back-lands. Because of this constant movement it was difficult for anyone to say at any given time just how many Maroons there were. This is not surprising in view of the fact that the size of the Jamaican population in those days was not accurately known. It was not until 1844 that a proper census was taken.

The historian Bryan Edwards said that the Spaniards in 1655 had 1,500 slaves who became Maroons, but this was just a guess. G.W. Bridges in his *Annals of Jamaica* said that Juan de Bolas alone had about 150 fighting men, but his general population figures are also not considered reliable. Dallas, another historian, said that the number of Maroons who surrendered in 1739 did not amount to 600. In 1770 Dallas estimated they consisted of 885 men, women and children.

There were five Maroon towns: Trelawny Town in St. James, Accompong Town in St. Elizabeth, Scotts Hall in St. Mary, Charles Town and Moore Town in Portland. The Charles Town and Moore Town Maroons were called the Windwards.

A census of Maroons in these towns for 1773 showed:

Trelawny Town	-	414
Accompong	-	103
Charles Town	-	219
Moore Town	-	143
Scotts Hall	-	49
TOTAL	-	928

Judging by the salaries of the Superintendents, the Trelawny Town Superintendent appeared to be the most senior, and the most important, of the lot. In 1769, he received two hundred pounds per annum, while the Superintendents of Accompong, Charles Town, Moore Town and Scotts Hall each got one hundred pounds.

Trelawny Town was Cudjoe's own domain. It stood on an uneven ridge and the houses were built on little heights with gullies running between them in various directions. The houses were constructed on a foundation of posts which were set four or five into the ground. They had thatched roofs, earthen floors and a yard made of clay and ashes rammed so hard that it was smooth and as solid as cement. The chiefs sometimes had larger houses with shingle roofs and wooden floors.

The Trelawny community included Furry's New Town, which was joined to the Old Town by a steep narrow path running for half a mile through a wood. Because it was situated on a high ridge, Cudjoe's domain was blessed with a cool, healthy climate. In the morning, cool, rolling fog drifted over hill and valley, and when the sun melted it away

> a magnificent view of the surrounding country side was revealed; a countryside of descending mountains and woods stretching away to the far-off sea.
> *DALLAS, History of the Maroons.*

Accompong Town, lying to the South in St. Elizabeth was also included in this region.

The Maroons flourished in this hard, beautiful country. Their diet and the years of strenuous, outdoor activity produced men who were not only strong but of magnificent physique. Dallas said that they excelled all the other types of Africans in Jamaica, being "blacker, taller, and in every respect, handsomer". They were further described by him as being

" erect and lofty; vigour appeared upon their mus-
cles and their motions displayed agility. Their eyes
were quick, wild and fiery (and) they possessed most,
if not all, of the senses in a superior degree".

There were people who said that the Maroons had an
acute sense of smell and they could track down parties of
runaway slaves, even when they were a long distance away,
simply by following the smell of their wood fires.

Bryan Edwards, who disliked the Maroons intensely,
could not refrain from admiring their superior physiques.
He said:

> Their mode of living, and daily pursuits, undoubtedly
> strengthened the frame, and served to exalt them to
> great bodily perfection.

> Such fine persons are seldom beheld among any other
> class of Africans or native blacks. Their motion dis-
> plays a combination of strength and agility. The mus-
> cles (neither hidden nor depressed by clothing) are
> very prominent and strongly marked. Their sight with-
> al is wonderfully acute, and their hearing quick.
>
> *History of the West Indies*

Unlike other observers however, Bryan Edwards did not
think much of their sense of smell, and he thought their
sense of taste was "depraved" because on one occasion some
of them preferred to drink new rum fresh from the still
rather than the wine which he offered them!

After the treaties no effort was made to educate the
Maroons or instruct them in any gainful activity suitable to
a peaceful existence. It was believed by many that the
Superintendents placed among them were men of little or
no education and that the posts were sinecures. The
Maroons were not well acquainted with English and spoke
the same rough dialect used by the slaves. This was
described as a combination of African dialects with a mix-
ture of Spanish and broken English.

Dallas said that as far as religion was concerned they held the vague belief that:

> Accompong was the God of the heavens, the creator of all things, and a deity of infinite goodness; but they neither offered sacrifices to him nor had any form of worship.

Edwards stated that they worshiped with "enthusiastic zeal and reverential ardour", that they believed in "Obi" and their Obeah men had great power among them. We can infer from these vague descriptions that the Maroons kept their religious practices very much to themselves, and that Europeans were able to learn very little about them.

The 1739 treaty had cheated the Trelawny Maroons in more ways than one. For instance, one third of the 1,500 acres which they had been given was rocky land. Much of the rest was poor earth covered with fern and foxtail grass. Only about 100 acres was really good land worth cultivating. Because of this the Maroons could not afford to rely on crop-growing alone. They kept pigs, cattle and horses which could feed on the acres of grass and even in the woods. They specialised in mares from which horses were bred for sale.

On the cultivable land the Maroons grew plantains, coffee, cassava, cocoa, corn, yam and several types of fruit and food trees. Chief among these was the avocado pear. They also planted pineapples in their hedges.

The women did much of the cultivating. They cleared the land for planting by putting fire around the trunks of trees until they were burnt through in the middle and fell of their own weight. Edwards thought little of their ability to cultivate. He described their grounds as always being in a shocking state of neglect and ruin. He claimed to have seen only small patches of Indian corn, yams and a few straggling trees, and appears to have ignored the fact that most of the land was worthless.

While the women planted, the men attended to the livestock and hunted. They caught birds and land crabs but their chief game was the wild boar which abounded in the interior of the island. They had a way of curing the flesh without salting it, and the resulting dish was called "jerked pork". The Maroons had a special fondness for jerked pork and also for ringtail pigeons. They loved to entertain and when important people came to see them their tables would be spread with wild boar, land crabs, pigeons and fish. Young Maroon girls might be offered for the further entertainment of the visitors and the occasion would usually develop into a hearty and boisterous affair.

Learning the ways of peace and recognising the need to augment their meagre revenue through trade, the Maroons quickly grasped the value of money and became accustomed to its use. They sold horses, foodstuff, livestock and jerked pork to the settlers and in the market-places. Some of the men hired themselves to the planters and new settlers to clear land and plant.

To earn extra money they made tobacco. Apparently they did mot grow the plant but bought tobacco leaves from estates and sometimes carried them for as much as 20 or 30 miles in bags knitted from tree bark and fibres. The bag rested on the back of the bearer and was attached by a cloth or fibres to the forehead. After the tobacco leaves had been cured they were twisted into long ropes, rolled into balls and carried down to the estates for sale. The finished product probably resembled the "Jackass Rope" (rope of tobacco coiled into round bundles) which Jamaican farmers still make.

With the money they earned, the Maroons bought salted beef, alcoholic drinks, firearms, and ammunition. They didn't spend much on clothes or on the trinkets which unsophisticated people usually load themselves with.

Maroon men were allowed to have more than one wife. Most men kept only one, however, as having several wives could be an expensive business. For one thing, it was the custom that if a man gave a present to one wife he was bound to give a present of equal value to any other wives he possessed. The Maroons also consorted quite freely with slave women on the estates which they visited. The planters turned a blind eye to this practice as they believed that children born from a Maroon father would be stronger and therefore more valuable.

Edwards regarded the Maroons as a brutal people. Ignoring the excesses of the planter class to which he belonged, he spoke of Maroon cruelty to captives and to their women and children. He based his belief that they were cruel to their women on the fact that Maroon women did heavy agricultural work and the men were able to have more than one wife. Using his own Christian, English, middle-class background as a yardstick, he therefore concluded that the women were bound to be wretched. He does say, however, that Maroon wives did not quarrel with each other, but this he put down to the fact that the miseries of their situation left them neither the leisure nor the desire to do so. He concluded that they were cruel to their children because he was told that some Maroon fathers, when drunk, were known to seize an infant which was crying too much and dash it against a rock.

One of the ways the Maroons had of earning money was to capture runaway slaves. The treaty promised that Maroons who brought in runaways "would be satisfied for their trouble as the Legislature should appoint." In other words they would receive a reward. After a time, however, some of the more hardened hunters grew more callous that they didn't seem to care whether they returned a man alive, or only brought in his head.

One of the reasons for this may have been that runaways became more fierce in their resistance to capture, perhaps preferring death to punishment and continued enslavement. At any rate the planters were not very happy

over the killing of runaways, for slaves were valuable property and of no use to their owners dead. To give the
Maroons an added incentive to refrain from killing, a law
was passed promising a bonus in addition to the usual
reward for every fugitive brought back alive. This bonus
was called "mile money".

But capturing runaways and rebels was not just a way
of earning money. It provided a very necessary release for
the turbulent spirits of a people whose whole way of life
had been founded on strenuous physical activity and dangerous pursuits. The freedom to range over the unsettled
interior without hindrance, the continued use of the great
wilderness as a hunting-ground, and the exciting and
rewarding game of hunting fugitives, were calculated to
satisfy the aggressive needs of the young Maroons and keep
them quiet and submissive to the colonial government.

One example of their service against rebels appeared in
the Journal of the Assembly of Jamaica for 1752. In connection with the death of the notorious rebel, Quaco Venter,
it was recorded that George Currie, an officer at
Accompong Town, had many times gone out after Quaco
Venter and his gang. In February, 1752 he captured
Beauty, one of Quaco Venter's wives. Shortly after, while
he was at Lluidas Vale, Currie set his party on the trail of
Quaco, and a fortnight after Beauty's capture, he was shot
dead by Currie's men. The Committee of the House which
considered the action thought that the killing of Quaco
Venter was "a very extraordinary service, as he was a dangerous rebel (who) killed many, and was a great terror in
the area". The Committee recommended that one hundred
pounds be paid to Currie.

Eight years later, the Maroons of Trelawny Town and
Accompong were paid four hundred and fifty pounds, "for
their services in the capture and destruction" of rebels during the great rebellion of 1760. 1781 found Scotts Hall and
Moore Town Maroons complaining that they had not been

paid an additional two hundred pounds for taking the notorious outlaw Three Finger Jack. They had captured several of Jack's men who had been brought to trial and executed. A petition of Bernard Nalty of November 14th, said that he had expended and laid out "divers sums of money in subsisting himself and sundry Maroons under his command in search of the notorious runaway called Three Finger Jack, and his party". He had also expended sums to support the Maroons and himself when attending at Yallahs Bay in St. David, at the trial of five runaways of Jack's party. The House resolved to pay the Maroons the additional two hundred pounds.

Even though they had now become slave hunters, the Maroons still maintained vigorous and friendly relations with estates slaves, and the young Maroons were never slow to mix with attractive females. They were allowed to hold dances in their towns whenever they liked, provided the dances were in the daytime. A limited number of slaves could be invited but they had to return to their estates before night.

Sometimes, a Maroon would fall in love with a slave and persuade her to leave the estate. Also, contrary to their reputation as hunters of runaways, Maroons would often try to harbour fugitives. To put a stop to these practices, another law was passed which said that any Maroon who persuaded a slave to leave an estate, or who harboured runaways, could be punished by being transported. Maroons found guilty of these offences could be sold as slaves to people in other Caribbean islands or on the American mainland.

There were many laws which gradually whittled away the independence of the Maroons. No party of them on the hunt for runaways could be larger than twelve, including the leader. No party could set out without the written permission of the Superintendent, nor could it remain out longer than twenty days. Maroons could not be hired by

Europeans without a written agreement and any debts which they owed, or which were owing to them, had to be settled by two magistrates. They were, nevertheless, to be protected from flogging or any other ill-treatment.

It must be emphasized that many of these laws had not been in the original treaties signed by Cudjoe and Quao. The English found it hard to break the proud, independent spirit of the Maroons, and laws were passed whenever a situation arose which indicated that they needed to be curbed. The sum total of these laws soon gave the distinct impression that the Maroons were being treated as a conquered race rather than as a people who had voluntarily agreed to make peace at the request of their antagonists.

There is no doubt that the clauses in the treaty which obliged the Maroons to hunt down rebels and runaways changed the entire character of their society. Before the treaty they were regarded as the refuge of any enslaved person who had the will and the courage to break the chains and strike out for freedom. They were the sanctuary of human dignity for the thousands of enslaved Africans, the symbol of resistance against oppression and inhumanity. Now the treaties reversed their role. They became a kind of mercenary force for the government, not so much dedicated to the protection of free men against criminals and the lawless, but dedicated to the destruction of enslaved men who desired to be free. The noble idea which had cast the Maroons in the role of enemies of oppression and fighters for freedom was almost dead. They carried themselves with the same dignity and fierce pride, but the spirit that had made them great was in danger of withering.

CHAPTER 19

THE RISING STORM

The Maroons may not have been fully aware of the manner in which they were being hedged around by numerous petty laws, but it was not long before they began to grow restless under increasing restraints. At first they channeled their energies and aggressions into the pursuit and capture of runaways and into brisk combats with desperate bands of rebels. In these exercises they helped to keep Jamaica safe from the constant threat of slave rebellions. It was the Maroons who killed the great Coromantee rebel leader, Tacky, in 1760; and Three Finger Jack in 1781.

An example of their usefulness was demonstrated during a critical period of 1766. A group of Coromantees had risen in Westmoreland and thrown the whole parish into a turmoil. Several planters and settlers were killed. Finally a force of colonists caught up with the rebels in the mountains after a long march. There was a brief fight which was terminated when the Coromantees, in typical guerrilla fashion, withdrew into the forest. The colonial force was so worn out with fatigue that they were unable to follow.

Just then a body of Maroons appeared. They had heard of the fight while they were out hunting hogs, and since a fight was to be preferred to almost anything else, they left off the hunt and hurried to the spot where the engagement had taken place. The colonial troops were still unable to move but they pointed out the path which the Coromantees had taken and the Maroons immediately set out in pursuit. They were superb trackers and it was not long before they came upon the Coromantees and engaged them in a death struggle.

By sunset the Maroons had killed or captured two-thirds of the Coromantees and scattered the survivors in the bush. Not content with this they embarked upon a relentless pursuit of the fugitives over the next few days and brought in most of them. For this they received the thanks of the House of Assembly.

This sort of service by the Maroons was used by several writers of the time to justify the policy of allowing them to remain as a separate body. These writers stressed the fact that as a sort of police force they were of incalculable value to the safety of the colony and that they were always willing to support the Government. The historian Dallas pointed out that the Maroons were assembled to assist in repelling the threatened French invasion of 1779 and 1780 which Admiral Rodney's naval victory over Count D'Estaing helped to avert.

In spite of this, there sometimes was more than a suspicion that the Maroons did not "pull their weight." Bryan Edwards, the great detractor of the Maroons, gives two examples from the period of the slave rebellion under Tacky in 1760. He says that a party of Maroons arrived on the scene of action two or three days after the outbreak. The colonial troops had just defeated the rebels in a pitched battle at Heywood Hall. They had killed eight or nine of them, and driven the remainder into the woods. The Maroons were sent after them with the promise of reward for each rebel killed or captured.

They wandered about the woods for a couple of days and then returned with a collection of ears which they claimed to have cut from the heads of rebels they had slain. They were paid for these trophies but Edwards says that it was subsequently discovered that they had not fought with or killed one rebel, and that the ears had been taken from Tacky's men who had fallen in the Heywood Hall fight and been left unburied.

A few days later, a body of Maroons and a detachment of the 74th Regiment were stationed at Down's Cove, a remote place surrounded by deep woods. In the middle of the night they were attacked by Tacky's men. The sentries were shot and the huts in which the soldiers slept were set on fire.

The soldiers ran out into the open. The light of the flames exposed them to the full view of the enemy and dazzled them so that they could not see the rebels. Tacky's men poured in a shower of bullets from all sides and some soldiers were killed. Major Forsyth, in command of the detachment, formed his men into a square and by delivering a brisk and continuous fire, managed to drive off the attackers.

During the whole fight the Maroons could not be found. Their absence was so conspicuous that Forsyth was inclined to believe at first that they were the ones who had attacked him. He found out later that as soon as the rebels attacked, the Maroons had thrown themselves flat on the ground and had remained in that position without firing a shot until the rebels were driven off.

To a certain extent their behaviour on this occasion was probably the natural reaction of trained guerrilla fighters and because of it they suffered not a single casualty. However, it also seemed to imply that in actions of this sort the Maroons were not prepared to sacrifice themselves unduly for their employers. In this respect they were certainly more sophisticated than other "native" troops, who gave their lives with great courage for the maintenance of a colonial power whose glory they could only share as servants.

Edwards believed that the behaviour of the Maroons during Tacky's rebellion showed that "the whites entertained an opinion of them which no part of their conduct at any one period confirmed". He felt that this erroneous opinion of their value was due to the strong impression which their fierce and powerful appearance had on all who saw them; an impression which reduced the colonists almost to a state of awe.

In spite of the many opportunities which they had to work off excess energies, the restlessness among the Maroons continued to grow, and showed itself in many ways. In April, 1774, Captain Davy, then chief of the Scotts Hall Maroons, was engaged with some of his men in one of the frequent hunts for runaways. They were accompanied by a group of rangers under Captain Bennett Smith and the whole party was operating in the Hellshire Hills in southern St. Catherine. They carried out an exhausting search in the rugged Hellshire heights but finding no runaways, descended to the coast and embarked on some boats with the intention of searching nearby Pigeon Island and the Keys that lie off Old Harbour.

Between Old Harbour and the Keys they came upon a dozen merchant ships lying at anchor, and somehow a rumour spread among the Maroons that there was a plan to ship them away from Jamaica on these vessels. Captain Davy and his men had been drinking and were in a very aggressive mood due to their failure to capture any runaways. They landed at a wharf belonging to William Thompson and saw some slaves handling cargo for one of the ships. Davy and his men went up to the slaves and accused one of them of being a runaway. Davy asked the man who his master was, and the man, evidently in no mood to be bossed around by Maroons, pointed in the general direction of the piazza of the warehouse where Thompson was standing and said that his master was over there.

At this time there was a great deal of ill-will between the slaves and the Maroons. The slaves resented the apparent zeal with which the Maroons hunted runaways, forgetting the days when confidential slaves and Black Shots had helped the colonists against them and marked their valuable provision grounds for destruction. Moreover, Maroons, despite their frequent love affairs with slave women and the offspring they left scattered about the estates, had developed an overbearing attitude towards the slaves and a feeling of superiority.

The slaves on the wharf were probably resentful both of the arrogant bearing of the Scotts Hall warriors and the fact that they were on the hunt for runaways. When the slave who was accused of being a runaway answered Davy in a truculent manner, Davy, inflamed by liquor, frustrated by his failure to find runaways and upset by the rumors of transportation, raised his cutlass and chopped the man down.

Immediately a yell of protest went up from the bystanders and the captain of one of the ships that lay close by the wharf shouted to Thompson that the Maroons were killing one of his men. Thompson ran on to the wharf and was followed by some of the seamen who were standing nearby. They jumped on Davy in a group and the Maroon captain, struggling fiercely with one of the ship's masters, dropped his gun.

Thompson seized the gun just as Davy broke free from the seamen and ran up the street. Thompson yelled at him to stop but Davy ran on. The wharf-owner raised the gun and fired a warning shot over Davy's head. As the shot rang out a Charles Town Maroon named "Sam Grant" leapt from a house and fired at Thompson. At that moment a slave stepped in front of Thompson, was hit by the bullet and was killed.

As the slave fell, Sam Grant bolted up the road, reloading his gun as he ran. He raced past curious people who had gathered at windows and doorways attracted by the shots and the shouting, and on past a company of soldiers who were stationed close by. Behind him ran a small boy shouting "Murder!" and "Stop him!" Others soon took up the cry and followed in pursuit of the fleeing Maroon.

Sam Grant ran for about a mile with the hue and cry behind him all the way. Suddenly a young English sea captain off a Bristol ship jumped in the road in front of him with a whip coiled in his hand. The captain's name was Townsend. "Let me pass", cried Sam. "I don't want to hurt you". But Captain Townsend stood his ground, his heavy whip upraised. Sam had now re-loaded his gun and as he approached Townsend he bent his forearm, brought the barrel down upon it, and fired point-blank. The bullet blew off the Captain's thumb, hit him in the throat and killed him instantly. Sam leapt over him, ran up the road and escaped.

He apparently took refuge in Moore Town and Robert Brereton, one time Superintendent General of Maroons, was ordered by the Governor, Sir Basil Keith, to go to the town and bring him out. When Brereton arrived and tried to take Grant, the Moore Town Maroons "broke into open rebellion". He reported that he was met by over three hundred Maroons under arms (certainly an exaggeration), who turned their backs on him insolently when informed of his mission. They claimed they were being ill-used by the British. Brereton eventually persuaded them to sign a written agreement that they would deliver up Grant to the governor in a week; but they never did. So poor Brereton had to make a second trip to Moore Town, and was this time successful in getting hold of Sam Grant who was taken to Spanish Town.

Sam was tried for murder before a magistrate, but fortune smiled on him. He was acquitted of the charge of murder when doubt was raised as to his intention of really killing Captain Townsend, considering the unorthodox and highly difficult manner in which he had fired his heavy gun by resting it on his forearm. The earlier and obviously accidental killing of the slave who had stepped in front of wharf-owner Thompson apparently was not held against him. It is presumed that Captain Davy of Scotts Hall also escaped without serious censure. Sam Grant later became Major of Maroons and Chief Commander at Charles Town.

Incidents like the one in which Sam Grant was involved should have served as a warning that the relationship between the Maroons and the colonists was detoriating. Since the treaties of 1739, the Maroons had roamed about quite freely in spite of the regulations which tried to control their movements; but apart from individual incidents there was no official trouble with them as a group until 1773.

In that year the property adjoining the treaty land was being surveyed and the Maroons, fearing that their lands might be . encroached upon, complained to their Superintendent. He invited observers to come along to see that they were not cheated.

In March 1792, a petition from the Trelawny Maroons was laid before the Assembly, saying that most of the one thousand five hundred acres of Trelawny Town consisted of very high rocky mountains, totally unfit for cultivation. The rest had been under cultivation since 1739, and being of a light texture was now exhausted, and was totally inadequate and insufficient to support the present number of inhabitants. As a result, trespass on adjoining properties were taking place, causing distress and confusion. The petitioners asked for something to be done.

The document was signed by Montague James, John Jarrett, Zachary Bayley and James Lawrence, and was certified by John James, Major Commandant of Maroons, and John Montague James, Superintendent of Trelawny Town. The petition is a striking example of the wholesale adoption by the Maroons of the names of leading colonists in their area.

The Superintendent was now a man of great power among the Maroons, greater than the treaties had envisaged.

Part of the reason was that he was practically the only literate person in a community of illiterates. Also he had fairly ready access to official places and could get things done for his charges.

The Maroons of Trelawny Town (Cudjoe's old community), had a special affection for their Superintendent, based not on his ability to read and write, or upon his contacts with government officials, but upon his physical strength and powers. This Superintendent's name was John James and he was the son of Captain John James of the Corps of Rangers which had fought with great distinction in the war against Cudjoe.

The senior Captain James had also been a Superintendent and the Maroons had always respected him as a gallant enemy. In 1763, therefore, when Governor William Lyttleton appointed the younger James as their Superintendent, the Trelawny Town Maroons were very pleased.

In addition to being his father's son, James Junior soon endeared himself to the Maroons because of his impressive physique and athletic ability. He could run barefoot over the rough, broken Maroon country with as much speed as the fastest Maroon. He could hunt, shoot and fight with the best of them and it was said that nothing he pursued ever escaped him. He was especially adept at hunting wild boars.

Sometimes when fights broke out among the Maroons and they began to swing their cutlasses at each other, he would jump into the fray, knock down the most belligerent of them and put them in irons. Afterwards he would preside over their punishment, sometimes using his authority to lighten their sentence if he thought it too severe. If he had been a Maroon in the old days before the treaties he would have made an ideal gang chief. As it was, the Maroons gave him the veneration that men who love strength, courage and martial skill usually reserve for a champion.

141

Apart from his physical accomplishments James was genuinely concerned with the welfare of the Maroons. He arranged and settled payment for work which they did for the colonists, smoothed over differences and made sure that no one imposed upon the Maroons, and that they in turn imposed on no one. He was a competent administrator who understood and liked the people among whom he worked.

Although not highly educated, James was a man of independent means and moved easily among the European society of the island. He was said to have had an excellent disposition and a forbearing temper. In 1791, about 28 years after he had been appointed Superintendent of Trelawny Town, James was given the rank of major and was promoted to the position of Superintendent-General in charge of all the Maroon towns of the island. His son was appointed to his old post as Superintendent of Trelawny Town.

So it was that three generations of the James family influenced affairs at Trelawny Town, and with the promotion of Major John James to Superintendent- General of all the Maroon Towns, the James clan was now placed in a dominant position over all the Maroons of Jamaica.

Under the strong hand of the James family the position of chief became almost redundant, a mere title which declined in prestige as chief followed chief. In the 1790s the captain of Trelawny Town was an old man named Montague. By the time Montague took over as chief the office had sunk to the point where the holder merely presided over a few ceremonies which had become virtually meaningless.

Montague's official dress consisted of a gaudily laced red coat and a gold laced hat with a plume of feathers. Only Maroon captains and officers could sit on seats in his presence. Others of lower rank either stood or squatted on the ground. Montague was the first to be served at meals. No woman was allowed to eat with him and he was served by young men.

142

He presided over council meetings and when it was necessary to keep order he spoke in an authoritative tone as became a chief. His voice was often ignored, however, because he was affecting a power which he did not possess. When there was anything really important to be done or decided it was to the Superintendent that the Maroons had to go. The young men looked upon Montague with some amount of contempt, but they went through the motions of respect because he bore the title of chief.

Some time after Major John James was made Superintendent-General of the entire Maroon community it was noticed that he began to lose interest in his job. He spent less and less time in residence among the Maroons and seemed to be giving increased attention to a property which he owned and which lay about 25 miles from Maroon Town (Trelawny Town).

A Superintendent of Maroons was required by law to live in the town under his jurisdiction. He could not be absent from this town for longer than a fortnight without the Governor's permission, and if he neglected his duties he would be subject to a court-martial. The same rules applied to the Superintendent-General but when the law of residence was brought to his attention, he ignored it. He simply complained that his salary was insufficient and went on about his business.

The Maroons grew restless at his continued absence and neglect. They tried to force him to return by complaining repeatedly to the House of Assembly but their complaints dragged on for years and James did not appear to be influenced by them. He really had no desire to lose his appointment but in addition to the attractive profits which he was making from his real estate activities, he had acquired a taste for the more sophisticated pleasures of colonial society which were not to be found among the Maroons.

Finally the Assembly grew tired of James' barefaced insubordination and relieved him of his office. His son was also removed from the post of Superintendent of Trelawny Town and an officer of the regular army, Captain Thomas Craskell, was appointed in his place.

James was furious and many people sympathized with him, but it was the Maroons most of all who were saddened by the news. They had only meant to force his return by their complaints, not to have him discharged.

To make matters worse, Craskell turned out to be the exact opposite of James, having neither his athletic ability nor his sympathetic understanding. The Maroons complained that when the young men quarrelled and fought among themselves, instead of interfering and breaking up the fight as James would have done, Craskell would head for home as fast as he could. His personality and manner of doing things enraged the Maroons. Insubordination increased rapidly and the chiefs who had by now lost practically all authority, were powerless to stop the rising tide of indignation and restlessness.

Seven or eight of the junior officers of Trelawny Town who had been greatly attached to James took over the leadership of the community and promoted the opposition against Craskell. They paid frequent visits to James and much to his satisfaction complained of the new Superintendent's incompetence and joined him in ridiculing Craskell. They still hoped to get rid of Craskell and have James restored.

While he was in charge of the Maroons, James' popularity and disarming manner lulled them into a state of wellbeing in which they did not seem to be aware of the encroachments of colonial law. With James' removal, however, a whole host of irritating circumstances seemed suddenly to make themselves felt. Among the chief complaints now made by the Maroons were unfair treatment by the colonists and the lack of sufficient land to sustain their growing community. They became violent and aggressive and an atmosphere was created which gave scope to the more lawless elements among them.

Two of the roughnecks went down to Montego Bay one day in 1795 and stole two pigs. They were arrested, tried, found guilty and sentenced to be whipped at the tail of a cart. The trial and the sentence were in strict accordance with the law and with the terms of the treaty. But the authorities made the mistake of carrying out the punishment in the presence of the slaves in the common workhouse, and of allowing the whipping to be done by a runaway slave who had been captured and returned by the Maroons. This was sweet revenge for the slaves in the workhouse and especially for the runaway who wielded the whip.

The news of the whipping spread rapidly among the slave population in the area, and as the two Maroons made their way home they were ridiculed in the streets of Montego Bay and laughed at on every plantation through which they passed. It made no difference that these two men were looked upon by their fellows with little respect. Their humiliating punishment was still a blow to Maroon pride and prestige, and the whole Maroon community felt that they had been made the laughing stock of the slaves.

This was just the excuse that their discontented spirits needed. A group of them went immediately to Captain Craskell and demanded that he take some action. If Craskell made any attempt to appease them it certainly did no good for in the middle of July, very shortly after the whipping incident, they drove him out of Trelawny Town. They warned him not to return, and informed him that if he and his colleagues wanted to make trouble they were ready for them. In fact, if Craskell and his friends did not come seeking them, then the Maroons would take the initiative.

Craskell later wrote that they were completely sober when they spoke to him.

It was reported that on July 16th Maroons from

Trelawny Town went to the south of the island for a supply of gun powder. They did not get any, however, primarily because of the anxiety they displayed and the price they offered. The difficulty experienced by the Trelawnys in obtaining adequate supplies of gunpowder was to be a crucial factor in the months of fighting that lay ahead.

CHAPTER 20

FLASHPOINT

After fifty-seven years of peace during which the freedom and independence of the Maroons had been gradually whittled away, a violent reaction to the creeping domination of the Colonial Government had finally set in.

Panic spread rapidly among the colonists and wild rumours flew about. It was said that the Trelawny Town Maroons had called in all their patrols and roving bands and had sent their women into the woods. One particularly wild rumour said that, in order to rid themselves of all encumbrances, the Trelawnys had made up their minds to kill their cattle and any of their children that were a hindrance to them. It was also rumoured that they had threatened to destroy some of the neighbouring plantations and all the Europeans on them; that they planned a two-pronged attack on the parishes of Trelawny and St. James, and that they expected to be joined by a number of the slaves and by their fellow Maroons from Accompong Town.

In fact, there was a feud going on between the Trelawnys and the Accompongs at the time. It seems that the Accompongs had taken possession of the original treaty of 1739 signed with Cudjoe and had claimed the right to keep it. The Trelawnys on the other hand had asserted that they had a right to the treaty, as Trelawny Town had been Cudjoe's headquarters and their fathers had been Cudjoe's personal followers. They repeatedly demanded that the Accompongs return the document and at about the time when the trouble with the colonists started, the Accompongs had indeed given it to them but apparently on the promise that it would be returned. Once having got their hands on it, however, the Trelawnys refused to give it up.

Far from giving help to the Trelawnys in 1795, therefore, the Accompongs were angry with them and testified in public that they disapproved of their conduct. Just to make doubly sure that everyone understood their position, they renewed their agreement with the colonists as laid down in the treaty and had all their young people baptized.

On July 18th, 1795, the magistrates of the parish of St. James wrote to the Governor, the Earl of Balcarres, telling him of Craskell's expulsion from Trelawny Town and of all else that had happened, including the many rumours. They also sent a message to the Maroons in which they suggested that four of them meet with four magistrates in an attempt to settle their differences. When the message was received in Trelawny Town, Montague, the chief, was not present, but some of the more belligerent spirits, who were said to have been drinking rum, dictated a letter to one of Craskell's men saying they wanted nothing but battle. They signed Montague's name to the letter, and it was sent off with only a few of the Maroons knowing about it.

As soon as he heard of the trouble which was brewing, ex-Superintendent Major John James made his services available to the Government. With his usual blunt courage, James, accompanied by two men, went to Trelawny Town. He suggested to the Maroons that they ask the Custos to come to the town with three others in order to hear their grievances. The Maroons agreed and they selected Captain Smith to take a letter to the Custos.

Meanwhile 400 militia men from Trelawny had assembled. They started marching towards Maroon Town and were about three miles away at the foot of some steep hills

148

when they saw Smith approaching. They noted that he was a man of magnificent physique and marvelled at the agility with which he came bounding down the slope towards them, flourishing a spear in his hand.

> "They observed a single man winding along the activities, with singular agility, and brandishing a lance to show that he had no other arms.
>
> This was a Maroon captain of the name of Smith, a young fellow of exquisite symmetry, whose limbs united all that was requisite both for strength and activity; the superiority of his gait, as he descended the side of the mountain, and the wild grace with which he flourished the lance over his head, excited the highest admiration".
>
> *DALLAS — A History of the Maroons*

Smith told the commanding officer that he was the bearer of a message inviting the Custos and chief magistrate of Trelawny, John Tharpe, Esquire, to lead a deputation to the town for a conference.

When the Custos received the message he agreed to go. In addition to Tharpe, the deputation consisted of Messrs. Stewart and Hodges, members of the Assembly, and Jarvis Gallimore, Esquire, a militia colonel. They journeyed to Trelawny Town on July 20th accompanied by a party headed by Colonel Thomas Reid of the St. James Militia, and also by Major James.

About 300 armed Maroons received them. They were in a very belligerent mood and some of them appeared to be under the influence of rum. The deputation was a little alarmed at first but settled down as John Jarrett, one of the Maroon Captains, began to state the grievances.

There were three main grievances: the indignity suffered by the Maroons when the two men accused of hog stealing were allowed to be whipped by a runaway; the need for more land, as the original treaty land, limited at best, was now worn out and could no longer support them; and the desire to have Major John James re-appointed to his old post.

As an immediate move towards easing the tension, someone in the deputation proposed a collection of money among themselves to give to the Maroons. Everyone gave something except Colonel Gallimore, who thought that such a gesture would appear to be nothing more than a reward for violence. Instead of taking money from his purse Gallimore took some bullets from his pocket and, showing them to the Maroons who were standing around, said: "This is the reward you deserve, and no other coin shall you get from me".

The deputation promised to bring the Maroons' grievances before the House of Assembly which was due to meet early the next month, and in spite of Gallimore's blunt words, left the town feeling that the situation was well in hand.

Everyone was convinced that the crisis was over. The 83rd Regiment of Foot, which had been detained from sailing for Haiti where a British expeditionary force was helping the French to fight the rebellious Haitian slaves, was allowed to proceed. The militia was sent home. Governor Balcarres ordered Craskell to go to Spanish Town and directed the Trelawnys to send their chief captains to submit to him by July 31st.

But suddenly new rumours again spread panic among the colonists. This time it was being said that French agents were bringing the revolutionary doctrines of Haiti into the island and spreading them among the Maroons and the slaves with the object of overthrowing the colony. People called attention to the truculent behaviour of the Trelawny Maroons and to recent complaints by the slaves of St. James and Trelawny.

It is impossible to understand colonial Jamaica in the days of slavery without taking into consideration the constant fear of insurrection which conditioned even the most peaceful activities. Much of the fear was based on hard reality but it was greatly intensified by the imagination and by perhaps a suppressed feeling of guilt. The events in Haiti persuaded the colonists that disaster was near at hand unless they took strong and immediate action.

On August 3rd, a council of war was held and Governor Balcarres was given the powers of Martial Law. He sent off a boat to order the transport bound for Haiti with the 83rd Foot to alter her course and head for Montego Bay.

On August 4th, the 83rd Regiment of Foot landed at Montego Bay. It consisted of over 1,000 men under the command of Colonel William Fitch. The day before, over 200 well-mounted dragoons under Colonel Sandford, and a detachment of 100 men of the 62nd Regiment were sent into Trelawny. At the same time Colonel Walpole with 150 dismounted dragoons embarked for Black River to command the forces in St. Elizabeth and Westmoreland. On the morning of August 4th, Balcarres left Spanish Town for Montego Bay to take command of the entire operation.

Meanwhile the message from Balcarres to the Trelawnys to send in their chief captains by July 31st had arrived rather late. Nevertheless, the Trelawnys chose six of their most eminent men to wait on him in Spanish Town. The six men obtained passes but when they arrived at Llandovery near St. Ann's Bay, they were stopped by the commanding officer of the militia and arrested. They were brought before Balcarres when he reached St. Ann on August 5th and he ordered them to be put in irons, apparently for coming in late.

When the Trelawny Maroons heard of this they were bewildered at what seemed to be a bare-faced breach of faith. They immediately sent messengers to tell their brethren who lived outside the town what had happened. Some of them also attempted to persuade the slaves on several neighbouring estates to join them, but were unsuccessful.

151

When he arrived in Montego Bay, Balcarres sent a message to the Trelawnys on August 8th which said:

"You have entered into a most unprovoked, ungrateful, and a most dangerous rebellion.

You have driven away your Superintendent, placed over you by the laws of this country. You have endeavored to massacre him.

You have put the magistrates of this country at defiance. You have challenged and offered them battle.

You have forced the country, which has long cherished and fostered you as children, to consider you as an enemy.

Martial law has in consequence been proclaimed.

Every pass to your town has been occupied and guarded by the militia and regular forces.

You are surrounded by thousands.

Look at Montego Bay, and you will see the force brought against you.

I have issued a Proclamation offering a reward for your heads.

That terrible edict will not be put in force before Thursday the 13th day of August.

To avert these terrible proceedings, I advise and command every Maroon of Trelawny Town, capable of bearing arms, to appear before me at Montego Bay, on Wednesday the 12th of August instant, and there submit themselves to His Majesty's mercy.

On so doing you will escape the effects of the dreadful command ordered to be put in execution on Thursday the 13th day of August; on which day, in failure of your obedience to this summons, your town shall be burnt to the ground, and forever destroyed.

And whereas it appears that other Negroes besides the Maroons of Trelawny Town, were there under arms, on the day that town was visited by John Tharpe Esq., and several other magistrates of the parish of Trelawny, you are strictly commanded and enjoined to bring such stranger Negroes to Montego Bay, as prisoner, on or before the before mentioned Wednesday, the 12th day of August instant".

After he wrote his summons, Governor Balcarres ordered the regular troops and militia to occupy all the known paths leading to Trelawny Town from the surrounding parishes.

On August 9th, the troops and militia moved into their positions as ordered. Regular troops and militia under the command of Colonel Sandford were stationed at Spring Vale and Wemyss Castle, four miles north of Trelawny Town. Sandford later sent detachments to Parnassus and Blue Hole. The 83rd Regiment of Foot under Fitch was marched to Vaughansfield, one and a half miles from the town, and there the Governor set up his headquarters.

Among the outlying Maroons who received news of the imprisonment of the six Trelawnys by Balcarres earlier in August, were two men named Johnson and Smith who had been allowed to settle with their families on the back-lands of estates in Westmoreland. There were other Maroons living in the area but they had no connection with Trelawny Town.

Johnson and Smith were held in great respect by the Trelawnys. When they heard the news they hid their women and children in the woods, and went to the Town with their young men. They advised the townsmen to make another attempt at a peaceful settlement. On August 11th, therefore, in answer to Balcarres' call that they should surrender their arms and submit to him by the 12th, the Trelawnys sent 37 of their men led by Colonel Montague himself. They intended to use this group as a test to see how Balcarres would treat them. If they were reasonably well treated, then they had made up their minds to submit.

The group surrendered their arms at the Vaughansfield headquarters. With the exception of Montague they were all made prisoner and their hands were tied behind their backs. One of them committed suicide before he could be confined. Two others, Palmer and Parkinson, were chosen to return to Trelawny Town to tell the others to come down.

153

When the Trelawnys heard what had taken place they decided to fight. They were quite convinced by this time that Balcarres intended to destroy them.

There can be no doubt that this was Balcarres' intention. The continued success of the slave rebellion in Haiti against the veteran troops of France and England, the re-awakened fear of the "terrible Maroons" and the deep-seated uneasiness of the slave-owners, had all contributed to produce a state of hysteria among the colonists. The Governor's irresponsible actions against the two peace missions of the Trelawnys mirrored this state of growing panic. Balcarres' strategy was to completely intimidate the Maroons by ruthless measures, but he underestimated the degree of toughness that still survived among the Trelawnys.

On the 13th August, Montague and the other prisoners were put into jail in Montego Bay. At first some of the north-side colonists, who had not been infected by the new wave of panic, thought that the Trelawnys had been unfairly treated, but in the general hysteria which soon gripped the island, all voices eventually became united in the belief that the Trelawnys must be brought low.

From the start there had been an element in Trelawny Town, mostly made up of older men, which had deplored the growth of an aggressive and hostile spirit in the community. This element had argued for a peaceful existence even at the cost of some humiliation. Many of them had probably been creamed off in the two deputations, and those who remained no longer had a chance of being heard in Trelawny Town.

Johnson and Smith returned to their settlement only to find that, in their absence, a group of Westmoreland militia had burned their houses and laid waste their fields. Feeling now that the colonists had determined on war, Johnson and Smith gathered their families and returned to Trelawny Town.

The Trelawny Maroons burned their houses and at

midday on August 12th, 1795, left the smoking ruins of Trelawny Town and set out for the settlement of Schaw Castle. They could go no farther north, for Colonel Sandford and his men were in front of them at Spring Vale, Wemyss Castle, Parnassus and Blue Hole.

The Trelawnys stood alone. They had received no help from the slave population, had been abandoned by their Accompong brethren and, in addition, were greatly outnumbered. They had a limited supply of food and gunpowder and about two or three hundred fighting men. They were facing 1,500 regular troops supported by several thousand militia men who had access to unlimited supplies.

In their favour, the Trelawnys had a great tradition of courage and skill as guerrilla fighters and an unsurpassed knowledge of the tremendously rugged countryside which their ancestors had used so well. They were also fortunate at this time of crisis in being able to produce first-class leaders.

Having made up their minds to fight they went into action immediately.

CHAPTER 21

WHIP AND SPUR

The rainy season had begun.

On August 12th, the day on which their town was burned (the New Town which had been built by Furry), the Trelawnys attacked a free coloured company which was hurrying to join Balcarres at his headquarters at Vaughansfield. The company was only a mile away from Vaughansfield when the Trelawnys hit them. On the same day they fired on an advanced post of militia a mile to the north of Trelawny Town. In both these clashes men were killed and wounded.

Also on August 12th, the Earl of Balcarres ordered Colonel Sandford, who had waited to the north, to move in on the New Town, then wheel to the right and occupy the adjacent provision grounds. Balcarres believed that this would put Sandford right behind the Trelawnys. He hoped to move his own force up to the Old Town and so trap the Trelawnys between Sandford and himself.

At this point it would be well to remember that what was loosely called Trelawny Town consisted of two settlements, the Old Town to the south which had been founded by Cudjoe and the New Town to the north founded by Furry. Both Towns were connected by a narrow defile half a mile long.

Colonel Sandford had been led to within striking distance of Schaw Castle, where the Maroons had withdrawn,

by one of the outlying Trelawny Maroons who had decided
to help the colonists. Sandford was in a position where he
could plainly see the Maroons on the heights between himself and the New Town when he got Balcarres' message.
All morning the Trelawnys had been making gestures of
defiance and blowing their horns at him, inviting him to
come up and get them.   Late in the afternoon he moved
out. With him, commanding the militia, was Colonel
Gallimore, the man who had been a member of the deputation sent to Trelawny Town to hear the grievances of the
Maroons and who had offered them a gift of bullets instead
of money.

The first part of Balcarres' order said "move in on the
New Town" and this Sandford proceeded to do. The
Maroons watched him coming up the hillside with his
mounted dragoons, militia and volunteers and after awhile
they moved back through the New Town into the defile
which lay between the Old Town and the New. Their movements appeared unhurried and deliberate.   They concealed
themselves among rocks and trees in the defile and waited.

Sandford reached the New Town without incident. The
column halted and the men began searching in the smoul-
dering huts.

A dragoon entered a hut which was still burning and
found a book entitled "Wake's Catechism": a manual of
instruction in the form of questions and answers pertaining
to the principles of the Christian Religion. It is difficult to
imagine what such a book was doing in the burning hut of
a Maroon warrior. In all likelihood it had been looted along
with other things from some settler's house. The book was
partially destroyed, only about two-thirds of it remaining.
The dragoon dusted it off and put it in the top left-hand
pocket of his tunic, and thus, is remembered in the annals
of the Second Maroon War, as a lucky man who must have
had a special guardian angel.

Another man who is remembered for his good fortune on

this occasion was Private Thomas Johnson of the Trelawny Leeward Troop, a militia cavalry unit belonging to the Western Division of Horse, which was made up of mounted troops from the western parishes of Hanover, Westmoreland, St. Elizabeth and Trelawny. Private Johnson was one of the troopers assigned to escort the baggage.

The officer who brought Balcarres' message ordering Standford to advance on the New Town and occupy the adjacent provision grounds, told the Colonel that there was no road to his right, and no provision grounds; so Sandford decided to ignore the second part of Balcarres' order, which was to turn to his right, occupy the adjacent provision grounds and wait.

Sandford was next informed that the Maroons had retreated to the ruins of the Old Town, and as he felt that it was too dangerous to halt indefinitely in the New Town, he decided not to wait for orders, but to push on to the Old Town towards which Balcarres should now have been advancing. Sandford was warned by his black attendants not to proceed any further, but it is said that the whole detachment held the Maroons in great contempt and marched forth confident of certain victory.

Sandford entered the defile at the head of the dragoons, followed by Colonel Jarvis Gallimore who led the Volunteers and the militia. The column was stretched out in a long, thin line and took up nearly half the defile. The Trelawnys, hidden on either side of the trail, waited until the soldiers were almost two-thirds of the way through. Then they struck.

Maroon sharpshooters on the left fired a volley which swept the column from one end to the other. Immediately the mounted men whipped their horses to a gallop.

Colonel Sandford riding out in front came within sight of a place where the trail divided into two paths, both leading to the Old Town. At this moment another volley swept the column. Sandford was hit and fell dead out of his saddle.

Colonel Jarvis Gallimore, galloping ahead of his Volunteers and militia, was knocked from his horse by a bullet and was never seen again. The dragoon with the copy of Wake's Catechism in the top left-hand pocket of his tunic received a sharp jolt in the chest from a bullet, but maintained his seat and kept on riding. Men fell all along the line.

Quartermaster McBride was shot from his saddle, six privates of the 20th Light Dragoons and eight men of the 18th Light Dragoons were killed as they rode. Behind them 13 militiamen and eight Volunteers were tumbled from the backs of their racing mounts.

In the wild scramble to break out of the trap, Private Thomas Johnson of the Trelawny Leeward Troop, still trying to escort the baggage assigned to him, rode into a hail of bullets. One shot went through "the rim of his belly", a second smashed into his thigh, a third struck his saddle, and a fourth perforated the brass barrel of his carbine. But Trooper Johnson clung grimly to his galloping horse.

A number of "respectable gentlemen of the Militia" perished in the ambush: Captain H.W. James, Lieutenant George Waterhouse of the Trelawny Leeward Troop, Henry J. Rusea, C.B. Etty and Patrick McGibbon; Dr. Begg, Lieutenant Job Dale, Quartermaster A. McDonald, Thomas McCullock, Peregrine Case, John Betterton Jr., and George Love of the Trelawny Windward Troop. Apart from those who were killed outright, scores like Trooper Johnson were wounded.

When the soldiers saw Sandford fall they were seized with panic. No officer came forward to take control and there was complete chaos. It seemed that the one thought in the head of every man was to escape as quickly as possible. Dragoons lashed and spurred their mounts and the men on foot raced madly for the Old Town which stood on open, elevated ground and was plainly visible. But if they had hoped to find Balcarres in the Old Town they were to be greatly disappointed. There was not a redcoat in sight.

According to an official report, when Sandford and Gallimore fell, the command devolved on Captain Butter of the 18th Dragoons. To attempt to turn about and retreat to the New Town would have been highly dangerous. It would have meant going "through a tremendous ravine", over a narrow, rugged, nearly impossible road, overhung with rocks and lined by the enemy.

So, it was forward: "to dash over mountains; an unexplored rocky country". Butter and his party "rushed on...", crossing an almost inaccessible land at full gallop. *(Lives of the Lindsays — BALCARRES.)*

The whole body of men broke into the Old Town at top speed, rushed through without stopping and took the nearest way south to the Vaughansfield headquarters. Every man contended for the front of the race and as many as had loaded guns or could bother to load them, kept up a scattering fire to right and left as they went; but they shot at imaginary enemies, for not one Maroon was to be seen. To add to the distress it began to rain.

At nightfall the disorganized mob, tired and demoralized, arrived at Balcarres' Vaughansfield headquarters. Some of them shot off their guns in their joy at having escaped alive. The dragoon who carried Wake's Cathecism dismounted from his horse and removed the book from his pocket. He looked at it curiously and discovered that the bullet which had struck him had penetrated it to within three leaves and was still there, resting against the last three leaves. The book had saved his life.

Private Thomas Johnson of the Trelawny Leeward Troop also slipped from his horse, wounded and badly shaken but thanking God to be alive. He recovered completely from his wounds.

Amid the noise and confusion at the headquarters and a fear that the Maroons might attack, Governor Balcarres slipped on a wet plank, fell and received a blow to his eye. Some of the men thought he had been shot and panicked, but Balcarres managed to regain his equilibrium and put a stop to the uproar. The troops were kept on the alert all night but no Maroons appeared, for the simple reason that the Trelawnys were busy celebrating their victory. For much of the night they drank rum and made merry in the ruins of the Old Town.

Of the soldiers, militia and Volunteers caught in the ambush, thirty-seven had been killed and many wounded. The Trelawnys on the other hand had not lost a single man. From the men who had fallen in the defile they took watches, knives, pencils and whatever else they could find. They also found and took Colonel Gallimore's gun. Perhaps they remembered the gift of bullets which he had made to them only a few days ago, and the words which he had spoken.

Gallimore's body was never found. It was believed that he had only been wounded when he was struck from his horse and that he had managed to crawl off into the bushes and hide himself in some recess, where he had died later from his wounds or from loss of blood. The Trelawnys had returned his gift of bullets.

That night as they celebrated, the Trelawnys drank so hard that sixty of the young warriors are said to have passed out completely. They lay insensible until two o'clock the next day when, with the help of the women, they were taken into Petty River Bottom, Cudjoe's old stronghold, which lay a little to the south.

Balcarres reported later that the Trelawny infantry had not kept up with Sandford's rapid advance. They had therefore not been caught in the ambush and "made their retreat unmolested, after staying in the New Town all night".

Writing to the Countess of Hardwicke on September 1st, 1795, Balcarres said:

"I have been exposed to fatigue and open air on the high Maroon mountains of Jamaica for this month past, and engaged in an arduous and bloody war with the Maroons. If I had not attacked them as I had done, my firm opinion is that the island of Jamaica (would have been) inevitably lost... I had a bad fall at the close of Colonel Sandford's rash business...
It jumbled my brain for two days, but I fortunately could retain my command".

Colonel William Fitch

Maroon ambush of Colonel Sandford's force, which took place between the Old Town and the New Town

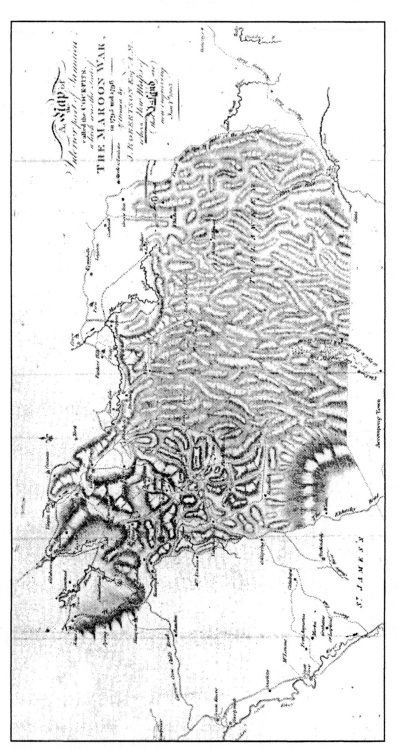

Map of the Cockpits drawn by J. Robertson in 1803, showing the area of the Maroon war in 1795 - 6

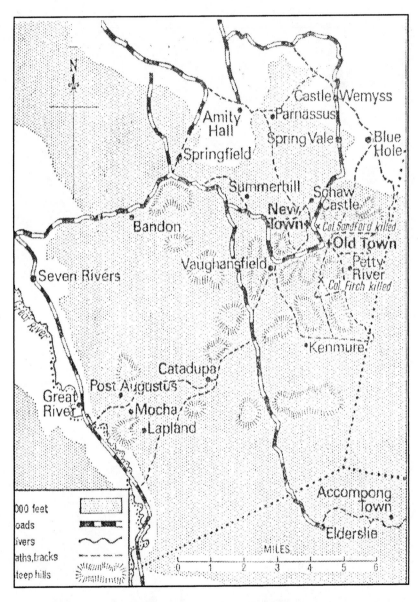

Details of the Cockpits,
based on J. Robertson's map

Privates of the 17th Lancers
(Light Dragoons)

Major-General
George Walpole

Colonel
Skinner

CHAPTER 22

THE STRUGGLE IN THE WILDERNESS

Apart from the trail through the defile, the Old Town could be approached from three other directions which were all easier to traverse. The way leading from Vaughansfield to the southwest was the easiest. A second way led by a circuitous route from the New Town and joined the Vaughansfield Road near the Old Town. A third ran in from the East through Tacky's defile.

Aware that all four approaches made the Old Town too accessible and therefore too vulnerable, the Trelawnys withdrew into Petty River Bottom where they had already sent their women and the drunken warriors. They actually moved into the long, narrow entrance passage to the Cockpit, which had been named Guthrie's defile after Colonel John Guthrie who had made the treaty with Cudjoe. The Trelawnys fortified the entrance and made it as impregnable as they could.

Balcarres was now determined to surround the whole area which included the Old and New Towns, and the Cockpits around Petty River Bottom. He hoped to reduce the Trelawnys by starvation.

On August 13th, he issued another proclamation from Vaughansfield in which he said:

> "I have determined to send out parties of persons accustomed to travel in the mountainous parts of the island, assisted by armed persons of colour and

163

Negroes to discover and destroy (the Maroons') haunts
and retreats, for the better encouragement of whom I
have resolved to grant the following rewards:-

- For every Maroon capable of bearing arms, brought
  in prisoner — 20 pounds.

- For every Maroon woman or young child brought in —
  10 pounds, (For Maroons who were slain while resist-
  ing capture, the same rewards were offered, on sufficient proof being presented).

- For James Palmer and Leonard Parkinson, who have
  behaved in a manner singularly atrocious (they had
  been among the group who surrendered at
  Vaughansfield and had been chosen to persuade the
  other Maroons to come in; but had not returned) - I
  offer an additional reward of 80 pounds, amounting
  in the whole to 100 pounds for apprehending or
  killing Palmer, and an additional 30 pounds amounting to 50 pounds, for apprehending or killing
  Parkinson.

Reinforcements of regular troops and militia were called
up and were employed for several days in destroying the
provision grounds in and about the two towns. Every now
and then, the troops engaged in the work would lay down
their tools, pick up their guns and fire crashing volleys into
the gullies and the bushes which, according to the historian
Dallas, "made the woods re-echo and the Maroons smile."

No doubt the volleys were meant to discourage ambushes or lurking Maroons, but it was all a waste of powder and
shots, for the Maroons remained safe in the narrow
entrance passage to Petty River Bottom.

On the heights less than a mile from the Vaughansfield
headquarters, their lookouts watched all that was taking
place and communicated the news from height to height
and back to their stronghold by means of the abeng horns
with their wonderful alphabet of sounds.

Johnson had now taken over command of the Trelawnys and Smith was one of his chief captains. They were confident and in spite of the destruction of their provision grounds managed to keep themselves supplied with food from outlying areas. Patrols well-trained in woodcraft and in the art of camouflage slipped almost at will through the surrounding lines of soldiers.

Governor Balcarres somehow got the idea that the Maroons were going to defend the Old Town. He was not aware that they had abandoned it, so he planned to launch a general attack upon it. Part of the plan was to drag up a field-piece from his headquarters, through the ruined provision grounds and on to a precipitous height on the site of the New Town where he had stationed some Light Dragoons.

To achieve this plan, a path had to be cut. It was the height of the rainy season with three or four hours of rain each day, and it took two days working in violent rains before the field-piece was dragged into place and mounted.

Colonel William Fitch of the 83rd Regiment of Foot was in charge of the party working up from the headquarters. Fitch was a tall, elegant man, descended from a wealthy and respectable family in America. He was described as being "endowed with all the advantages that could accrue to a generous mind from a polite and liberal education possessing that manliness of person which when added to the affability of his address and the suavity of his manner, endeared him to his friends as the gentleman and scholar". He was a brave, competent professional soldier, and his men loved and respected him.

At one time while the gun was being dragged up and Fitch was busy giving orders to his men, a Maroon patrol under a warrior named Dunbar lay in hiding 30 feet away from him. Dunbar said afterwards that he would have fired on Fitch and his men but had no cover through which to make an immediate retreat from the large number of

165

soldiers who were near at hand.

In spite of the swarm of troops guarding the country-side, the intrepid Dunbar passed near the Vaughansfield headquarters at eleven o'clock on the night of August 30th and burned down some building six miles away on the road to Montego Bay.

Balcarres now mounted a three-pronged attack on the Old Town.

On the morning of August 23rd, the army moved out in three columns. Two columns under Colonels Incledon and Hull advanced south from the New Town and from the east through Tacky's defile. The third column led by Colonel Fitch, in which Balcarres himself marched, set out from Vaughansfield.

One account said the columns maintained a profound silence on the march, and Hull's column was within 200 yards of the Old Town before it was discovered by the Maroon sentinels. Another account however said that as the men marched they fired into the woods at frequent intervals, hoping to kill or intimidate any lurking Maroons; but they neither saw, hurt nor intimidated anyone, and when they reached the Old Town they found it empty.

All the fanfare, noise and show of force had been for nothing. In fact the whole exercise was rendered somewhat ridiculous by a small scouting party of about a dozen Maroons, which stood observing everything from a high rock overlooking the town, but some distance away. After watching for a while, they began taking long shots at the soldiers with great coolness and insolence. They succeeded in wounding three men, one of them severely, before going leisurely away.

Balcarres found no one to fight in the Old Town, but a detachment of the 20th Dragoons, which Colonel Sandford had commanded, made a minute search for his body and found it. They buried the remains with military honours. The bodies of eighteen men who had fallen in the ambush were also found and buried, but there was no trace of Colonel Jarvis Gallimore.

It will be remembered that Major John James, the former Superintendent-General of Maroons, had volunteered his services to the government at the start of the trouble. He was still awaiting trial for failing in his duty and was perhaps trying to rescue his reputation and restore himself to the good graces of the authorities.

He led a Volunteer party into the pathways used by the Trelawnys. They were on the trail of a Maroon patrol and James finally took them close to the mouth of Guthrie's defile. He then advised them to go no further. "They can now see you," he said, "and if you advance 50 paces more they will convince you of it."

As soon as he had said this an abeng horn was blown and a voice asked if Major James was with the Volunteers. "If he is," said the voice, "let him go back, for we don't wish to hurt him; but as for the rest of you, come on and try battle if you choose." The Volunteers were hungry and tired and in no mood to accept this kind of challenge, so they turned back.

On the return journey they came upon a post held by a detachment of regular soldiers. James, taking his importance and popularity for granted, got into a violent argument with a sentry and the officer commanding the post who did not know him. James evidently got the worst of it and was so humiliated that he withdrew his services and apparently left the area of hostilities. He had not been feeling well for some time and shortly after, with his mind preyed upon by all the accusations that had been brought against him, his health broke down altogether. He died the next year.

Balcarres had never trusted James, feeling that he was in league with the Maroons. He also believed that the gentry of St. James and Trelawny were closely associated with them. In a letter to the Duke of Portland on October 27th, 1795, Balcarres said:

> "Most of the gentlemen (of St. James and Trelawny) have connections with the Maroons, and almost the whole of them pay contributions to those fellows to induce them not to injure their properties.
>
> The most dangerous man in that country (St. James and Trelawny) is Major James. He has been all his life the head of the Maroons, and (some of the leading men of those two parishes) are connected with him by marriage and consanguinity. He rules the whole with a rod of iron. His niece, a young lady of twenty, is married to the Custos, Major-General Palmer, aged about eighty. (Palmer) is the senior Major-General of the Militia.
>
> The second Major-General is Mr. Reid, who is a younger man, and more active, but overbearing; hated the whole Militia, and is equally under the rod of Major James and the Maroons".

Governor Balcarres was determined to carry out his plan of confining the Maroons in a circle and to achieve this he used large numbers of slaves to chop down trees and build a cordon around the area. He put Colonel Fitch in charge of this operation and left to make further arrangements for carrying on the campaign.

The troops in the area were reinforced by a strong body of militia drawn from St. James, Westmoreland and Hanover and supported by a large group of "Confidential Black Shot" recruited from several plantations. The whole force was under the command of General Reid. Operating from the Vaughansfield headquarters Reid launched another fruitless and ludicrous attack on the Trelawnys.

Detachments were placed in ambush along the pathways leading to the Petty River Bottom Cockpit in the hope of surprising Maroon foraging parties and patrols. At the same time a force of 300 men was sent out to make an attack on Petty River Bottom. Instead of marching straight to their objective, however, they turned left somewhere along the way and presently found themselves in the Old Town where Colonel Fitch was stationed. Fitch told them that he thought they were a "bunch of fools" and made it plain that he didn't want them around, so they returned to Vaughansfield.

The militia detachments which were lying in ambush along the Maroon trails hoping to come to grips with foraging parties, had no better luck. Heavy rains damaged their gunpowder, kept them soaked and made life thoroughly miserable. The men were relieved every two weeks but the whole business was so useless, uncomfortable and exhausting, that the majority of those who were relieved refused to return to duty. One man, a Captain Oldham, actually died of fatigue. These militia detachments failed to surprise any Maroons, perhaps for the simple reason that the Maroons knew where they were all the time.

At the Old Town, meanwhile, Fitch was receiving visits from the Trelawnys. Groups of them would climb to the heights above his quarters and call down to him. At first Fitch wasn't sure what to do, and then one day he decided to ask a group of them to come down and talk to him. He promised that they would not be hurt or detained. They asked him to withdraw his sentries and when this was done, some of them came down. Among them was that peerless patrol leader, the elusive Dunbar.

Dunbar and the others told Fitch that the Trelawnys were willing to stop fighting provided they were given a full pardon and an assurance that they would not be transported. If there was one fear the Maroons had, it was the fear of being transported.

The colonial government seemed to have kept this fear hanging over them and one recalls the fury of Captain

Davy, chief of the Scotts Hall Maroons, when he heard rumours of a plan to ship himself and his men away from Jamaica. The Maroons had a deep love for the country and the thought of being banished from it was almost worse than death.

As he talked with Dunbar and the others, Colonel Fitch grew confident. He told them that he did not have the power to grant any specific terms but he could at least promise them their lives and would write to Balcarres about their offer. They tried to persuade him to exceed his authority and make detailed terms with them, but Fitch, growing more confident, told them that he was a professional soldier and not deeply involved in the rights and wrongs of the situation.

Speaking candidly and perhaps a little boastfully he said that if they wanted peace or a truce he would be glad to conclude one with them, but if they wanted a fight he was ready for that too. If he was not fighting them there in the Cockpits he would be over in Haiti fighting rebellious slaves. One way or the other it made little difference to him. Fitch felt he had the upper hand and he was playing it for all it was worth.

Seeing that he was not going to relent, the Trelawnys told him that they would agree to surrender if he would give them his word that they would receive favourable terms; and if he would let two of them go to visit the thirty-seven Maroons who had been locked up in Montego Bay by Balcarres at the start of hostilities. Fitch agreed to this and Dunbar and another man named Harvey were chosen to go to Montego Bay. They went to the Vaughansfield headquarters, left their guns and ammunition with General Reid and set out for the town.

Fitch waited for two days during which he continued to have friendly visits from the Trelawnys. At the end of the time Dunbar and Harvey returned bringing with them old Colonel Montague who had been staying at Vaughansfield, perhaps as some kind of hostage. Dunbar and Harvey gave the impression that all had gone well and that they would bring in the Trelawnys to surrender the next day. But they had brought back a few pounds of salt with them and this puzzled Fitch.

"If you are going to surrender tomorrow," he said, "it's unnecessary to take up all that salt." But Dunbar and Harvey pointed out that it was only a small amount, hardly enough to be divided, so Fitch let it pass.

When they arrived at the camp of the Trelawnys, Dunbar and Harvey told what they had seen at Montego Bay. They had seen their fellow Maroons on a ship in the harbour. This could mean only one thing: the dreaded transportation. There seemed no alternative now but to fight it out.

Fitch waited in vain for the Trelawnys to come in but not one appeared. It must have dawned on him then that the wily Dunbar, behind whom stood the shadowy figure of Johnson, had manoeuvred him into the peace talks in order to create the opportunity both to find out what had happened to the thirty-seven captured men and to form some opinion of what might happen if they themselves made peace.

Fitch was now determined to push the campaign with all his professional skill. He built advanced posts where the tracks used by Maroon foraging parties emerged. These tracks were the supply lines over which food from the outlying countryside was taken into the besieged Maroon camp and Fitch hoped that the presence of the posts would make it impossible for the tracks to be used any longer.

Fitch next turned his attention to the land which lay directly in front of Guthrie's defile and the Petty River Bottom Cockpit. The ground was covered with low trees between which grew a confusion of bush and plantains. This screen of bush and trees obscured the mouth of the defile, offered excellent cover for the Maroons and made manoeuvring difficult. Fitch decided to clear away all the vegetation. He turned hundreds of slaves into the area with axes and machetes and put two flank companies of the Westmoreland militia to guard them as they worked. One of the officers was a near-sighted lieutenant of infantry named Tomlinson who wore glasses.

From the Petty River Bottom fortress Johnson watched Fitch put his project into operation and then he called together his captains and lieutenants and made plans to defeat the move. First he sent out Captain Charles Shaw with a party to deal with the two militia companies guarding the slaves. Shaw set an ambush for them half a mile away from Fitch's quarters and they walked right into it. The Maroons fired a volley which killed seven militiamen and wounded many others. Ten slaves in the working party were also killed and the whole force, slaves and militiamen alike, fled in confusion out of the area.

In the retreat, Lieutenant Tomlinson of the Light Infantry lost his eyeglasses. As a result he missed the path taken by his companions and apparently stumbled into the arms of the Maroons. Some time later his head was found suspended by the hair from the bough of a tree.

CHAPTER 23

A TRAGIC HERO

A mile and a quarter to the south of Fitch's quarters was an advanced post consisting of huts surrounded by palisades. It was manned by thirty privates, two corporals and a sergeant, all under the command of Captain Lee of the 83rd Regiment of Foot, which was Fitch's own regiment.

Captain Lee was nervous because his post was overlooked by heights which were easily accessible to the Maroons. He sent a message to Fitch telling him that the post was not in a safe position and on the morning of September 12th, 1795, Fitch set out with a party to inspect the site for himself. He was accompanied on his inspection by Colonel Robert Jackson of the militia, Lieutenant Brunt of the 83rd Regiment, Captain Brisset and two Accompong Maroons.

When Fitch reached the post he took a look around and quickly agreed with Captain Lee that it was in a dangerous position. With characteristic energy and dispatch he decided to do something about it at once. He set out to look for a better site accompanied by Captain Lee, sixteen of Lee's soldiers, the two Accompong Maroons and some of the other men who had made the journey of inspection with him.

As the party proceeded, the countryside became rougher and more difficult. The mountains rose higher, the valleys were deeper and it began to seem that it would be impossible to find a better position in such country.

The two Accompongs were scouting ahead and presently came upon signs of the Trelawnys. They reported what they had found to Fitch and warned him not to go any farther as the signs indicated that the Trelawnys had just left the spot and were probably close at hand. Some of Fitch's companions were inclined to ridicule the warning until the Accompongs showed them the signs, which included the tops of some wild coco (eddo) which had recently been dug up.

In spite of this evidence the search proceeded. Colonel Jackson asked Fitch for permission to go ahead of the party with Captain Brisset. He wanted to reconnoitre the piece of ground which lay in front of them to determine whether or not it would be suitable for the new post. Fitch gave permission but told Jackson not to take longer than ten minutes. Fitch was actually on the point of giving up and had made up his mind that if in the next quarter of a mile he found no suitable place he would seek elsewhere.

Jackson and Brisset pushed on ahead accompanied by the Accompong Maroons. Fitch came on more slowly behind with the rest of the men. After walking for about one hundred yards Jackson, Brisset and the Accompongs came to a place where the trail divided into two. Both branches led steeply down into a valley. They hesitated for a moment and then Brisset and the Accompongs took one branch and, Jackson took the other. Jackson went a few yards down his branch and, perhaps not liking the look of it, turned back. He started down the other track behind Brisset and the Accompongs and had not gone very far when a volley of shots split the air and echoed and re-echoed off the precipitous sides of the valley.

Captain Brisset staggered away to the right and crashed dead among the bushes. One of the Accompongs gave a loud shriek and fell; the other dropped dead without a sound. Colonel Jackson was the only one left standing, saved perhaps by the fact that he was slightly behind his companions.

Farther down the trail Fitch, Captain Lee and the others had also been raked by the shots of the hidden Trelawnys. Fitch himself was hit and crumpled down upon the dead trunk of a fallen tree.

Captain Lee's men, shocked into action by the ambush, fired at places where the smoke from the guns of the Trelawnys still hung. Ahead, Jackson jumped off the exposed trail on to lower ground and raced back to where Fitch, Lee and the others had stopped. He found Fitch sitting on the tree trunk, one arm resting on the stump of the branch and his head propped on his hand. The other arm hung limply at his side and blood was running from the middle of his waistcoat.

Jackson grabbed the hand that hung at Fitch's side and spoke to him but there was no response. He drew his dagger and swore that he would kill both Fitch and himself rather than allow either of them to be captured by the Trelawnys.

The Trelawnys began to reload and Lee's men standing stunned and frightened in the trail, with their eyes searching the rocks and trees for a target, heard the clicking of metal as the Trelawnys cocked their guns. Jackson shouted at them to lie down and they threw themselves to the ground. Jackson tried to pull Fitch down from the log where he sat exposed but Fitch resisted. Jackson was still trying hard to pull him down when another volley exploded from the Trelawnys' guns.

Fitch was hit in the forehead above the right eye and fell dead. Captain Lee, Adjutant Brunt and several of the men were also hit. Once again Jackson was unhurt. He shouted at the men to move out quickly and they fled, helping the wounded along but leaving the dead behind.

Some of Lee's men who had been left behind at the post, hurried out to see what was happening when they heard the shooting. It was felt that if they had not come up when they did, none of the wounded would have escaped.

One of the survivors, a private of the 83rd Regiment, had multiple wounds. From his head and neck were taken "a piece of a brass gun barrel, four slugs, a piece of square iron and several small shot", all of which gave an indication of the sort of make-shift "bullets" used by the Trelawnys.

A few days later Captain Lee died of the wounds he had received. The ambush had taken the lives of eight men while seven had been wounded.

Three hundred militia and about two hundred Regular troops, horse and foot, were sent out in a determined search for the Maroons who had ambushed the party.

Colonel Fitch was deeply mourned by his men and by all who knew him. Lieutenant-Colonel Robert Jackson, who had been with him at his death, seemed especially affected. It was almost as if Jackson felt guilty at having fled and left Fitch behind, though he had not moved to save himself until it was clear that Fitch was dead.

Fitch's body could not be found at first, even after an apparently thorough search of the area where the ambush had occurred. But Jackson would not give up. Like a man obsessed, he searched and searched, and finally, towards the middle of November, two months after Fitch had been killed, he came upon a pile of rocks in a cockpit. Beneath it lay the remains of Colonel Fitch. The body had apparently been taken there and covered with rocks by the Maroons.

The remains were conveyed to the Old Town and buried beside Captain Lee, who had been interred there earlier. The funeral took place on November 15th and was attended by the whole 83rd regiment and the officers quartered at the Old Town. An article in a newspaper, noting that Fitch's remains had been "exposed to the weather for two months", said that:

"The sweetest tears shed on mortals are those which heaven bedews the unburied head of a soldier".

Other newspaper articles described Fitch as "an excellent man in all respects, devoted to the duties of the profession and esteemed by all who had the pleasure of serving under him... Much as might be said in honour of the memory of Colonel Fitch, it is not probable that the first of Writers, or the first of Orators, could speedily reconcile his Regiment to the loss of so excellent, so humane, so generous a Commander".

But Fitch's remains were not to lie permanently in the Old Maroon Town. They were removed and interred in the Montego Bay churchyard on Wednesday night, June 22nd, with military honours, by a detachment of the 17th Light Dragoons and the 83rd regiment quartered in Montego Bay. The procession moved from the barracks at 7 p.m., and during the march and until the funeral service was over, minute guns were fired from the fort and by the artillery of the Militia. The scene was solemn and affecting. Fitch had become the great tragic figure of the war; the fallen hero.

CHAPTER 24

WALPOLE TAKES COMMAND

With the loss of the fearless and energetic Fitch, another equally brave and competent officer had to be found to take charge of the campaign in the field. The choice was a fortunate one for the colonists. Colonel George Walpole, originally in command of the forces in St. Elizabeth and Westmoreland, was promoted to the rank of Major General and appointed Commander-in-Chief.

At the start of the war, Governor Balcarres, as Commander-in-Chief, had taken a leading role. This was quite in keeping with his military experience. Born in 1752, he had joined the army at the age of fifteen. In 1771 he was made a Captain in the 42nd Highlanders and in 1775, became a Major in the 53rd Foot. During the American War of Independence, he distinguished himself at the battles of Ticonderoga and Huberton, and he was promoted to Brigadier General in 1777. By the terms of the Convention made by General Burgoyne of the American army, however, he was compelled to surrender, and remained a prisoner until 1779. He was elevated to the rank of Major General in 1793, about two years before taking up his duties as Governor of Jamaica.*

With the Maroon war going badly, it seems that Balcarres decided to step back and give Walpole a fairly

---

*Balcarres died in 1825.

free hand in developing an offensive campaign. On appointing Walpole, Balcarres took the opportunity to inform the Duke of Portland of his lack of confidence in the two senior Major Generals: Palmer and Thomas Reid Jr. That was when he mentioned the strong influence which he felt Major John James, ex-Superintendent of Maroons, had over them. Balcarres told the Duke that it was impossible to continue the service under such commanders, "I was therefore forced to appoint Colonel Walpole to be Major General in the King's service until his Majesty's pleasure should be signified". Walpole's appointment gave him precedence over Palmer and Reid.

On September 15th, as soon as he received his dispatches, Walpole left Accompong Town alone and rode hard through a dangerous stretch of country to Fitch's old headquarters at Trelawny Town. He found Fitch's men tired and dispirited. Accommodation was bad and heavy rains flooded the area. Walpole tried to get the men to do something to improve their conditions but they would not budge. They felt that the struggle was useless and that it would never end.

Walpole realized at once that morale was so low that one more defeat might destroy it altogether. He decided not to launch an attack unless the odds for success were clearly in his favour and unless the results of a victory would mean a decisive turn for the better. He had studied the nature of the country in which the campaign was taking place and understood that while it was ideal for defensive purposes it presented terrible obstacles to an attacking force. He therefore set out to find a way to make the country work in his favour and to force the Trelawnys to fight on more equal terms as far as the terrain was concerned.

Balcarres' plan had been to build a cordon around the area but Walpole abandoned this idea when he realized that the skilful Maroon patrols could slip through any time they wanted to. Instead he began to develop the plan which Fitch had started, of building posts and clearing the countryside.

He increased the number of posts so as to cover the nearby settlements more effectively and used gangs of slaves guarded by strong advance parties to clear the heights surrounding his camp. These included the very high rise near his headquarters from which Dunbar and his men had called down to Fitch when they had made an attempt at peace talks. Walpole also began to complete the work of clearing the land in front of Guthrie's defile which Fitch had started.

On September 22nd, while Walpole was busy with his bush-clearing operations, Governor Balcarres rose in the House of Assembly in Spanish Town and told the members that he believed that the trouble with the Maroons had been instigated by French revolutionaries and had been premeditated for a long time. He seemed to believe that the Trelawnys had moved before the plans were quite ready and this, he told the members, had given him the opportunity to nip the conspiracy in the bud.

He reported that his troops had stormed and occupied the Maroon country, taken their towns and bottled them up in the barren wilderness. The truth of course was that the Trelawnys had burnt their New Town, abandoned their Old Town and made a strategic withdrawal to their immensely powerful stronghold in the Petty River Bottom Cockpit, from which they commenced to frustrate all the attempts of their enemies, inflicting numerous casualties, apparently without the loss of a single man.

The House granted a sum of £500 to the Accompongs for their good conduct and also to provide compensation for the two Accompong warriors who had been killed with Fitch. A proclamation was also issued offering a reward of £300 for killing or capturing any slave who joined the Trelawnys. These rewards were further increased by additional sums of money offered by the various parishes.

An act was passed allowing for two companies of free people of colour to be raised and providing for the families of the killed and the disabled. The government also made an attempt to get active help from the far-off Charles Town Maroons. Sam Grant, the man who had aided the escape of sea captain Davy at Old Harbour in 1774 and who had killed a sea captain while making his own escape, was now the Chief Commander at Charles Town. Sam Grant and his Charles Town Maroons were ordered by the government to take up duty in Kingston. They marched to the town but after a while began complaining that they were not getting enough food to eat. They packed up and marched back to Charles Town. The years had apparently not dimmed the distinctive character of Sam Grant but the action of the Maroons caused great alarm among the citizens of Kingston. While all this was taking place, Johnson and his Trelawnys continued to keep the troops busy.

Colonel Fitch and Captain Lee had died trying to find a new site for Lee's post. The post still stood where it was, a mile and a quarter to the south of the Old Town and dangerously exposed to Maroon attacks. It was now commanded by Captain White of the 83rd Regiment.

One night one of the sentries at this post thought he saw a shape pass him in the dark. He gave the alarm and at dawn two search parties scoured the area under White's direction. They saw no one and returned to the post. Captain White called for his coffee and went into his hut. A boy started towards the hut carrying the coffee. Suddenly there was a nerve-shattering burst of musket fire and shots smashed into the post. The boy with the coffee was hit and fell dead.

White gathered together his tiny garrison and beat off the attack. He managed to hold out until reinforcements arrived. Everyone was now thoroughly convinced that the post was in too vulnerable a position and three weeks later it was abandoned.

In the meantime Walpole's slave gangs were steadily chopping away the cover of bush from the surrounding country. While they worked he began to train his soldiers to use some of the Maroon tactics. They learned how to take advantage of whatever cover there was while they fired and reloaded.

When the heights were sufficiently cleared to make an ambush impossible, Walpole sent seventy Light Dragoons under Lieutenant Richards to climb up the hill on the right of Guthrie's Defile. They were to find out whether it was possible to descend into the Cockpit from that side. At the same time, in order to create a diversion, Walpole sent a sergeant with a squad of men to the left side of the approach to the Defile.

Lieutenant Richards and his men marched for about a mile and then began to climb the right hill of the Defile. Needless to say, the Trelawnys had long been aware of their movements and as the Dragoons moved up they began firing into them. Harassed by the accurate shooting of the Maroons and hampered by the precipitous nature of the ground the Dragoons could make no headway; but here Walpole's training began to show results. The Dragoons hunted for cover. They hid behind rocks, trees and stumps and so avoided casualties. From their concealed positions they fired back at the Maroons.

They were pinned down, however, and not being as careful in their shooting as the Maroons, they soon began to run out of ammunition. Richards sent a message to the sergeant on the left side of the Defile asking him to come up and cover his withdrawal. The sergeant started off at once. He was leading his men across the track which led into the Defile when he heard a horn sound deep in the Cockpit. Immediately he changed direction and led his men straight down the path into the Defile. They went straight into the jaws of death.

No one will ever know why the sergeant made this decision. It was suggested later that when he heard the horn he may have thought that Richards had managed to force his way into the Cockpit and so had charged into the Defile to help him.

Richards and his Dragoons, clinging to the hillside, waited in vain for their support. They shouted loudly in the hope of attracting the sergeant to their position but no one appeared. Just as they were beginning to wonder what was keeping him they heard heavy firing break out in the Defile and quickly guessed what had happened.

Taking advantage of the diversion which the sergeant had unwittingly created, Richards managed to get his Dragoons off the hill without too much damage, but the sergeant and several of his men were killed in the Defile and many others were wounded.

In his report later that day, October 20th, 1795 Richards said:

> "The working party of the 17th Dragoons was this morning attacked. None would have probably been killed, but for the obstinacy of a sergeant with a rein-forcement of 20 men who, in spite of the admonition of one of the white men (on duty with) the Negroes walked into (an) ambush

> A detachment of the 13th Light Dragoons having, by my orders, marched to cut off the Maroons in the rear, on gaining the southern declivity of the hill, at the foot of Montague James' grass-piece, discovered the Maroons, about 50 or 60 in number, retreating into their caves; the men quarrelling apparently, and the women distinctly crying".

Richards' account of the crying Maroon women and the arguing men, seen by the detachment of the 13th Light Dragoons, gives the impression that Walpole's relentless efforts were paying off. The embattled Trelawnys were beginning to feel the pressure.

Walpole's first attempt to come to grips with the Trelawnys had failed but he was far from discouraged. More important, however, was the fact that in spite of the continuing rains which normally had a depressing effect on troops in the field, his men seemed in better spirits. The gloom which had been cast on them by the death of Fitch was lifting. Walpole took advantage of the growing morale and redoubled his efforts. He built two more posts; one to the south-east at a place called One Eye which lay at the extreme end of the line of Cockpits, the other to the north-east of this on the banks of the Hector's River. Next he began to gather information about the country from surveyors and from the Accompongs. He made them give him details of the Maroon tracks and of the unfrequented springs in the area.

Having done all this Walpole took precautions against ambush or a surprise attack. Then he settled down and waited patiently for the rains to stop.

CHAPTER 25

JOHNSON'S RAIDERS

Early in October, Balcarres reinforced Walpole with detachments of regular troops under the command of Colonel Skinner, a very brave and able officer. There were now thousands of heavily armed and well-supplied regular troops and militia against Johnson's entire force of about two hundred and fifty Trelawny warriors, who were hampered by women and children and ill-supplied with food and ammunition.

In spite of this, Johnson was not content simply to remain on the defensive. He divided his force into two distinct groups. The larger formed a sort of garrison and was stationed in Guthrie's Defile and Petty River Bottom Cockpit under the command of Captain Charlie Shaw, the man who had frustrated Fitch's early attempts to clear the bush away from the front of Guthrie's Defile. Apart from guarding the Cockpit stronghold, Shaw was also responsible for the protection of the women, children and valuables of the Trelawnys. It was Shaw who broke up the attempt of Richards' Dragoons to climb the hill on the right of Guthrie's Defile.

The second and smaller group of Trelawnys was commanded by Johnson himself. This was a raiding force and operated outside the protection of the Cockpit fort. Johnson had no fixed headquarters. He shifted from one position to the next, depending on the location of the place which he intended to attack next. When the troops thought he was at one place on a certain day he would launch a surprise raid the next day twenty miles away.

To strengthen his small force Johnson pressed about forty slaves into his service. Those who fought well were promoted but, if in the next fight their standard of performance fell below Johnson's expectations, he would flog them.

Johnson imposed an iron discipline on his band of raiders and his own sons came in for the same harsh punishment as any other man if they deserved it. It was the only way in which he could successfully face the terrific odds against which he fought. The discipline produced good results, for not only did his men fight well but they were never surprised except for a few occasions when the out-sentries happened to be careless slaves. We may be sure that, if they were not killed or captured, these sentries paid dearly at the hands of Johnson for their carelessness.

Several of the slaves whom Johnson had pressed into his service were eventually killed in battle, but he said later that he only lost two of his Trelawny men.

Moving with bewildering speed, Johnson's raiders penetrated the surrounding lines of soldiers almost at will. They struck at the settlements of the colonists with fire and shot and then disappeared like phantoms. Leonard Parkinson, for whom Balcarres had offered a reward of fifty pounds, dead or alive, was one of Johnson's lieutenants.

It was said that, apart from the slaves, the raiders numbered no more than thirty-six. They were extremely active in September and October, and their first target was George Gordon's Kenmure settlement in Westmoreland where they set fire to the dwelling house and other buildings. At ten o' clock on the morning of the following day they burnt the houses and works on Jacob Graham's valuable coffee plantation known as Lapland. Mr. Trought's extensive coffee plantation at Catadupa was raided next.

Houses on Great River Penn, the property of John Shand were burnt; as well as the small settlement belonging to Messrs. Stevens and Bernard. The house of a carpenter named Dent, near Roehampton estate went up in flames, and when news reached the military that raiders were threatening some of the mountain estates, especially Mount Tirza, a party of Dragoons was sent from Black River to guard the area.

Dr. Brooks' settlement was set on fire and two men killed; Stormont's settlement was burnt; the trash house of Roger's estate at Darliston was destroyed by fire and so was Lewis' house. Nairn plantation owned by Samuel Waite was destroyed and on the same day raiders plundered and burnt Bandon, the residence of Dr. Largie, where they were seen digging in the slaves' provision grounds.

Raiders in ambush between Spring Vale and Shaw Castle fired at Messrs. Bell and Webb of Falmouth, missing Webb but wounding Bell. James Sadlow of the Trelawny Windward troop, riding from Spring Vale with a very large packet from Governor Balcarres to be delivered to General Walpole, was ambushed at the same place where Bell and Webb had been attacked. Trooper Sadlow was shot from his horse, a bullet going through his heart. The packet from the Governor was found torn to pieces near him, and the fragments were collected and sent on to Walpole.

The raiders swept through Mocho, Ginger Hill, Gowdey's and other places, destroying them all. A food convoy guarded by ten soldiers and bound for the newly established outposts at Mocho and Augustus, was surprised and wiped out. At first it was believed that one of the soldiers had escaped and hopes ran high; but when his body was later found half a mile from where his comrades had fallen, there was a general feeling of depression.

Governor Balcarres increased the reward for killing or capturing Maroons: "A reward of three hundred dollars (instead of sixty dollars or twenty pounds offered on August

13th) will be paid to any person or persons, slaves as well as others, who shall take or kill in rebellion any Trelawny Town Maroon man. And the service of any Negro or other slave, who shall take or kill any Trelawny Town Maroon or Maroons, will be taken into consideration by the House of Assembly."

In spite of this incentive, and the almost hopeless position of the Trelawnys, a fair number of slaves, and even some free men, risked everything to join them.

The raiders were getting a lot of provisions from Gordon's settlement at Kenmure (which was the first place attacked), so General Walpole established a post close to the settlement which effectively cut off access to the provisions. Two days later on October 11th the Maroons attacked the post, but a detachment of the 83rd regiment under Major Godley, was on hand and repulsed them with considerable losses. According to army reports twenty were killed. A letter published in a supplement of the Royal Gazette of October 1795 said: "The groans and moanings of the Maroons were distinctly heard, and their calling to each other for assistance."

Walpole reported to Balcarres that he thought the attack was a combined effort of raiders returning from the country (Johnson and Parkinson's parties) and another group sent out for the sole purpose of destroying the post. He believed the Maroons were prevented from reaching the main group in the Cockpits, as Major Godley's men reported that they passed up the hill, back towards Kenmure, "with the most horrid yells".

The following day, a party of militia, sent to destroy the provisions of a settlement close to the Cockpits, ran into Maroons loaded down with supplies which they had been collecting in different places: butter, mutton, pork partly cured in smoke, yams, plantains, cocos, etc. The militia attacked and the Maroon foragers were forced to abandon their valuable provisions in order to save themselves.

The militia pursued, keeping up a brisk fire. They saw blood on the pathways but had to stop when they came to a sink hole surrounded by precipices, which prevented them from advancing. The foraging party escaped with their wounded, but the militia destroyed the provisions at the settlement close to the Cockpits and set fire to a number of huts. As these began to burn there was a loud explosion, which was thought to have come from ammunition concealed in one of the huts.

Food had become one of the chief objectives for both sides. On the part of the Trelawnys every effort was being made, particularly by Johnson and his raiders, to supply the main body with a continuous flow of provisions. On the part of the soldiers there was a constant marching to and fro to cut off the foraging and raiding parties, and to seek out and destroy provision grounds. If force of arms could not subdue the resolute Trelawnys then starvation would. In spite of all efforts, however, raiding parties continued to penetrate the ring of troops.

A group of seven raiders burnt a dwelling house on Abingdon, the property of a Miss Dunbar, on the Eldersley road. They also set fire to Springfield Pen, the plantation of George McLennan, after collecting every portable article that could be of service to them, especially butter, salt, soap, candles, etc. They next burnt the house and destroyed the provisions at Mount Lebanon, a settlement belonging to Content estate. On October 16th they descended on Amity Hall at seven in the morning and burnt the overseer's house and the works. The overseer escaped but the book-keeper was killed.

Between ten and eleven the same morning raiders burnt Mount Parnassus, a settlement belonging to the late Robert Kerr; and at three the same afternoon fired the provision settlement called Mount Ararat (or Mount Ida) belonging to Isaac Lascelles Winn.

The Montpelier company under the command of

Lieutenant McLennan, whose Springfield Pen property had been burnt, marched from their station at Seven Rivers at two in the morning to join Captain Hamilton, commanding a detachment of Brown infantry two miles away at Wiltshire estate. The whole force, under Hamilton set out to intercept the tiny band of raiders who were reported to be on the way to Catadupa.

The raiders spent the night in the woods. Early the next morning, McLennan and his Montpelier company proceeded along a narrow path where they could only walk in single file, and came out on a coffee barbecue at Catadupa.

As McLennan set foot on the barbecue, Samuel Barnett, the leader of the Maroon party, appeared on the other side. An invalid girl belonging to Trought's coffee plantation at Catadupa, which had been raided, was making a fire in the middle of the barbecue. Barnett was walking towards her when he came face to face with McLennan.

The Lieutenant levelled his gun and the Maroon instantly grabbed the girl and placed her in front of him. McLennan advanced and Barnett, realizing he would soon be trapped, let go the girl and ran, stooping close to the ground keeping his head almost at knee-level. McLennan fired at the small of his back. The bullet hit Barnett who screamed, leapt about two feet in the air, and fell from the barbecue to the ground four feet below.

McLennan's militiamen came running out of the woods, shooting. The raiders dropped the loot they were carrying and dashed into nearby coffee bushes. Barnett was still alive. He had fallen at the feet of a slave belonging to McLennan, whom the Maroons had abducted from Springfield the evening before. Struggling up, he hobbled off in an opposite direction, leaving his weapons behind and shouting to his men to save themselves as he was done for.

Shortly after, seven very young Maroons accompanied by several runaway slaves, descended on Unity Estate and slew Mr. Nash the overseer. They set fire to John Reid's dwelling house near Unity and to Edward Flemming's house. The latter blaze was put out by Flemming's slaves. St. Ann militia rushed to Unity in the afternoon, and to Spring Vale next morning.

As a result of the series of lightning raids, and the destruction of houses and works, particularly on Amity Hall estate, militia guards were posted by Major General Thomas Reid, Jnr, on "respective properties adjacent to the woods."

Slaves provided the troops with a lot of information. One, named Simon, owned by John Simpson of Bounty Hall estate, ran away and joined the Maroons, and went with a raiding party of twenty to Chatsworth for provisions. On returning they encountered the Trelawny Light Company and engaged them in a fight, during which Simon was mortally wounded by Sergeant Adam Webb.

As Simon lay dying he informed his captors that the rebels had plenty of bullets but very little gunpowder. The main body was near the Old Town and the women had been sent to a place which he "described perfectly". Simon said watchmen on properties had been providing the Maroons with salt, and Leonard Parkinson had been sent out with a foraging party but had not yet returned. Parkinson's group had been responsible for the attacks on Amity Hall, Parnassus and other properties. Simon informed his interrogators of the route Parkinson had taken and plans were made to cut him off from the main body.

On Friday October 9th, a slave named Neptune, belonging to Jacob Graham, was captured at Cold Spring by a party of militia under Lieutenant-Colonel Barnes. Neptune was carrying a gun charged with three balls, a cutlass and a bag of ammunition. He said he had been with the Maroons for four weeks, two of them spent in Westmoreland with Johnson's Raiders. He had participated in the raid on Dr. Brooks' settlement at which two men had been killed.

Zell, an Ibo, belonging to Isaac Lascelles Winn of Winn's Mountain, said he was forced away with three other slaves by Maroons and went with them by way of Vaughansfield. He was made to carry salted provisions and yams taken from Amity Hall. Zell reported that the Maroons were short of provisions but had plenty of houses and water in the Cockpits. The path to their camp was well watched, and so narrow, that only two persons could walk abreast on it. The Maroons told him they would rather die than submit. They never went out in a body but only in small parties so as not to make too much noise. Many lived in caves. They were short of gunpowder and some had none at all.

Robert Montgomery, a mulatto slave from York estate, said he was with the Maroon youths, women and children under Montague James near Ginger Town. Gunpowder was so scarce that the youths guarding the females were only allowed a half of their usual charge; and those sent on foraging or fighting missions were only given a round and a half, or two rounds each. He reported erroneously that Johnson had died of wounds, and said that the measles and flux had carried off some of the younger children. Provisions were so scarce that the Maroons were doing away with girls under ten and infants. But Montgomery was not a reliable witness.

On the other hand a slave named Jamaica, the property of John Reid and Company, said he was employed for two weeks by the Maroons, cutting thatch and looking for wild yams which were very plentiful. The Maroons had all their children and had not killed one to his knowledge. There were several young ones at the breast and many of all ages. They had fowls but no other stock. Their weapons were kept very clean and they carried their gunpowder in cow horns which they put under their heads at night.

Slaves who had been captured by the Maroons, but who got away, reported that the Maroons were always afraid they might escape and reveal the locations of their hideouts. Robert

Montgomery of York estate was one who got away. He escaped to Captain Allen's post from a foraging party he was with, and led a strong party of the 83rd Regiment to the Maroon camp near Mocho where Parkinson was in command. But the raiders got away after firing a few shots.

A slave driver named Commodore, belonging to James McKean, carried off four slaves into the mountains to join the Maroons, threatening to cut off their heads (according to what they said) if they did not go with him. They escaped and informed the authorities. Commodore was captured, tried in the Slave Court in Montego Bay and convicted of rebellion. He was sentenced to be hanged in Market Street immediately, and his head to be cut off and placed in the most public place, as a warning. Commodore had twice before attempted to escape by putting to sea in canoes, along with other slaves he had persuaded to join him.

CHAPTER 26

PSYCHOLOGICAL WARFARE

The area of hostilities was literally crawling with troops. A typical day's report showed Kingston and St. Catherine detachments gone into the woods, a party of Regulars taking post at Mocho, reinforcements of militia guarding Catadupa, a belt of troops surrounding and ambushing the Maroon trails, a detachment of seventy infantry and forty cavalry marching from the parish of Vere to join the forces acting against the Trelawnys.

On November 6th, the Brown Company of St. James, marching from Willis' settlement, fell into a Maroon ambush. Soon after the engagement began the Maroons blew their horns, and were apparently reinforced. An officer of the company said that the Maroons were so well-concealed that he saw only one during the action. They were on both sides of the defile; to the right of the front of the column, and to the left of the rear.

The Brown Company held their ground but the firing was very heavy. According to the officer:

"I was at a loss to learn where all the balls came from for the last eight or ten minutes (of the fight). They were flying about like hail; and what rendered it worse was we could see none of the infernal rascals. We had seven men killed on the spot and four wounded; two of them mortally. Sergeant Hanlon is among the number; they were killed in the last five minutes of the

action. We retreated to Willis' house, where, had they
attacked us, we might have been cut off. We brought
off all the dead and wounded but one, whom we could
not find."

The officer thought the Maroons numbered eighty or one
hundred and had their women and children with them.
"They were on a steep hill, full of rocks and woods, when
they attacked us," he wrote. "I imagine they are all on
their march to the Black Grounds (in southern Trelawny)
and that we fell in with the whole or main body of them."

As soon as news of the action was received, troops hurried into the area: detachments from the adjacent posts
occupied by the St. Ann's, Clarendon and Trelawny militia,
and a part of the Trelawny Leeward Troop. They searched
the adjacent hills but met no Maroons, and in the evening
fell back to Dromilly and the neighbouring frontier estates.

Early in November Lieutenant Hamilton, commanding a
detachment of St. James Militia at Catadupa, four miles
from Trought's settlement at Mocho, was informed that
raiders who had burnt several settlements in St. Elizabeth
and Westmoreland and killed a Mr. Gowdie and his
nephew, were returning loaded with spoils and provisions.
Johnson was in command and the raiders had been sighted
in Mocho Pen, part of a Cockpit lying between Mocho plantation and Catadupa, and terminating in a narrow defile at
each end.

Hamilton was joined at Post Augustus on Saturday,
November 8th, by Captain Lewis Williams, who was on his
way to Vaughansfield with a detachment consisting of the
Westmoreland Brown infantry and Black rangers; and also
by the brothers William and Robert Russel from St.
Elizabeth with some Volunteers. Hamilton's post was not
properly secure. Maroons had burnt his huts not long
before when he was out on patrol, and ten of his men were
sick. Nevertheless, leaving ten men to guard the post with

its sick soldiers, he took forty men and went with Williams' on Sunday morning, November 9th, to seek Johnson.

They went through Mocho to Vaughansfield, and then through the first defile for a distance of about two miles, before stopping and going into ambush, expecting Johnson and his force to pass that way. After waiting for a few hours the scouts reported that no Maroons were in sight. Hamilton was worried that Johnson might get behind them and attack his weakly-defended post, so he returned to Post Augustus with his men.

Captain Williams and his detachment pushed on. They saw fresh tracks which indicated that Johnson had returned from St. Elizabeth, probably the evening before. They also saw fresher footsteps, suggesting that their presence had been detected by Johnson's scouts who would by now have reported to him. But, Captain Williams was a young man and he felt it would be worth any risk to come to grips with the terrible Johnson. He made up his mind "to follow at all hazards, despite the bad defile ahead", and later apologised for his rash conduct in a letter to Major General Walpole.

At about 11 a.m., when Williams and his contingent were about a mile from Mocho, they ran into an ambush. Johnson had been waiting patiently for them. What saved them was the fact that Johnson was almost out of gunpowder.

When the Maroons started shooting, Williams withdrew from the trail into the woods. A few shots were exchanged. Each side could occasionally see the men of the other side among the rocks and trees. There was a long pause during which nothing much happened. Williams wisely took advantage of this stalemate and at about 1 p.m. retreated to the open ground at Mocho Pen. He waited there for Johnson.

At two in the afternoon, Johnson attacked. Because of his shortage of gunpowder he had to use psychological warfare.

His men came from the woods and gave the soldiers a volley, and the shooting back and forth started. The Maroons shouted abuse at the soldiers, and every now and then, blew their horns and gave the impression that they were being reinforced by a fresh group of men. Six times they blew their horns, and each time the soldiers thought they saw a fresh group of Maroons coming up, threatening to surround them.

Above the noise of battle Johnson's voice could be heard, abusing the soldiers and ordering forty men to go to one side or another; giving the impression that he had a large number of men. The Maroons displayed a great deal of recklessness. Early in the conflict, Johnson deliberately exposed himself as he went up and down, exhorting his men, scorning to take cover. He caught sight of Captain Williams whom he knew personally and began to abuse him. One of the Russels from St. Elizabeth fired at a Maroon whom he thought was Johnson "and laid him dead on the spot". A "Mulatto" Maroon named Harvey, boldly running out to retrieve the body, was shot down. Six other Maroons came out "and exposed their persons in a manner hitherto unexperienced, and were killed". Johnson had actually been wounded and, according to another story, drew a knife, cut out the bullet, and went on directing his men.

The soldiers noticed that the Maroons appeared to be short of powder. The sound of the guns and the effects of the bullets indicated that very little gunpowder was behind each shot. One shot fired at only thirty yards distance entered the fleshy part of a man's thigh but did not go through.

By about five in the evening Williams' ammunition was almost finished and it was beginning to rain. He decided to pull his men out of Mocho Pen, pass through the Western defile and get back to Catadupa before night. When Johnson saw what he was doing, he ordered forty men to go round the hill, shouting: "Cut them to pieces, don't spare one". Perhaps by then he had nothing to fight with but cutlasses.

According to a military report: "the retreat was so well timed and ably conducted that the entrance of the defile was gained at a critical moment, after a severe contest with the (Maroons), who attempted to cut off the retreat The Maroons allowed Captain Williams and his party to retire in good order, bringing off their wounded to Catadupa". One may conclude from that statement that Johnson had run entirely out of gunpowder.

On the way to Catadupa, Williams met Lieutenant Hamilton advancing with a party to his assistance. WIlliams' losses were slight considering the length of the engagement: two killed and four wounded. He thought his men had killed perhaps eleven Maroons, and seven for certain; and that there must have been many more wounded. A baggage slave who concealed himself under a rock during the action, saw four dead bodies removed by the Maroons into the woods, "over whom there was much wailing and lamentation." Many cherished the hope that Johnson was among the slain. But he was very much alive.

The parish of Westmoreland was so pleased with the performance of Williams' contingent that they proposed making them a "handsome gratuity", and hoped that other Western parishes and the whole country would follow their example. On November 19th the Westmoreland vestry presented Williams and his men, drawn up on parade, with 1,050 dollars, for seven Maroons killed; and gave 30 dollars to three armed slaves, who were with them "and whose good behaviour entitles them to the praise and remembrance of the community."

If an impartial judge had observed that battle however, the prize would have gone to Johnson. He had successfully ambushed those who had set out to ambush him and had fought with very little ammunition. By outrageous courage and the use of psychological tactics he had tricked the enemy into believing that he had ample reserves of men at his beck and call, and had finally forced them to retreat.

CHAPTER 27

FEAR AND FORTITUDE

The war had become a fearful and desperate business. It was to be a comparatively brief war, but before it was over, twenty actions would be fought in which nearly five thousand troops (about 1,520 of which were highly-trained regular soldiers), supported by Mosquito Indians and savage Cuban hunting dogs, would strive mightily to overcome less than three hundred Trelawny Maroon warriors (about 250).

In addition to the regular infantry and horse and foot militia, the 13th, 14th, 17th, 18th and 20th Light Dragoons, and the York Hussars also took part in the conflict. The 17th Light Dragoons were experienced in colonial warfare. They had served in the American Revolutionary War and were attached to Sir Banastre Tarleton's British Legion, a mixed force of cavalry and light infantry. As a part of the Legion, they were involved in the successful siege of Charleston in 1780 and in a series of other victorious battles in the south which ended, however, in Tarleton's defeat at the battle of Cowpens in 1781.

Walpole, who had been given a very free hand by Balcarres, had three infantry divisions at his disposal, but he chose to train the 17th Light Dragoons in wilderness warfare. They learned to fight on foot and work in pairs or groups, "one man taking charge of another's (weapons) when he required both hands for climbing". Most important however, was that, like the Maroons and American Indians, they learned to take advantage of cover. Writing to Balcarres on December 22nd, 1795, towards the end of the war, Walpole reported that his whole detachment had behaved creditably; but he had to make special mention of the 17th Dragoons, because their "undaunted bravery" in action made such an impression on the Maroons, that it was instrumental in bringing about their submission. He said the Maroons spoke of the 17th "with astonishment", which was indeed great praise coming from those fearless warriors.

The 17th wore blue jackets with white facings, white breeches and Hessian boots.

The war had its quota of deserters. On November 16th, when the Clarendon Brown Infantry was ordered to march into the woods, six of the privates decided they had had enough of the fighting. On the night of the 16th, privates John Robertson, George George, Samuel Wright, Johnson, James Garvey, John Freeman and George Davis deserted their post.

They were apprehended, tried for desertion on Wednesday, November 25th at a court martial held in a Falmouth hotel, and sentenced to death.

In the afternoon, the proceedings of the Court and the sentence were sent to the Commander-in-Chief, Governor the Earl of Balcarres. The documents were accompanied by a petition from the President of the court martial, the Honourable Colonel Shirley, and the members of the Court, praying for mercy. Balcarres' reply, written from Spanish Town on November 27th, was received on Sunday afternoon. On Monday morning, November 30th, the 20th Light Dragoons and a part of the Leeward Troop were ordered to parade in the main street. The prisoners, under custody of the main guard and preceded by the President and members of the Court Martial, marched to the centre of the horsemen; and then all proceeded to the review grounds.

Before the assembled Horse and Foot, the prisoners were brought forward to hear the Governor's message, which said in part:

> "The Commander in Chief approves of the proceedings and sentence. Such is the punishment the Law has decreed to men who basely and dishonourably desert their Duty, when their country calls on their services to act in arms against the Enemies.
>
> The lives of those unhappy men are most justly forfeited.
>
> A relaxation of discipline at the present crisis, would stamp discredit upon the conduct of the Commander in Chief, and it becomes difficult indeed, in his responsible situation, to extend the Royal Mercy to men who have brought themselves into so terrible and afflicting a situation.
>
> The Prisoners have pleaded their character and their Youth.
>
> If young men of good character desert their Colours in the hour of danger, by whom is their country to be defended?
>
> By whom are their own families and those who are dear to them to be protected but by those who have Courage, Fortitude and Strength, to meet the common Enemy and to afford such protection?
>
> Neither their Character nor their youth can alone operate to save them; but the eminent and distinguished services of the soldiers of their Colour, have made a deep impression upon the mind of the Commander in Chief, and will act more powerfully in their favour.
>
> This together with the strong recommendation for mercy presented in their behalf by the members of the Court Martial, and the Custos and gentlemen of their parish, has obtained their PARDON, which they are permitted to plead upon their knees, at the head of the

Regular forces and Militia, now stationed in
Falmouth."

The six dejected prisoners were probably certain that
they would be shot, and had to sweat through the reading
of the Governor's message up to that point where the word
PARDON was said. Their relief can only be imagined.

After the ordeal they were ordered to join their detachments, with the hope that by "zealous and diligent dis-
charge of their duty they would expiate their offence, and
be restored to the favour of their King and country".
Balcarres' statement was read at the head of every troop
and company of militia in the island.

Johnson drove himself and his men to the breaking
point. He must have realized quite early that, in the
absence of any significant assistance, his less than three
hundred men could not hold out forever against the thousands arrayed against them. The fighting men alone might
have gone on to the bitter end, but the increasing distress
of the women and children, always in peril, hungry and on
the move, could not be set aside.

Courage and endurance were not enough. In the final
analysis it was a matter of food and gunpowder. The trails
were closed, the provision grounds were guarded and
Walpole, with access to all the supplies and fresh men he
needed, was closing in, relentlessly.

Most of the reports and evaluations we have of the
Maroons came from their enemies, or from frightened or
calculating slaves, who were prepared to tell what they
thought their masters wanted to hear. So it is not wise to
go entirely by what was said and written. We have very little of the Maroons' own side of things.

Jumbo, a slave belonging to Richard Haughton Reid of
Hanover, said he was carried away in October 1795 by a
party of Maroons, commanded by Johnson, Dunbar and

Smith. He described Johnson as "the most cruel, savage and enterprising man" amongst the Maroons. "Even his own party disapproves of his conduct at times, but he has more authority than any other commander, and his devastations would have extended far beyond what they did (but) for the wound in his leg."

Early in December Colonel Skinner with one hundred and thirty men of the 16th and 83rd regiments marched from Cold Spring to the Mocho Post. One hundred and twenty men of the St James Militia under Colonel James marched the same morning to Post Augustus at Catadupa, then on to Mocho also.

Many slaves accompanied them for the purpose of opening a line of communication between Cold Spring, Catadupa and Mocho, and also to destroy an immense quantity of ground provisions which grew in the "greatest exuberance" at Mocho.

The use of slave gangs was an important element in the campaign. They were drawn from estates in the area, which were also obliged to provide provisions for the troops. Early in the conflict, Governor Balcarres found it necessary to get tough with estate owners who were not cooperating. On September 13th he wrote from Falmouth to Major General Reid, Colonel Hall and Colonel Jackson to say: "Where the estates neglect to send their quota of Negroes and provisions, they must be forced to send double the quantity... All must be given up rather than the above be infringed on in the smallest degree".

Two days after reaching Mocho, Colonel Skinner with a large body of Regulars and forty Shot explored the woods from Mocho, through Lapland to Catadupa, and destroyed several detached provision grounds. The day before, ten raiders descended on John Gray's house at Industry estate. Gray, awakened from sleep, jumped out of his bed and dashed through the back door into the garden. The Maroons fired two shots at him, but he escaped, clad only in his night shirt, and ran hard to Bull Penn, owned by James Peterkin.

The raiders set fire to Gray's trash houses, and also burnt the shed and dwelling house of his neighbour, a man named Cooper. They slew a driver who was blowing a shell horn to alert the neighbours. Slaves put out the fires, and the neighbours, accompanied by a detachment of the St. Ann Militia stationed at York, and a troop guard from John's Hall, hurried to Industry. But the raiders had vanished after plundering the stores of rum, provisions, clothes and a small quantity of gunpowder. It was reported that the head of the raiding group was wearing two watches and carrying a spy glass.

The frantic troop movements were accompanied by some mishaps. Sergeant Charles Gray of the Artillery Company of the St. James regiment, part of a detachment ordered to march to Vaughansfield, mounted a mule to take him on the journey. The mule was restive and ungovernable, and threw him. Before he could disengage himself from the stirrups, the animal delivered such violent blows "in the region of his stomach and bowels that inflammation set in." Despite the best medical attention available, Sergeant Charles Gray died 24 hours after receiving the mule's kicks.

Sam Cunningham, First Major of the Western Division of Horse, exerted himself so strenuously in the back-breaking Cockpit Country, that he died of fatigue. The report of his death said that: "his anxiety in his country's cause induced him to attempt exertions which his constitution proved inadequate to." Major Cunningham's death from fatigue was regarded as much a sacrifice in the line of duty, as if he had been cut down by a bullet. He was buried with the military honours of his rank, attended by a party of his own regiment and a detachment of the St. James Foot. His fellow officers bore his remains to the grave, while minute guns were fired by the artillery.

While all the fighting and manoeuverings were taking place in and around the Cockpit country, in the wet month of October, Lieutenant Colonel Quarrell, a member of the Legislature, who had been serving with the troops in the mountains, fell ill, and was advised to go to the sea coast to regain his health. There he met a Spaniard and began to converse with him about the state of the island. The Spaniard told him that some years before, when the British abandoned the Mosquito Coast, the Spaniards tried to take possession of it by military force, but were prevented from doing so by the determined opposition of the Indians. They lost three regiments in a few months chiefly because of ambushes and surprise attacks. In desperation they imported thirty-six dogs and twelve chasseurs (dog handlers) from Cuba to see if they could be of any use against the Indians. The dogs were successful in preventing any more surprise attacks or ambushes and finally the Indians were driven out of the territory.

Listening to the Spaniard, it occurred to Quarrell that perhaps this was exactly what was needed in Jamaica to help overcome the Maroons. He persuaded the Speaker and several members of the House of Assembly to lay a scheme for the importation of dogs before the Governor. The House approved the scheme and Quarrell offered to go on the mission himself provided he were given a ship and a letter from Balcarres to the Spanish Governor of Havana requesting permission to purchase two hundred dogs.

The government agreed and a schooner, *The Mercury*, was sent down to Bluefields at the western end of the island to take Quarrell on his mission. *The Mercury* had twelve guns and a crew made up of "four British seamen, twelve Curaçao Negroes and eighteen Spanish renegadoes." Quarrell was given a letter addressed to Don Luis de las Casas, Governor of Havana. He went on board accompanied by a friend, Captain Gilpin of the militia, and two servants. He was still ill and had a fever when *The Mercury* sailed from Bluefields at the end of October.

At about the time Quarrell sailed, General Walpole began to press home his carefully planned offensive against the Trelawnys.

CHAPTER 28

WALPOLE'S WAR OF ATTRITION

While it rained, Walpole had studied the information which he had gathered from the surveyors and the Accompongs. Now he knew the locations of the springs of water and he knew where the Maroon trails ran. With this knowledge he planned to cut off the Trelawnys from their meeting-places and from the vital supplies of water.

There was one big flaw in the plan, however, and that was the fact that Petty River Bottom, the Maroon stronghold, had a never-failing spring of water. The plan to cut off the sources of water would not be fully effective until the Trelawnys and their women and children were driven out of Petty River Bottom. To achieve this, Walpole decided to concentrate most of his attention on Shaw rather than on Johnson's raiders.

Lieutenant Richards' attempt to scale the wall of the Petty River Bottom Cockpit had failed, so Walpole had to find another way. As soon as the rains stopped the work of clearing the bush from the countryside was pushed forward. When the heights above Walpole's headquarters were cleared, it became obvious that they almost overlooked the Cockpit. A big gun mounted up there could drop shot into Petty River Bottom.

Walpole ordered his men to drag a big howitzer on to the height. The gun was mounted, the gunners found the range and shot after shot went crashing into the Cockpit.

It was almost a repetition of what had happened sixty-one years before when Captain Stoddart pulled his swivel guns up into the Blue Mountains and bombarded Nanny Town.

The Trelawnys were helpless to stop the procession of bursting shells. There was no place to hide. Charles Shaw gathered up his people and took them out of the Cockpit which for so long had been a refuge, but which had now become a trap.

A short time later General Walpole and his men marched through the dreaded Guthrie's Defile and entered the Cockpit. Petty River Bottom had fallen. Shaw sent the women and children to a remote Cockpit which lay outside of the parellel formation of Cockpits of which Petty River Bottom was a part. Then he occupied a Cockpit adjoining Petty River Bottom and ordered his men to fortify the slope which was most exposed to attack. They threw up a line of breastworks made of old stumps and plantain trees, and settled down behind it to get what sleep they could.

The next morning a new supply of shells was brought up for the howitzer. The gunners pointed their piece at Shaw's fortified slope and fired for range. Soon they were dropping shells into the line and sending earth and rocks flying among the Maroon warriors. The range was too great for the Trelawnys to use their muskets, so once more they were forced to abandon their position. They scrambled up a tremendous height to the left until they were almost out of range of the howitzer. The shells now fell at random and they were able to settle down for a while. But another problem soon presented itself. The hot sun and hard morning's work had dried out the Trelawnys. They began to feel very thirsty.

One of the Trelawny women climbed down from the heights with a container. She filled it with water, put it on her head and started back up the slope. A young Cornet of the elite 17th Dragoons named Oswald Werge, saw her. Instead of trying to intercept her, he followed quietly behind, keeping out of sight until he was sure where the path led.

He reported back to his commanding officer and a storming party was at once assembled. They climbed quickly up the path, launched a fierce attack on the Trelawnys and sent them tumbling down a very steep precipice. Shaw held his men together and kept them moving. They went past Putty Putty Bottom which was a small, secluded valley where there was a cave and a natural well of water. They kept going until they reached Ginger Town Bottom on the north range of Cockpits, a place so remote that only a very few Maroons had penetrated to it.

Ginger Town Bottom was close enough to the well of water in Putty Putty Bottom and was also within easy reach of the provision grounds of the slaves in the Trelawny mountains. It was an excellent place for a headquarters and Shaw halted his tired men there and made camp. But he realized that he had to stem Walpole's advance, so he retraced his steps almost at once and launched a series of attacks at the troops with his tiny force. Walpole's men were now entrenched on the slope which they had taken from Shaw. It was a strong position and with their superior numbers they repulsed all the attacks of the Trelawnys; but Shaw achieved his objective by stopping their forward drive for a while.

Somewhat later, operating out of Ginger Town Bottom and looking for food, Shaw and his men ran into a body of militia. They killed and wounded some of them and scattered the rest, but their movements were becoming increasingly curtailed by the mass of militia and Kingston troops which now began to throng the area. Everywhere they turned they were faced by armed men who always seemed to outnumber them. No longer could food be brought back freely to their camp and Shaw and his people began to feel the pangs of hunger. It was hardest on the children.

Goodin, a Mocho slave, captured by troops on Sunday December 6th, reported that he was with the Maroons when they were driven out of their Cockpit stronghold; and he described his experiences.

Struggling to express himself in English, Goodin said they settled in a place towards the rising sun, burnt a house, carried off two cows and killed them by a pond. The meat was shared out and some given to the children then they took some water, which was very scarce.

They usually got water from the wild pines and from ponds near the mountain settlements. He saw no springs in the mountains. Three times they raided the Unity provision grounds, but were unwilling to go too far towards the rising sun.

They dug bitter yams and cured long thatch for food, and always kept lookouts in trees to watch for the enemy. Marching usually at the time the soldiers ate dinner, they always carried their clothes and things with them. Whenever they plundered clothes from the enemy, they burnt their old worn-out clothes; but they were usually badly in need of clothes.

The women carried the baggage. They had a place for the women's huts and a place to dress victuals, which was near the women's huts. The children were guarded but they did not always have sentries at night. There were constant complaints of hunger, as bitter yams were scarce. An old gray-haired man who could hardly walk, and was not allowed to go with the foraging parties, stayed with the women and took care of everything. Everything was brought to him to share.

They were short of gunpowder, and took away some of the guns they had given to the "Country Negroes" to give to the boys; telling them that if they ran away from the soldiers they would kill them. Some carried no guns because they had no powder. The powder horns were not filled to more than "two or three fingers breadth deep".

The bullets they had were made of hammered pans. They cut up old bills to make bullets; heating one in the fire and cutting it with another. They wore the caps of soldiers killed in the first battle.

Goodin's quaint language paints a gloomy picture of the condition of Shaw's people.

Having driven Shaw out of Petty River Bottom, Walpole now began to cut the Trelawnys off from the Cockpit water supply. He drove a road from north to south, through the springs in the Cockpits; then posted troops at the springs so that the Trelawnys were unable to use them.

The capture of Petty River Bottom and Walpole's success in cutting off the springs left Shaw and his people in a desperate position. A period of drought had set in and all the water which the rains had left in the hollows of the rocks was soon exhausted. Fortunately, the Maroons were experts in the art of survival and they were helped considerably by the tiny reservoirs which nature provided in a plant called the Wild Pine. Each leaf of the Wild Pine is shaped like a spout and at its base there is a natural bucket reservoir which can hold about a quart of water. Protected from the sun and the wind, the water in each leaf remains for an indefinite period and is kept pure and cool. According to Balcarres:

> "The Wild Pine (Tillandria Maxima), the black and grape withes, (which are about two inches in diameter) and the roots of the cotton tree, all furnish a supply of water to the thirsty wanderer in the wilds of Jamaica. Six feet junked off the smaller part of the root of the cotton tree, where it tapers to the thickness of a man's thigh, will yield several gallons of water. (The Wild Pine) takes root on the body of a tree and the leaves of it are so formed as to catch the rain and conduct it to a reservoir at the base, where, being never exposed to the sun, it is found delightfully fresh and cool".

The reservoirs in the leaves of the Wild Pine kept the Maroons going for a while but eventually even these were exhausted and their suffering from hunger and thirst became acute.

With Johnson licking his wounds in Westmoreland and Shaw bottled up in the Cockpits, there was relative peace for a couple of weeks. Taking advantage of this lull a party of men set out for the place where Colonel Fitch had been ambushed. It was then that Jackson found the remains of Fitch and those who had fallen with him. It was now late in November, and the line of operations in the area of conflict extended over twenty miles in length, and ran through tracks and glades and across hills.

The country had spent 500,000 pounds in the struggle against the Trelawnys. This did not include the loss sustained by individual proprietors which was caused by the need to release their employees for duty with the militia, and by the destructive work of Johnson's raiders.

In many areas cultivation had been suspended and law courts shut down. According to Edwards "the whole island seemed more like a garrison, under the power of martial law, than a country of agriculture and commerce, of civil judicature, industry and prosperity."

In spite of the fact that the troops were beginning to have some success, the colonists remained despondent. Like their predecessors who had had to deal with Cudjoe they felt that the fighting would never end. The historian Dallas said:

> Neither the energy and determined activity of Lord Balcarres nor the skill, bravery and success of General Walpole seemed to avail in this war. The whole range of cockpits was open to the enemy; if annoyed in one (cockpit) they chose another and the contest had all the appearance of being an endless evil, or rather, one that threatened the entire destruction of the island.

So what might on the one hand appear to be a great success when Walpole drove Charles Shaw out of Petty River Bottom, might, when viewed in another light, seem to be nothing more than the decision of the Trelawnys to leave one Cockpit for another in order to escape the "annoyances" of the troops. In addition, the casualties inflicted on the Trelawnys were insignificant while the colonial forces lost many men, including top-ranking officers like Sandford, Gallimore and Fitch. After nearly five months of fighting a vastly outnumbered and ill-equipped foe, their best troops failed to bring matters to a conclusion, and overall was the constant fear that the example of the Trelawnys might encourage the slaves either to join them or to attempt an outbreak of their own.

If this had happened the economy of the island would have suffered greatly. Credit from Great Britain, which was strongly tied to the successful production of sugar, would have dropped steeply. There was also reason to believe that the enemies of Britain would have taken advantage of the chaos to supply arms and munitions to the rebels and perhaps even to make a determined bid to capture Jamaica.

In the depressed atmosphere which existed a Council meeting was called in Falmouth to decide what should be done. General Walpole hurried from the Cockpits to attend the meeting. It was proposed that a mission be sent to the Trelawnys to persuade them to make peace. This was in accordance with the precedent set nearly sixty years before when peace had been made with Cudjoe and Quao.

Walpole spoke out strongly against the proposal. He said that a peace obtained by supplication would both increase the arrogance of the Maroons and cause a great loss of faith and confidence among the colonists. He assured the Council that the campaign was going well and that he and his men would eventually save the country.

CHAPTER 29

JOHNSON AT BAY

Walpole was acutely aware that Johnson over in Westmoreland was a constant threat. His vigour and activity made it necessary to keep a strict watch on his movements. But Walpole couldn't spare enough troops to set up posts in Westmoreland and hold down Shaw at the same time, so he decided to bluff Johnson. Pretending to be making plans for the establishment of a grand depot in Westmoreland, he gave orders for provisions to be purchased. He went about the whole business with the appearance of great secrecy, but hoped all the while that Johnson's informers would carry the false news to him.

By November 18th, Walpole had managed to established posts at the Hector's River and Mouth River and was covering the eastern section with militia from Clarendon and Vere. He was worried about the south, however, especially in the region of the Nassau mountains. He did not have enough troops to guard it properly. The weather had been dry in that area and the people lived in fear of Johnson for they knew that their drought-ridden estates would burn easily.

To keep Johnson busy Walpole made feints into the area where the raiders were thought to be. One of these feigned movements was carried out by a strong force made up of several companies of Regular soldiers and about fifty Confidential Black Shot under the command of Captain Drummond.

Early in December Johnson was operating with his raiders south-west of the Cockpit country in the St. James mountains near Chesterfield.

Jumbo, the slave who called Johnson the most cruel, savage and enterprising of the Maroons, said that on the day he was captured by the Raiders he was taken to their town which was about a mile in the woods from Cold Spring. They remained there until all the food in the neighbourhood was exhausted, then removed to a wood a short distance south of Mocho. There they lived, unmolested and with plenty to eat, until the battle with Captain Williams at Mocho Pen, when Black Harvey and four others were killed and Johnson was wounded in the leg. They removed when large detachments of troops began constantly passing up and down between Mocho and Augustus. Their camp was abandoned just a few days before it was found and burnt by the Regulars. Johnson established a new camp on the Chester River near Chesterfield estate. Jumbo and other slaves were made to carry the baggage.

Johnson raised two runaway slaves to the rank of Captain. One was a Coromantee named Cudjoe belonging to a Mr. Fowler, and who later had part of his jaw shot away; and the other was Casacrew, belonging to Whittaker's estate. Johnson had great confidence in them. The Raiders had plenty of clothing, balls and slugs but were very short of gunpowder. Jumbo reported that the supply of gunpowder which they had obtained when they raided Gowdy's place had long ago been expended.

In December, a detachment of the St. James Militia under the command of Lieutenant Findlater, marched from Post Augustus at Catadupa into the woods, on one of the many missions to seek out and destroy the elusive enemy. On the third day, while going through Lapland on the way back to their base, they heard the haunting notes of Maroon abeng horns coming from the direction of Chesterfield.

They hurried there and found that the Raiders had set fire to Chesterfield estate in three places, but as the cane was wet very little damage had been done. They saw about thirty Maroons and pursued them closely, but "they were too nimble in their flight for the party," and got away.

The next day, Drummond (who apparently had been raised to the rank of Lieutenant Colonel) marched from Post Augustus to find Johnson's settlement, which he had been informed was in the vicinity of Chesterfield, southwest of the Cockpit country in the St. James mountains. His force consisted of a detachment of the 16th Regiment, supported by Findlater with seventy militia men, and forty-eight Black Shot under McLean and Feariss.

They tracked the Raiders from ten in the morning. At three in the afternoon, the Black Shots, who were in front, ran into two Maroon sentries. One of them, who was called Cheshire, was shot twice. In spite of that, he engaged a Black Shot in a ferocious cutlass duel, until he fell and was slain.

Drummond's party, realizing they were near Johnson's settlement, rushed forward. The Black Shots, leading the attack, charged up a hill. At the top, they were met by Johnson's men coming up from the other side. Both groups started shooting and kept it up for about ten minutes, until the Maroons, running short of ammunition, were forced to give way.

Johnson drew back to another position, and Drummond sent in his Regulars who poured heavy and sustained fire into the Raiders. Under cover of this fire the Black Shots charged again. Johnson began to retreat, fighting every foot of the way.

At about this time a detachment of Dragoons and St. Elizabeth militia rode up, attracted by the firing. The rolling powder smoke and thick undergrowth obscured their vision, and in the excitement, they fired into the Black Shots instead of at the Maroons. Fortunately none of

217

the Black Shots was hit, but their forward drive was stopped.

Outnumbered and out-gunned, Johnson took advantage of the general confusion and pulled back his men. He retreated over precipices, and the troops said his Raiders left a trail of blood. Both sides fired at whatever "objects presented themselves." At 5 p.m. the Maroons stopped shooting altogether, having apparently run out of gunpowder. Fortunately for Johnson, night began to fall, and with his detailed knowledge of the difficult terrain, he was able to extricate his forces with his usual skill.

The battle had taken place within gun-shot of the Raiders' camp, and all the young men were by turns engaged. The old men left the camp with the women and children, and were joined after the action by the surviving warriors. The whole group moved to a place of greater safety for the night, and the next day marched to find the main Maroon party by way of Auchindolly. They met them on the third day, about two miles to the south-east of the Old Maroon Town.

After the battle, Drummond buried three Regulars and one Black Shot who had been killed, collected the wounded with their arms and ammunition, and made camp in the woods for the night. A Kilmarnock cap which had apparently been worn by a Maroon, was picked up on the ground where the firing first began. It had a shot hole through both sides. The musket of Cheshire, the sentry who had been killed, was also picked up and identified as belonging to the 83rd Regiment.

Drummond also found a settlement of about one hundred and four huts which he burned. Seven graves, around which the earth appeared to be recently turned up, were uncovered. One contained the body of a grey-haired man apparently wrapped in linen. It was later learned that he was one of Johnson's captains, killed in the battle with Williams and Russel at Mocho, and that he was dressed in clothes looted from Gowdy's house, which the Raiders had plundered and burnt.

Drummond returned to Post Augustus the next morning. His men carried the severed head of Cheshire, the sentry, which was taken into Montego Bay that night and publicly exposed.

Once more Johnson had escaped, but the weight of numbers and equipment was beginning to tell. Whereas he had roamed unchecked in the past, striking at will, he now found himself increasingly occupied with extricating his Raiders from difficult positions.

Jumbo believed that if Johnson had not been defeated at Chester River, he would have attacked and destroyed Belvedere (owned by General Reid), Hazelymph, Greenwich, Wiltshire and Montpelier. After that, said Jumbo, he had intended to move against the parish of St. Elizabeth, using as guides, some slaves from Gowdy's and Whitaker's who had joined him.

Jumbo said that around the time of the Chester River fight, Johnson was joined by ten Nanny Town Maroons under their Lieutenant; all able young men, well-armed, but also short of gunpowder. They encouraged Johnson to carry on, and promised to assist him if they could get powder.

This evidence of support for the Trelawnys from other Maroon communities was mentioned several times by Balcarres in his letters. Writing to Sir Adam Williamson on July 28th, 1795 he said: "Parties of the Trelawny Maroons have been seen on their way to the Blue Mountains". To the Rt. Hon. Henry Dundas in October, 1795 he said:

> "The Maroons to Windward are in a state of inactive rebellion. They refuse to obey an order from me. They stop people on the roads; they have out their sentinels; they have bought gunpowder and have built their huts

in the heart of the Blue Mountains. If we do not attack
them it is understood they will not attack us; and
should the Trelawny Maroons succeed, everything to
Windward may be in the worst situation".

In December he told the Duke of Portland that:

"The Charles Town Maroons, although they have disobeyed my orders to come in a body to Kingston, have,
notwithstanding, come in by small and detached bodies. They are an infinitely softer and more docile people than those of Trelawny Town. The Nanny Town
Maroons are closely connected in relationship with the
Trelawnys. They have not come in, either in a body as
they were commanded, or in parties; and have sullenly
rejected the bounty of the Assembly. They have openly
declared that if the Charles Town Maroons will go into
rebellion, they will join them, regardless of the causes
of that rebellion. They have actually built huts out of
their own district, within the range of the Blue
Mountains (a country of immense strength), as if
preparing for hostilities, either in the event of the
Trelawny Maroons proving successful, or of a rebellion
taking place among those of Charles Town. This body
being equally depraved with the Trelawnys, is more to
be dreaded from the ease with which it could be supported from San Domingo".

Commenting to the Duke of Portland about the "nature and conduct" of the Trelawnys, Balcarres said:

"They had manifested great fortitude, great general-
ship, and had preserved a secrecy in their manoeuvres
unparalleled among European soldiery. The velocity of
their movements and their knowledge of the ground
were so superior to ours as to make them be considered
almost unconquerable. At the same time their concealment of their women, their old and infirm people, and
their children, showed that their haunts were still
totally unknown to us".

Jumbo, the slave of Richard Reid of Hanover, who escaped from the Maroons after being pressed into Johnson's service, and gave a wealth of information to the military, said that after the Chester River fight, Johnson's party fell in with a settlement of about thirty-five "Congo Negroes" far south, in a south-easterly direction from Chesterfield estate. The settlement was so well-cultivated and improved that Jumbo thought they must have been there for some time.

Jumbo said he escaped from the Trelawnys on Christmas Day, and left them "in want of many necessaries of life." Food was scarce and meals precarious and scanty. The women all seemed willing to submit, but when the group was in danger of being discovered from the crying of a child, some were resolute enough to be capable of stifling the child.

Jumbo had gone with a few Maroon men and many of the women to forage for provisions from the Castle Wemyss grounds; and there he made his escape. He was interrogated on January 2nd, 1796 in Montego Bay, at which time he told the story of his adventures.

On the morning of the day on which Drummond returned to Port Augustus, after the Chesterfield fight, Maroons set fire to buildings on Green Vale estate in Trelawny. The Kingston Second Grenadiers hastened to the scene and exchanged two or three volleys with the Maroons before the latter retreated, leaving a large part of their plunder behind.

The raids seemed endless, and General Walpole, trying to keep track of them, and of the constant troop movements, must sometimes have been very frustrated. As he strove to win the much-needed decisive victory over the Trelawnys, Lieutenant Colonel Quarrell was over in Cuba, making every effort to bring a new force into the struggle.

CHAPTER 30

THE HOUNDS OF HELL

The schooner *Mercury* anchored off the coast of Cuba at a little straggling village called Batabano situated near a three-mile stretch of morass which separated it from the sea. Colonel Quarrell disembarked and had to walk along a small causeway almost covered by water in order to reach land.

The commander of the company of infantry and detachment of horse stationed at Batabano looked at Quarrell's papers and provided him with four horses for his companions and himself, and a guard of two dragoons. Quarrell rode to Besucal, a town of 5,000 inhabitants which lay in the mountains on the road to Havana. He arrived at night and felt so sick that he declined to accept the hospitality of the lady Governor of the town, the Marquisa de St. Filippe et St. Jago, and stayed in a wretched house instead.

The next day he visited the Marquisa's Palace and told her about the Maroon war and asked her help in persuading some of the Besucal people who were chasseuers (dog handlers) to go to Jamaica with him. He then rode on to Havanna arriving there on November 3rd. The Governor, Don Luis de las Casas, received him and gave him permission to purchase dogs.

Quarrell had brought with him a copy of the proclamation offering rewards for killing or capturing Maroons. He had this translated into Spanish and sent copies to the mountains of Besucal in the hope of attracting the chasseurs who lived there.

The chasseurs were described as men "with a Spanish countenance, swarthy but animated, above the middle size, thin but not meagre." Their job was to pursue and capture persons guilty of murder and other offences and to accomplish this they used the famous hunting dogs that Quarrell had heard about. "They were a very hardy, brave and desperate set of people, scrupulously honest and remarkably faithful." With a few ounces of salt for each man they could support themselves for many months eating only the vegetables and roots which were to be found in the woods. It is said that they drank nothing stronger than water but that they always smoked cigars except when out hunting, as the strong tobacco smell would have warned fugitives of their approach.

They habitually wore checked shirts open at the neck, a wide pair of checked trousers and a light straw hat with a round shallow crown and a rim seven or eight inches wide. On their feet they wore a pair of untanned leather shoes and in addition they skinned the thighs and hocks of the wild hog and thrust their feet into the raw hide as far as they could force them. This pliant hide took the shape of a short, half boot which fitted very closely on the foot. It could last for a march of weeks or months, but once taken off it would shrivel up and become dry and useless.

Chasseurs usually wore a small crucifix around their necks and were armed only with a long, straight machete or couteau, longer than a dragoon's sword and twice as thick. It resembled a flat iron bat, sharpened at the lower end. The handle was without a guard but it was shaped to accommodate the fingers. The chasseurs used the flat sides of this weapon to administer merciless beatings to their dogs while they were being trained.

The fully-trained dogs of the chasseurs were perfectly broken and would not kill a fugitive unless he resisted.

When they came upon a fugitive they would bark at him until he stopped. Then they would crouch near him, terrifying him with ferocious growling if he stirred, and barking so as to attract the chasseurs to the spot. Chasseurs might hunt with two dogs but they were obliged to keep three which they maintained at their own cost.

The dogs were kept chained at home and when walking out with their masters were muzzled and put on a leash. They were tough and hardy and were the size of a very large hound with erect ears which were cropped at the points. Their noses were pointed but widened greatly towards the base of the jaw.

The dogs were attached to the belts of the chasseurs by cotton ropes which were fixed to the collars around the animals' necks. When pursuing a fugitive the chasseur would slip the rope from his belt, secure it around his waist and drawing his machete, push forward nearly as fast as his dog.

The Besucal chasseurs had about seventy well-trained dogs. They agreed to go to Jamaica with each man taking three dogs and to use every means necessary "for hunting and seizing negroes". They also agreed to stay for three months during which time they were to be given any assistance they required, and be paid £200 each (£100 down and the rest at the end of the three months) plus expenses. If the Government needed their services for longer than three months they would have the option of either making a new agreement or getting a free passage home. They agreed to split the reward money for any captured Maroons with the troops who assisted them.

After some complicated negotiations and numerous intrigues and adventures with Spanish officials and soldiers, Quarrell finally gathered together forty chasseurs and one hundred and four dogs, of which only thirty-six had been properly trained. The rest, being only partially trained, were likely to kill anything they pursued. They would leap at the throat or at some other part of a fugitive and never let go till they were cut in two.

Early one morning men and dogs were taken through two hundred yards of shallow water to reach the *Mercury*, and were all on board by sunrise. While clearing the harbour, the *Mercury* was driven aground by her pilots and almost at the same time a storm sprang up. The schooner weathered the storm and on the third day most of her ballast was thrown overboard. Then her anchors were taken out and by means of a process called warping she was towed off the bank. Once in deep water a course was set for Jamaica and on December 14th, the day after the fight between Captain Drummond and Johnson, she arrived in Montego Bay.

Lieutenant-Colonel Quarrell had been away for seven weeks but his mission had been successful. The chasseurs and their dogs were landed and their wild and formidable appearance spread terror throughout the town. The muzzled animals with their heavy rattling chains charged ferociously at every object, pulling along the chasseurs in their fury so that they could hardly be restrained.

The people fled the streets. They locked themselves into houses and even closed the windows while the savage dogs went by snarling and sniffing and pulling their masters along. But even as they fled from the dogs, hope sprang anew in the hearts of the colonists and joy spread throughout the land; for surely not even the Trelawnys would be able to withstand such savage beasts.

Lieutenant-Colonel Quarrell was "congratulated, thanked and extolled" by the colonists and dispatches were immediately sent to General Walpole at his headquarters in the Old Town announcing the arrival of the dogs. On landing, Quarrell was told that very little progress had been made with the war. The troops had suffered great losses, the militia were exhausted and the number of them reporting for active duty had dropped off considerably.

Word of the arrival of the dogs spread so rapidly that in two hours General Reid in command of the Great River Post heard the news. It was a part of Reid's force under Drummond which had fought with Johnson on December 13th. After the fight, Johnson had threatened to burn Belvedere, which was Reid's estate. Reid wrote to Quarrell describing the action between Drummond and Johnson and asked that the chasseurs and their dogs be sent to him as quickly as possible. He assured Quarrell that he would hold himself responsible to Walpole for not having awaited his orders in connection with the dogs.

Post Augustus had been designated by Walpole as the rendezvous where his troops were to be assembled for an all-out attack on the Trelawnys. On receiving Reid's letter, Quarrell at once sent his chasseurs to this rendezvous.

On the way the chasseurs made two halts in order to feed their dogs. At the first stop several dogs were set on an ox. They pinned him down, and one of the chasseurs cut his throat with a sharp machete. The dogs pushed each other aside to get at the squirting blood and soon they were half covered with it. The blood, mixed with the dust of the road which they had picked up, gave the dogs an even more ferocious appearance which was well calculated to inspire terror. The slaves on the estates through which they passed left their work and fled in all directions.

The chasseurs made their second stop at Seven Rivers where they planned to spend the night. General Walpole, eager to see what Quarrell had brought back, journeyed from his headquarters to Seven Rivers in a post-chaise and arrived there at seven o' clock. He was accompanied by Colonel Skinner who had been appointed to lead the attack on the Trelawnys.

The chasseurs had been given guns upon their arrival at Seven Rivers. They had received them reluctantly and had consented to some kind of drill. Now, as Walpole watched, they fired their guns upon receiving a command and then advanced. As soon as the guns went off the dogs leapt forward with the greatest fury, and their masters, pulled forcibly along at the ends of the cotton ropes shouted wildly.

Some of the dogs were maddened by the continuous shouting. They turned around, seized the guns in the hands of their keepers and tore pieces out of the wooden stocks. They strained forward towards where Walpole stood beside his chaise. The chasseurs pulled hard on the ropes and only just managed to stop them before they reached the General. Even so Walpole had to climb into the chaise for safety and if the chasseurs had not exerted every ounce of their strength the dogs would have attacked his horses.

Walpole was happy to observe the strength and ferocity of the dogs. He was now confident that he would be able to end the conflict without having to resort to making terms which would lessen the dignity of the government or cause the colonists to lose face. The chasseurs were told that they would be required to join the troops in an attack on the Trelawnys. They objected strongly as they wished to come to grips with the Maroons alone and in their own way. They were told, however, that they must submit themselves to Colonel Skinner under whose orders they had been placed.

Johnson, meanwhile, had returned to a position a mile east of his old haunt after the fight with Drummond. From there he felt sure that he could mount his attacks and raids with more advantage. Covered by the woods and independent of the now doubtful security of the Cockpits, he thought himself equal to any force which could be brought against him. When he heard of the arrival of the chasseurs and the dogs, however, with the by now exaggerated reports of their size and fierceness, he decided to leave his new position and join forces with the rest of the Trelawnys.

CHAPTER 31

THE FATAL PEACE

In all the months of campaigning, no real victory had been won over the Trelawnys. Walpole had succeeded, however, in severely curtailing their movements and in reducing them to near starvation. The militia under Colonel Skinner had been chiefly responsible for checking their raids on the provision grounds in Trelawny. Walpole himself had forced them to withdraw into the remote Cockpits where the coming of dry weather made it difficult to find water. The troops at Post Augustus and Mocho had managed to keep Johnson away from the areas which they were guarding, and the posts established at the Mouth and Hector's rivers with the Clarendon and Vere Militia under Colonel Robertson and Major Shaw had successfully opposed the Maroon inroads to the East. Now Christmas was approaching and the whole colony was crying out for an end to fighting.

Christmas was the period when a strict watch was kept over the slaves in case the high spirits let loose by the festivities might cause them to get out of hand. Everyone was astonished that the Trelawnys had been able to fight so long against such overwhelming odds, and the colonists were soon alarmed by a rumour that a large body of Windward Maroons and slaves intended to join them. Crop time was near and the ripe canes were dropping their dry blades. It would only take a few rebellious slaves to start a fire that could sweep through whole districts aided by the strong prevailing winds.

Pressure was brought on Walpole from every hand to make peace. He was very reluctant to do this but knew that sooner or later he would be forced to. His great concern therefore was to find a way of coming to terms with the Trelawnys without losing prestige. The arrival of the chasseurs and their dogs gave him the perfect instrument with which to bargain. His plan was to convince the Maroons that although he was now joined by a force which could not fail to drive them from their positions, he was willing to adopt mild measures rather than proceed with a plan which could only have the most terrible results.

Walpole sent off Colonel Skinner to find Johnson but ordered him to keep the chasseurs and dogs in the rear so as to indicate to the Maroon leader that they would not be used unless the efforts at peace failed. At the same time Colonel Hull was ordered to advance from the Old Town against Shaw's party and Walpole directed him to offer them terms of peace.

Hull was in command of a very strong force consisting of a part of the 62nd Regiment, detachments of the 17th Light Dragoons and other elements of the regular army. He left the Old Town on December 18th.

Some months before, when Colonel Fitch had been alive and in command at the Old Town, he had allowed Dunbar and Harvey to visit the imprisoned Maroons at Montego Bay. The two Trelawnys had returned bringing old Colonel Montague with them. Montague had gone on to Petty River Bottom where he stayed with Shaw when Johnson detached his Raiders from the main body. Shaw was in charge at Petty River Bottom but in deference to Montague's age and position he conceded a sort of nominal command to the old chief. After hearing of the arrival of the chasseurs and their dogs, Johnson sent a message to Montague and Shaw asking them to meet him near the Old Town.

Shaw's people were now in grave trouble. They were living practically from hand to mouth. The iron ring of soldiers and militia had cut off most of their water and food supplies, and measles had broken out among them. Their women and children were in a pitiable condition, and Johnson's order to meet him must have come as a relief after the weeks of virtual seige.

From their remote Cockpit hide-out Shaw's people were moving up to rendezvous with Johnson when they ran into Hull's powerful force, which had marched about six miles from their headquarters at Old Town. They met at a place called Pond River.

When Hull realised that he had made contact with Shaw's party he sent back a runner with an order that the baggage be brought up quickly. The runner was a slave named Cato. He was one of those characters for whom freedom-fighters and under-dogs have an instinctive hate. He was the slave who upholds the tyranny of his masters, not simply by accepting it, but by actively helping them to maintain their power to enslave men. Throughout the whole campaign Cato had been a most faithful guide. It was Cato who had discovered the hide-out of the Trelawnys and during the actions at which he had been present he had behaved with great bravery. Cato was a marked man, and as he ran swiftly down the trail with Hull's message, a Maroon sharp-shooter spotted him. The Maroon took aim at the moving target, fired and brought down Cato like a hunted hog. The colonists regarded his death as "unfortunate".*

When they met at Pond River, Shaw's Maroons were on the side of a steep hill; Hull's soldiers were on the opposite slope and between them lay a narrow glade. Hull's orders

---

* *In March 1796, Walpole wrote to Balcarres strongly recommending that he place "before the Assembly the case of the family of Cato, a slave of Mr. Samuel Vaughan's (who) during the whole campaign (had) been a most faithful guide. It was by his means that we discovered the retreat of the Rebels, and he behaved by every account with*

had been to make peace, but when his advance guard came suddenly upon the Maroons they were apparently so surprised that they opened fire. Shaw's men promptly returned the fire. Hull's officers yelled at their men to cease and to take cover behind the trees. They called repeatedly to the Maroons to stop shooting, telling them that General Walpole wanted to make peace, but the Trelawny warriors kept up a straggling fire. When the Maroon captains realised that the soldiers had stopped firing they leapt up from cover and were seen skipping among the rocks, commanding their men to hold their fire.

Finally there was silence. A Maroon captain shouted across to the soldiers asking if Walpole was there. Someone replied that he was not but was being sent for, and that in the meantime Colonel Hull had been authorised to make peace. A long dialogue now took place between the two groups during which the Trelawnys made it quite plain that they were suspicious of the whole business. Then Oswald Werge of the 17th Light Dragoons (the man who had follow the female Maroon water-carrier up a hill and found the way to Shaw's line above Petty River Bottom) came out into the open, threw down his weapons and descended to the foot of the hill. He started across the glade, calling to the Maroons to meet him, saying that the war was ended and neither side should be afraid to meet and shake hands.

A Maroon named Fowler rose out of the rocks and bush, went down the slope into the glade and shook hands with Werge. On Werge's suggestion they went through the ritual of exchanging hats and jackets, reminiscent of the exchange that had taken place between Cudjoe and Russell fifty-seven years before.

---

singular *bravery during the action. He was unfortunately killed by a Maroon in an ambuscade on his way back to bring up the luggage." The St. James commissioners recommended that annuities of ten pounds be granted to William and Francois, the sons of Cato, during their respective lives.*

Charles Shaw, Commander of the Trelawny group, now came out into the open and descended into the glade. He was followed by two of his captains. He assured Hull that his people would not attack if the soldiers did not advance. Night was now falling and a decision had to be made as to how the two forces should spend it. Between them in the glade lay a spring, and it was agreed that each side should detail two sentries to guard it. In this way it was felt that neither side would have the advantage of the other.

The night passed quietly until about 2:00 a.m. when both sides began to feel very thirsty. The Maroons called out to Hull and suggested that he withdraw his sentries a little way until they could get some water. This was done and then the Maroon sentries were withdrawn until the troops supplied themselves with water.

At daybreak the Maroons were told that Walpole was on his way. In the meantime Hull invited them to send some of their captains to meet an equal number of his officers at the spring, but the suspicious Trelawnys refused.

Walpole arrived early in the morning accompanied by General Reid, Commander of the Great River Post. They were met by old Montague and his captains and according to the historians, peace terms were proposed by the Maroons and accepted by Walpole. This seems extremely unlikely, since it was the troops who had come seeking peace. In all likelihood it was Walpole who suggested the terms and persuaded the Maroons to accept them. The Maroons were never good at this sort of negotiation and were always at the mercy of the skilled colonial administrators.

The proposed peace terms were that the Maroons should beg His Majesty's pardon on their knees, that they should go to any place to which they were sent and settle on whatever lands the Government, Council and Assembly might think proper to allot them, and also that they should give up all runaways. Walpole added a fourth, important term which was between the Maroons and himself and for which he took personal responsibility. He promised them that they would not be banished from Jamaica.

Once the preliminaries were settled, the Trelawnys were given a certain amount of time to allow them to go back for their women and children in their remote hide-outs. Before they left, Walpole warned them of another party of troops which had been sent from a different direction to co-operate with Hull and which was therefore not aware of the peace. To safeguard them against attack in case they ran into this party Walpole gave them a letter to Colonel Stevenson, the commander, telling him of the terms which had been made.

Some of the Maroons set off accompanied by about thirty of their women who were carrying the baggage and provisions. They were commanded by Captain Smith who had Walpole's letter with him. The route which they followed took them straight towards Colonel Stevenson.

As they were climbing a hill Stevenson's men appeared above them and the Maroon women ran off in different directions. The men shouted at them to stop, but they kept running and presently Stevenson's men opened fire.

The Maroons sought for cover and Smith found a cleft stick into which he fixed Walpole's letter. He ran from opening to opening between the trees waving the stick with the letter, hoping that someone would see it and recognise its significance; but Stevenson's men kept on firing and advancing. With the bullets flying around him, Smith held up his cleft stick and retreated as they came on. When he saw that his efforts were having no effect he raised his gun and ordered his men to fight back. A brisk battle developed during which a militia captain and several of the troops were killed, and many others wounded. Using the protection of the woods with great skill the Maroons fought off Stevenson's thrust, and the militia, after thoroughly exhausting themselves, retreated. It was clear from this action that while the Trelawnys were prepared to consider peace, they were far from being beaten.

On December 18th Johnson set off with the larger part of his force to seek Shaw in the Old Town. He left a small party to take the baggage and the women and children who had joined him to a secure place in the southernmost Cockpits. He had made up his mind that if the peace treaty which the colonists seemed ready to make was not to his liking or proved to be only a ruse, he would abandon the Cockpits, force a way through Walpole's troops and find friendlier territory.

He planned to cross the island with the entire Trelawny Maroon Community, going by way of the Cave River to the south and east of the Cockpits, and then descend on the estates in the mountains of Clarendon. Clarendon was the old home of the Trelawnys from which Cudjoe had migrated many years before, to escape the same kind of military pressure that Johnson was now experiencing. The Maroons still had relatives among the Clarendon slaves and they were likely to be more kindly disposed towards them than the slaves in the north and west.

Had Johnson been able to make this move, the seat of war would have had to be transferred to Clarendon. For Walpole it would have meant fatiguing marches, new quarters and camps, a new terrain to be mapped out. It might also have meant that the fertile Clarendon estates would have been destroyed. Fortunately for the colonists, Shaw and Montague ran into Hull before they could join with Johnson, and Walpole was able to convince them that his desire for peace was sincere. So Johnson never got the opportunity to put his plan into action.

When Johnson heard of the peace made by Montague and Shaw he realised that, whether he liked it or not, the war was at an end; for the group that followed Montague and Shaw consisted of the majority of the Trelawnys. Johnson therefore made up his mind to submit and share the fate of the others. He began gathering his people to lead them in, but it was a slow process.

Colonel Skinner, unaware of the events that were taking place, left Post Augustus on December 19th, with a part of the 16th Regiment, a detachment of the 83rd and the Cuban chasseurs and their dogs. His orders from Walpole were to find Johnson and offer him peace.

Skinner marched to Johnson's old position and when he failed to find him pushed on with redoubled vigour in the hope of overtaking him. The chasseurs begged him to allow them to advance to the front of the column but he kept them in the rear as Walpole had ordered. Although Skinner did not know it at the time, he was within two miles of the small force which Johnson had left to protect his women and baggage, when, at 2:00 p.m. on the 19th, a courier overtook him with a message from Walpole.

In the message, Walpole told Skinner of the meeting with Shaw and Montague and the proposals for peace. He ordered him to return at once. When the chasseurs heard the news they protested loudly, for they had been expecting at any moment to come up with Johnson and engage him in a fight, from which they hoped to get great rewards. But Walpole had to be obeyed and they turned back with Skinner's column.

As soon as Governor Balcarres heard of the peace agreement between Walpole and Shaw's Trelawnys, he left Major-General Donald Campbell in charge of the troops on the south side of the Cockpits and rode north to Wemyss Castle. Ever since the death of Colonel Fitch, Balcarres appeared to have taken very little active part in the campaign. He seemed to have left everything to the very capable General Walpole. Now, however, the situation demanded his presence.

At Wemyss Castle on December 28th, Balcarres ratified Walpole's treaty and fixed January 1st, 1796, as the date on which all the Trelawny Maroons should surrender. The Trelawnys had four days' grace.

Considering the circumstances, it was too close a date. Shaw's Trelawnys who had gone off to bring back their women and children had had to fight their way past Stevenson's militia in spite of having Walpole's letter in their possession. This must both have shaken their confidence and delayed them somewhat. In addition, when they reached their destination, several of them found their families so sick that they were unable to travel. Some of the women had been lost when Walpole had driven the Trelawnys out of Petty River Bottom and of these only one could be found.

Apart from this, the Trelawnys had a natural distrust of the colonists brought about largely through experience. Old Colonel Montague, legitimate chief of the Trelawnys, remembered the time at the outbreak of hostilities when Balcarres had called on his people to submit, and he had gone down in good faith to Vaughansfield on August 11th, 1795, with thirty-six of his fellows, only to see his men tied up and thrown in jail. He remembered also that in July, 1795, six of the most eminent of the Trelawnys had been put in irons when they gave themselves up to Balcarres, a few days after a deadline which he had set.

Recalling all this, Montague now tried to stop the Trelawnys from going in, even though he had been the one who had entered into the treaty with Walpole. The old chief was at last beginning to realise what his people were up against. But it was too late.

Smith and Dunbar went in as early as December 24th, but many other Trelawnys, in spite of their willingness, could not overcome their distrust. Each man wanted his neighbour to go in first to see what would happen to him. One man would go down and if everything seemed all right would then return and get his family. In this manner they trickled in.

On December 28th several Trelawnys arrived and Walpole read them Balcarres' ratification of the treaty.

They made certain to ask him if the terms of peace would be fully honoured and he assured them that they would be.

The deadline of January 1st laid down by Balcarres came and went, but the vast majority of the Trelawnys still had not come in. The day seemed to go unnoticed, much to Walpole's disappointment. Balcarres, either ignoring or simply unable to appreciate the difficulties which faced the Trelawnys, chose to interpret their failure to meet the deadline as a sign that they had decided to continue the fight. On January 5th, therefore, he ordered Walpole to advance against them with the chasseurs and the dogs.

On January 12th messengers sent by Johnson contacted Walpole while he was on the march. They told him that Johnson and his party would be going to the Cockpit "within the posts" (this may have been Petty River Bottom) and that he was requesting a supply of provisions for his starving people.

In spite of Johnson's message, Walpole continued to advance. On January 14th, twenty-four Maroons came in and another messenger from Johnson arrived saying that the large number of sick people in his party had slowed him down. He would therefore not be able to reach the post that day, but would arrive the next morning.

Before the 14th was over forty-nine more Maroons arrived and the next day Walpole met Johnson coming in with another fifty or sixty. Several other groups followed until three hundred and twenty-six were accounted for.

The number of Trelawnys who submitted by January 16th totalled four hundred, including women and presumably children. But there were still some who remained at large.

By order of Balcarres, the Trelawnys who came in were marched down to Montego Bay under escort. They were sent off in groups at different times but Walpole kept several with him, chiefly those who belonged to the families of Johnson and Smith, for he believed that they could influence the others to come in.

Once Johnson was sure that the fight was over, he had turned his immense energies to the preservation of his people. He seemed to sense the mood that Balcarres was in and realised that for each day that there were Trelawnys still at large, the danger to the whole community would increase. What he did not know was that it was already too late.

He teamed up with Smith and together they were tireless in their efforts to roundup the Trelawnys. They were successful in bringing in many, but there were two notable exceptions: Palmer and Parkinson.

Palmer and Parkinson had been among the thirty-six men led by old Montague who had surrendered their arms at the start of the conflict and been promptly flung in jail by Balcarres. Later they had been chosen to go to Trelawny Town to tell their fellow Trelawnys to submit, but instead they had urged them to fight. As a result they had been charged with advising the Maroons to set fire to their towns, and a big reward had been placed on their heads.

Like Montague, Palmer and Parkinson had not forgotten Balcarres' treachery, and now, as they hid in the hills overlooking the military headquarters and watched the Trelawnys being marched off in groups to Montego Bay escorted by troops, they were sure that more treachery was intended. With the small group which remained with them they fled southward into the remote Cockpits, leaving behind a white flag at Pond River.

Johnson and five Maroons had gone out to find the missing Trelawnys. They stayed out for six days, which was the time allowed them, and returned with six Trelawny warriors and a great many women and children. They also brought back the news about Palmer and Parkinson and their withdrawal into the remote Cockpits.

The white flag which had been left at Pond River was found by Smith, who showed it to Walpole, and boasted that he could bring in Palmer and Parkinson, "as easy as kiss your hand." He asked to be given a search party of eight Maroons and a detachment of troops without the dogs. Walpole was willing to let him have it but Balcarres, who was at Dromilly, refused.

Johnson and Smith again went out and on February 11th returned bringing thirty Maroons, but they did not find Palmer and Parkinson. Two days later, on February 13th, Walpole sent out Lieutenant Gubbins in command of a detachment of the 13th Light Dragoons, accompanied by some of the chasseurs with their dogs and a few Accompong Maroons to act as guides. They were not well supplied with provisions, as no one seemed to realise how deep into the mountains Palmer and Parkinson had penetrated.

The party entered the woods at One Eye on the St.Elizabeth side. They marched for several days and soon began to suffer from thirst and the fatigue of the rough journey. Even with the help of the dogs they could find no Trelawnys. Becoming footsore and utterly weary, they finally returned to base.

But Walpole could not afford to give up. Palmer and Parkinson, because of their refusal to submit, had become a dangerous symbol of the old truculent, free and independent Maroon spirit. At all cost they had to be brought in.

On February 16th Walpole left the Old Town in another attempt to find the missing Trelawnys. He was accompanied by Colonel Skinner and about eighty men of the 13th Light Dragoons and the 16th Infantry as well as the Spanish chasseurs and their dogs. Johnson and Smith went with them. They passed through Elderslie, Accompong Town and Aberdeen and on February 29th were guided to a hill about a mile and a half north of Aberdeen where smoke had recently been seen.

They marched until 4:00 p.m., then halted and made camp. Walpole was reluctant to go any farther with the whole group because of a shortage of water. He detached a party consisting of nine men of the 13th Light Dragoons under Quartermaster Wilkinson, a Spaniard named Zeny, Francis Robertson, surveyor, Lambert Tate, surgeon, some chasseurs and Maroon Captain Smith.

Smith conducted the party a little way and then returned to the main body as Walpole had ordered. Robertson, the surveyor, also turned back after a while. The rest pushed on and eventually came upon a runaway slave. One of the Spanish dogs was loosed and sent after the runaway. Desperate, the man turned to face the charging beast and cut him twice with a cutlass. But the dog leapt in again, seized him by the nape of the neck and held him. When questioned, the runaway said that he and two others had deserted Palmer and Parkinson a few days before. He promised to lead the party to the Trelawny camp.

Early on the morning of March 3rd they set out. They marched the whole day, passed through Johnson's old camp which was now deserted, and then, as both men and dogs were exhausted, made camp for the night. The next morning they continued the march to within a mile of the camp of Palmer and Parkinson.

Lambert Tate, the surgeon, accompanied by the prisoner, went forward under a flag of truce. They came to within a quarter-mile of the camp when they were stopped by a Maroon sentry. The sentry sent for Palmer and Parkinson, but after waiting for about five minutes, Tate moved on when he saw no sign of the Trelawny leaders.

He passed several Maroons and runaways. Some of them abused him and some looked on in silence. When he reached the top of a hill which led to the mouth of a defile Tate was again stopped by armed Maroons. He looked beyond them and saw twenty men armed with guns and cutlasses.

The sentries led him to the camp which lay at the bottom of the hill. There he came face to face with Parkinson and talked to him. Parkinson agreed to send his nephew back with Tate to hear the terms. They made a quick journey to Walpole's camp and returned with Johnson and Smith, who finally persuaded Palmer and Parkinson to submit.

Johnson dispatched four Maroons with the news. On March 16th, they reached Walpole and told him that Johnson was coming with the missing Trelawnys. On March 21st, Parkinson and thirty-six of the Trelawnys submitted to Walpole, bringing forty-four stands of arms with them. The next day thirteen more Trelawnys and several runaways came in.

Almost a month earlier, on February 24th, 1796, a statement had been issued from Kings House in Spanish Town on behalf of Governor Balcarres, which said:

"The Commander-in-Chief has the pleasure of announcing that, owing to the energy of the country and the valour and zeal of His Majesty's forces, both Regulars and Militia, the Maroon Rebellion is brought to a most honourable and happy termination. Although the embers may remain and must be attended to, the great work is nevertheless accomplished, and the Militia may return to their homes with those honours which they have so justly deserved.

The whole of the Trelawny Maroons are safely secured as prisoners, with the exception of twenty-one Maroon men, and some women, who are still in the woods. Of those twenty-one some are sick, and others severly wounded. The remainder keep out merely from a consciousness of the atrocity of their crimes.

The last three engagements under the respective commands of Captain Drummond of the 16th Regiment, Colonel Hull of the 62nd, and Lieutenant Colonel Stevenson of the Trelawny Militia, contributed much indeed, to the happy event that has taken place. And the Commander-in-Chief returns his thanks to those officers, and to the parties they commanded, for the gallantry and good conduct which they displayed on those occasions.

He desires to make his acknowledgements to the Hon.
Major-General Walpole, for the indefatigable zeal and
ability which he has manifested in the service".

Balcarres' statement also praised the Major Generals of
the Militia and the Commissioners for their efforts and
assistance, and then concluded:

"Martial Law, having been unanimously continued for
the purpose of returning the troops to their homes, the
Commander-in-Chief intends that the movements of
the troops in the neighbourhood of the Maroon Town,
shall commence on the 4th of March; and as the last
division marches into Spanish Town on the 18th, on
that day Martial Law shall cease, unless very powerful
and indispensible reasons should occur for continuing
it..."

A poem entitled "On the Termination of the Rebellion"
and dated March 29th, 1796 appeared in the Supplement of
the Royal Gazette, Saturday March 26th to Saturday April
7th. It said:

"The Conflict's past; peace deigns once more to smile,
Upon the labours of our fruitful isle;
Returned to hell, Rebellion shuns the day,
While Concord spreads around, her golden sway;
O! Could her spirit soften all mankind'
Diffusing through the earth a kindred mind,
Vice to o'er throw; while virtue's heavenly form,
Allays with Godlike force, war's baleful storm.
Vain with! Perhaps, the mass of human crimes,
Demands the awful judgements of these times,
Pursuing evil's spacious weak-man road;
Provoking the just wrath, hardened! of God;
Blind to approaching horrors, onward driven,
Till prayers, too late, are offered up to Heaven.
Let us, preserved, from a ferocious band'
By boundless conduct, consecrate the land;

Confess our benefits, by honest zeal,
In striving to promote the public weal.
Let those entrusted to a master's care,
Possess of every good, their proper share;
View with compassion's eye, their lonely lot,
Nor leave for calumny, a single blot".

CHAPTER 32

BALCARRES' DEFENCE

On February 26th, 1796, General McLeod got up in the
House of Commons in London, and said that the circumstances which he had to relate had filled him with a degree
of horror that was impossible for him to express, and that
almost disabled him from performing the task he had
undertaken. He held a newspaper in his hand in which he
said was a statement that had to be cleared up at once. It
was a gross charge against a nobleman for whom he had
the highest respect, and materially affected the character
of the British nation. The general then read an article in
the newspaper entitled "A Letter from Jamaica," which,
after giving a general account of the war against the
Maroons, proceeded to state that one hundred bloodhounds and twenty Spanish chasseurs had been imported
from Cuba to be employed against the Maroons.

At the end of the article, McLeod said he was sure that
while he was reading, his audience must have called to
mind the cruelties practised by the Spaniards in the conquest of South America. It was a known fact that the
Spanish planters had amused themselves by hunting down
the natives with blood hounds, allowing the dogs to tear the
bodies not only of men, but of women and children. Such
atrocities naturally filled the mind with horror, he continued, but what would be said if the British should introduce
such an inhuman practice into their Colonies?

244

Much had been said of the barbarities of the French, said Mcleod, but in their worst excesses, they set men to murder men; they never thought of employing dogs for that purpose. He had seen war in all its shapes, but nothing so dreadful as what he had just stated.

He did not himself believe there was any truth in the statement, but it was necessary to investigate the matter. He therefore wished to be informed by Ministers on the subject, and if it turned out to be true, much as he respected the Noble Lord in question, he would bring him to the bar of the House to answer for such conduct.

Mr William Pitt, the Principal Minister, said it was impossible for him to give a decisive answer; but nothing could be more foreign to the Ministers of His Majesty, George III, than the carrying on of a war by means of blood hounds to tear people to pieces. Mr Charles Yorke, a supporter of Balcarres, arose to say that the use of blood hounds to detect murderers was nothing new. They had frequently been used in England for the purpose. The way in which the Maroons carried on the war was most shocking; slaying without mercy all who fell into their power. The country where the fighting was taking place was mountainous and woody, but the Maroons knew every part of it, and could easily conceal themselves.

It was therefore very probable, concluded Yorke, that the hounds had been introduced for the purpose of detecting the Maroons, and not for the purpose mentioned by General McLeod. Mr. Charles James Fox said that no one could accuse the King's Ministers of intending to conduct the war by means so revolting to humanity; but as the facts had been stated the truth or falsehood of the matter should be ascertained.

A letter to the Editor of the *True Briton* newspaper, came out in defence of Balcarres. The writer said that General McLeod made the Earl of Balcarres appear to be a satellite of Tyranny, letting loose the bloodhounds of war to tear in pieces the deluded but innocent natives. But if the bloodhounds were employed by Balcarres against the Maroons, one must ask why.

In the first place, said the writer, the dogs had been employed to save from ambushes and treachery, the lives of gallant soldiers (witness the death of Colonels Fitch and Sanford), by discovering the retreats of an enemy bound by no faith, who had broken a treaty after laying down their arms, and who could only be looked on as concealed murderers, ready to leap out from caves, rocks and woods to pillage and destroy the innocent.

The writer reminded the General that the blood hounds were only dogs, endowed with a superior instinctive scent, by which they could trace and discover the concealed haunts of men, in the same way as a pointer or setter is trained to set at a partridge, and being allowed to do no more than find out its object. It was therefore as reasonable to protest against sending out a well-armed scout to discover where a treacherous enemy lies concealed, as to object to the use of the bloodhounds, particularly against an enemy impossible to get at by any other means.

The writer called Balcarres "a man of the mildest temper and most approved humanity", and revealed that, at that very moment, the colonists in Jamaica were considering the erection of a statue to the Earl, to be placed alongside Rodney's statue in Spanish Town, as the saviour of their property, and of the lives of themselves, their wives and their children. Without the zeal and active humanity of the Earl of Balcarres, the unfortunate island of Jamaica would have presented a second picture of the horrors of Santo Domingo.

"If it is a crime to preserve to England one of her most valuable islands," said the writer, "if it is a crime in a Civil magistrate to expose daily his own life in defence of the innocent against a band of concealed ruffians, and to trace out their haunts by every means calculated to spare the effusion of human blood, then the Earl of Balcarres stands eminently guilty. But it is a crime for which the people of England will be more ready to give him their cordial approbation, and an increase of honours, than to join with the General to reprobate his conduct".

Another letter, to the Editor of *The Sun* newspaper, also defended Balcarres, calling him a man of good conduct and uncommon placid temper and humanity. The writer described the difficult Maroon country, which he said allowed a handful of men to keep thousands in awe, having already cost the lives of two hundred and fifty soldiers. This unequal conflict suggested the idea of sending to Cuba for dogs to scent and point out ambuscades, thus saving the troops from destruction, and compelling the Maroons "to fight upon fair terms, or surrender".

Both writers (they may have been the same person) were mistaken in their assessment of the true nature of th Cuban dogs, and how they would have been used had the Trelawnys not made peace. Lieutenant Colonel Quarrell, who procured the dogs, was well aware that they would kill a cornered man if he resisted; and that the majority, being half-trained, were likely to kill anything they pursued.

In addition, the writer to the editor of *The Sun*, appeared extremely naive in suggesting that the Trelawnys fight "upon fair terms", as if demanding, in the interest of good sportsmanship, that some two hundred and fifty Maroons, woefully short of gunpowder, should march into a wide open field to do battle with nearly five thousand trained soldiers, with access to unlimited supplies and massive reserves of men.

In fact, war implies the willingness to kill, and this "games approach" to warfare, as if it were a cricket match or a chess tournament, was not only insincere and self-indulgent, but was the sort of thinking that had caused the British army to suffer major defeats in North America.

Balcarres replied to General McLeod's accusations in

two letters addressed to Charles Yorke. He said that if he had to be charged at the bar he presumed it would be at the request of all the Commons of Great Britain, and not at the pleasure of General McLeod. He quoted from a letter written to him by General Walpole saying that if the services of the Spaniards and their dogs could not be retained, the Maroons would soon terminate the treaty.

Balcarres claimed that not a drop of blood had been shed by the dogs. They had been brought over at the request of the House of Assembly, who sent one of their own members to procure them, one of their own ships to convey them, and who bore all the expenses. It was strange, said he, that General McLeod should think that the use of bloodhounds by the Spaniards to attack and rob the peaceful Indians of the western world, was similar to the use being made of dogs (not bloodhounds) in Jamaica. The dogs had been brought in for defence and protection against "a banditti who had entered into a most dangerous and ungrateful rebellion." Their skill and ability in planting ambushes made it impossible to overcome them by ordinary means.

He said he had served the last war (probably the American War of Independence) with eleven nations of Indian savages, and he compared them to the Maroons, who, when engaged in warfare, plaited their hair, besmeared their faces and painted their bodies the colour of the ground or foliage. They concealed themselves and when discovered, twisted and turned to avoid their enemy's fire and threw their arms (weapons) in the air "with wonderful agility."

When it suited them, however, the Maroons discarded their ferocity and assumed the most mild and insinuating manners, "descend from their mountains to the plains, and mix with civilized society." Even so, the estate owners dare not refuse them anything they ask.

From a military point of view, continued the Earl, the Maroon land to the rear of their town was of "amazing strength," a "tremendous country," into which no Europeans had ever dared to penetrate. Their policy was such as to deter all Europeans from approaching it.

He thought the power of the Maroons could be compared with a fort on high ground which commands the plains beneath. They were so well aware of this, that the "bolder sister of a bold and noted Maroon, on the first day of the Rebellion, took the title of Queen of Montego Bay."

Balcarres said that in attacking the Maroon territory, his line of operation was more than twenty miles long, the last six miles of which was through tracks and glades which the military word 'defile' could not properly describe. He claimed that in spite of ceaseless exertions, his commanders had never been able to bring up a force equal in numbers to the enemy. Delay, in his opinion, would have been fatal, and was as much to be dreaded as a defeat.

Again addressing the question of why the use of dogs was in one case fair and in another unfair, Balcarres likened it to the laws and customs of war, which authorised a fort to fire red-hot shot, but denied it to a warship. The reason is obvious, he said: the one is for defence and the other for aggression. That was why he had refused to send dogs with the troops to Haiti to fight against Touissant L'Overture; because in that case territory was to be acquired, while in the case of Jamaica, territory was to be maintained, by every possible means.

Why, he asked, had the late Earl of Chatham made use of Indian savages in the war with the French in North America? Why did the great and illustrious Lord Amherst and Marquis Townsend use such an instrument? Because if they had not, the enemy would have used them. General Burgoyne supported the "use of savages" as a fair instrument of war; but if their neutrality could have been secured, the British Government would have thought their use unfair.

"I must be judged by my actions," the Earl wrote.."I

desire no screen, no shelter, but the honour of my own mind." He wished to publicly say "in the face of the world," that if it had been necessary to loose the one hundred and four dogs against the Maroons, he would have had no more remorse than someone would feel, if a murderer had entered his gates, and been torn by the house dog.

Balcarres also justified the use of the Cuban dogs, as a dreadful instrument of war, by asserting that the Maroons had taken an oath to kill all Europeans, and that all the prisoners who fell into their hands (at least apparently the European ones) were killed.*

The Earl was supported by the Jamaican House of Assembly, which, in a message presented to him, said:

> "We cannot but take this opportunity of expressing our acknowledgments of the eminent advantages derived by the importation of the Chasseurs and dogs, in compliance with the general wishes of the island. Nothing can be clearer than that if they had been off the island, the rebels could not have been induced to surrender from their almost inaccessible fastnesses. We are happy to say, that terror, excited by the appearance of the dogs, has been sufficient to produce so fortunate an event; and we cannot but highly approve that attention to humanity, so strongly shown, by placing the dogs in the rear of the army".

The chasseurs, however, were quite clear about their reason for being in Jamaica. They had come to set their dogs on the Maroons; to kill Maroons or capture them for reward. They were eager for action, and were so confident of success, that they begged to be put in front of the troops with their dogs, armed only with lances.

They probably took savage delight when people fled on the approach of their terrible hounds, and were disgruntled

---

* *Keeping prisoners was out of the question for the Maroons. Prisoners would have been an insupportable millstone around their necks. They had barely enough food for themselves and had to care for their women, children and old people.*

when ordered to march behind the soldiers. They greeted the news of the peace as a disaster, which would prevent them from proving their dogs against the enemy. In their state of acute frustration it was not surprising that they should run into serious trouble.

On Sunday evening, May 29th, they got into a terrific fight in Montego Bay with sailors from some of the ships in the harbour. Two sailors and one chasseur were killed, and several wounded. It was only the intervention of the police assisted by the military, which brought the desperate conflict to an end. An enquiry was held and a verdict returned against three of the chasseurs, for wilful murder. They were arrested and put in close confinement.

Balcarres and his supporters were never tired of accusing the Maroons of atrocities and of killing prisoners. The treatment of Fitch's body was frequently referred to. Yet the colonial authorities were scarcely less harsh in dealing with captured slaves who had joined the Trelawnys.

Jupiter, the property of Peter Franklyn, found guilty of joining the Maroons, was hanged and his head cut off and put on the mill house at Weston-Favel estate. Sampson, owned by Robert Fowler of St. James, was found guilty and hanged the same day. Joe Harvey, property of the heirs of John W. Harvey, was found guilty and hanged the next day. Bernard, belonging to John Gray, for joining the Maroons when they attempted to burn Industry estate, was sentenced to be hanged in the Montego Bay market place, his head cut off and placed on the mill house of the estate. The sentence was carried out the following day. The list goes on and on.

CHAPTER 33

THE BROKEN PROMISE

Although the great majority of Trelawnys had submitted to the terms of the treaty within a short time, three months had now passed, and apparently very few of the runaway slaves who had joined the Maroons were formally delivered up under their true identity. This provided Balcarres with the opportunity for treachery, for he now began to claim that the Trelawnys had violated the treaty.

Rumours began to spread that they were to be transported and Walpole immediately expressed concern. He told Balcarres that the Trelawnys had only been induced to make peace because of the promise he had given that the colonists would honour the terms of the treaty and that they would not be transported from Jamaica. He said he felt it was his duty to see that the terms were observed, and if he failed in this he would resign his command. Balcarres replied cynically that he thought the country had a right to every advantage afforded by the treaty and he would leave it to the Legislature to determine whether it had been observed or not.

With equal cynicism a special secret committee, composed of members of the Council and Assembly, was appointed to look into the matter. These gentlemen were obviously chosen because they could be relied upon to give the kind of decision that Balcarres and his supporters wanted. Walpole asked to be permitted to give his evidence to them, but they refused him, saying that the Governor had already given them all the information they needed.

The Committee met and made its decisions in ten resolutions. In the third resolution they went back to the period just before the fighting broke out, and stated their opinion that the Maroons under Montague who had surrendered at Vaughansfield as a result of the Balcarres proclamation, as well as the six Trelawny captains who had gone in a few days previously and been arrested at St. Ann's Bay on their way to Spanish Town, could not claim the protection of the treaty as they had submitted before hostilities began. It was recommended that they be transported.

In the fourth resolution they said that Smith, Dunbar and Williams, together with their wives and children and two others, who had come in on January 1st, were entitled to the benefit of the treaty since they submitted before the deadline. In the seventh and eighth articles, however, it was their opinion that all the Maroons who came in after January 1st, including Johnson and his party, should be shipped off the island. They justified this by saying that these Maroons had broken the treaty on two points. First they had failed to come in at the prescribed time, and secondly they had failed to hand over the runaway slaves who had joined them, allowing most of them to come in under the pretence of being Trelawnys. These were precisely the points that Balcarres had made.

Walpole and his friends objected strenuously to the decisions of the Committee. They pointed out that except for a small group of thirty or forty under Palmer and Parkinson, all the Trelawnys had surrendered within about two weeks of the time prescribed, and they again stated the reasons why this had happened. They emphasised the fact that the Trelawnys had submitted on the understanding that they would be protected by the peace terms. Walpole further pointed out that he had been very reluctant to obey the repeated orders of Balcarres to march the Maroons who had submitted to Montego Bay, as he had felt that it would increase the reluctance of those who still remained in the hills to submit; and this in fact was exactly what had happened in the case of Palmer and Parkinson.

All the field officers held the same opinion as Walpole. They felt that they had given the Trelawnys a pledge from which no Assembly in the world could release them. It was also pointed out to the Committee that the runaways had deliberately been allowed to come in as Maroons, otherwise they would have escaped; and they had subsequently been identified.

Despite the arguments of Walpole and his officers, the Committee was determined to get rid of the Trelawnys. They felt the colony would be more secure if they were removed from the island. They were supported in their stand by the Duke of Portland, Secretary of State for the Home Department, who wrote a letter to Balcarres saying that it would be best to dispose of the Trelawnys if it could be done with propriety.

Balcarres and his Committee were not too concerned with propriety, however. They were prepared to abandon all appearance of fair play and it is doubtful if they really considered it very important to keep their word with the Trelawnys.

The Trelawnys had been taken to Montego Bay and St. Ann's Bay after they had submitted. Now they were removed to Kingston, some being taken in vessels and some marched overland. They were to be banished, but the Committee recommended to Balcarres that those who had distinguished themselves by their "repentance and subsequent good behaviour" should be allowed to remain. Balcarres accordingly gave orders that Johnson, Smith, Williams, Dunbar and a few others with their families should be allowed to stay. To their everlasting credit these men refused to be "honoured" in this manner and asked to be allowed to share the fate of their people.

Smith in particular had an interesting excuse for not staying. He had four wives and, like the others, apparently extended the idea of family to include cousins and all other relatives. This would have meant that a considerable amount of people would have to be exempted from exile with him. Sensing trouble in this direction the authorities told Smith and the others that they would only be allowed to land with one wife and her children. Smith said he preferred to go rather than to abandon any of his wives and children.

In addition to wiping out the Trelawny menace once and for all, Balcarres wanted to make sure that the Maroons who remained were broken in spirit. Apart from the Trelawnys, the most fractious group was the Windward Maroons, especially the Charles Town Maroons under Sam Grant. These were the men who had been ordered by the government to take up duty in Kingston after Fitch had been killed and the war seemed to be going from bad to worse. After a few days they had marched back home without permission. Using this as an excuse, the Windward Maroons were persuaded (or ordered) to make a public submission on their knees on the March 18th, and to take an oath of allegiance to the King in the presence of Commissioners who were expressly appointed for the purpose.

For solving the Maroon problem so conclusively, the Assembly thanked Balcarres and voted him seven hundred guineas to buy a sword. Walpole was also given thanks and voted five hundred guineas to buy a sword. But his conscience would not allow him to accept it.

He wrote to the Speaker of the House, acknowledging the thanks of the Assembly and saying that his success was due in great measure to the "zeal, skill and gallantry" of Colonel Skinner and the rest of his field officers. Without their assistance, he said, all his best endeavours would have failed. In concluding, he said that he could not accept

255

the honour of a vote of money for a sword, since the Assembly had thought fit not to accept the agreement which he had entered into with the Trelawny Maroons, and since their opinion of that treaty had been written into their books in a different manner than he himself conceived it.

Walpole's letter angered the Assembly. They thought that it misrepresented their actions and that its language was "disrespectful and derogatory to the honour and dignity of the House". They ordered it to be struck from their minutes.

Walpole's principled stand on behalf of the Trelawnys, and his concern that his word given to them be honoured, shows him in a most noble light. However, he also was tainted with a certain callousness in regard to their fate, which, considering the circumstances, was quite understandable.

He had great respect for Palmer and Parkinson, and admired their strength of purpose and courage. He even told Balcarres that if Palmer and Parkinson did not accept the peace terms he would never be able to conquer them. Like just about everyone else who wrote about the Maroons, Walpole was impressed by their tremendous physical abilities, but in a letter to Balcarres of December 24th, 1795, he suggested a cold-blooded formula for destroying them:

> "If I might give you my opinion," he wrote, "it should be that they (the Maroons) should be settled near Spanish Town, or some other of the large towns, in the lowlands. The access to spirits (alcohol) will soon decrease their numbers, and destroy that hardy constitution which is nourished by a healthy mountainous situation."

The Spanish chasseurs, who had remained in the service of the government longer than the time specified in their contract, were voted seven thousand pounds and provision was made for them to be returned to Cuba.

The big problem that now remained was where to send the Trelawnys. It was suggested that they be sent to an unsettled part of North America which lay far from the coast so that they would not be tempted to try to return to Jamaica. Lieutenant-Colonel Quarrell suggested that they be sent to Canada and it was finally decided to send them to Nova Scotia on the east coast of Canada. Its capital, Halifax, was founded in 1749. The winter lasts for half the year and the frost-free season varies from less than one hundred days in the uplands to one hundred and forty days along the south shore. The temperature can fall in winter to as low as thirty-five below zero. Even though they were accustomed to their cool mountain regions, this change would be a radical one for the Trelawnys.

The plan for banishing the Trelawnys was approved by the Legislature but not formally adopted. Nevertheless a sum of twenty-five thousand pounds was voted to meet the expenses of transporting them from Jamaica, and a Law was passed making it a crime punishable by death without clergy for any of the Trelawnys to return or for anyone to conceal them.

Colonel Quarrell was selected to accompany the Maroons and was appointed Commissary General by Balcarres for the purpose. His job was to provide them with suitable clothes, food and accommodation while they were confined on board ship and for some time after they had been landed in their country of exile. He was also to buy sufficient land and tools to enable them to build houses and support themselves by farming. Balcarres ordered him to proceed with his charges to Halifax, capital of Nova Scotia, and to remain there until he received further orders.

There were some transports anchored in the harbour at the time which were bound for Europe. The Maroons were put on three of them: the *Dover, Mary,* and *Ann.* The 96th Regiment was embarked on the transports as guards, and on June 6th, 1796, the ships sailed from Port Royal in the company of a large fleet bound for Europe under the protection of *H.M.S. Africa* with the *Reasonable, Iphigema,* and *Scorpion.*

In April 1796, a little over a month before the departure of the Trelawnys, a bill was tabled in the House of Assembly to amend the Act passed in 1758 to Ascertain and Establish the boundaries of Trelawny Town, and to settle and allot one thousand acres for Accompong's town, and to ascertain the boundaries thereof. The bill sought "to appoint commissioners to sell the lands granted to the Trelawnys, with a reservation of so much thereof as may be necessary for the use of the troops that may be quartered there." It was resolved that the "said bill do pass."

*Leonard Parkinson,
one of the Maroon captains*

*The Earl of Balcarres, Governor of Jamaica at
the time of the Second Maroon War*

Cuban chasseur with dog

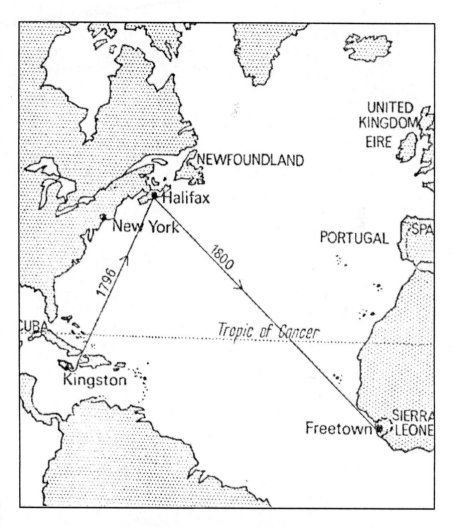

Map of Maroon transportation: from Port Royal
to Halifax, Nova Scotia, in 1796;
thence to Freetown in 1800

Halifax citadel, Nova Scotia

CHAPTER 34

EXILE

In his role as Commissary General, Quarrell was assisted by a deputy and by a surgeon specially appointed to look after the Trelawny Maroons. Balcarres also gave him letters of introduction to Sir John Wentworth, Governor of Nova Scotia, His Royal Highness Prince Edward, in charge of the armed forces in Canada, and Admiral Murray.

The voyage took six weeks and the Trelawnys were quiet and well behaved. In spite of the surgeon, seventeen of them died, which was small compared with the number of sailors and others who perished. During the voyage warm clothing was made for them out of linen, and this was cut in a uniform manner with a few distinctions to mark the officers.

The transports parted with the European-bound fleet off the American coast, and shortly after, on July 21st, the first ship carrying the exiles arrived at Halifax, to be followed by the other two on July 23rd.

When Quarrell landed he found that Prince Edward had issued an order that no one was to be allowed to disembark from the transports. Apparently unfavourable reports of the Maroons had reached the inhabitants of Halifax and they wanted no part of them. Quarrell, accustomed by now to such set-backs, delivered his letters to the Admiral, the Prince and the Governor and told them that they need have no fear of the Trelawnys. In addition, he wrote a reassuring report and circulated it among the principal inhabitants. It was not very long before they agreed to allow the Maroons to land.

The Prince went on board the transports to see the Trelawnys for himself. On the *Dover*, the soldiers of the 96th Regiment were drawn up at the rear of the quarter-deck. The Trelawnys, dressed in their linen uniforms, stood in line on each side of the whole length of the ship, with their women and children standing forward, all clean and neat.

While the band played, the Prince inspected them. He was very impressed by the height, bearing and physique of the Trelawny warriors and thought that some use should immediately be made of their strength and vigour. As soon as the Maroons were landed, therefore, they were put to work to help complete fortifications which the inhabitants were building as a protection against a French squadron which was raiding the Newfoundland fishing stations and threatening to land a force.

The fortress was quickly finished. One particular section on which the Trelawnys had worked under the direction of Prince Edward was named the "Maroon Bastion" and became a monument to the Trelawnys. They spent their money in the town and everyone was pleased with their industry. The Duke of Portland wrote giving permission for them to be settled in the province of Nova Scotia, provided it could be done without injury to the colony.

Five miles from Halifax on the opposite side of the harbour was a place called Preston. The Governor of the province suggested that the Trelawnys be settled there. Quarrell did not want them to be settled in a body as he thought it would cost the Jamaican Government too much. He also did not want them to be located too near to Halifax as he feared they might be tempted by jobs in the town and so neglect the cultivation of the land.

During this period Quarrell fell ill, for the third time

since leaving Jamaica. It was probably the same illness from which he had suffered when stationed with the troops in the Cockpit country and that had plagued him while he was hiring chasseurs and dogs in Cuba.

When he felt better, he went to have a look at Preston. He found it to be a very barren place which had been occupied twice before; first by disbanded soldiers and then by American slaves who had abandoned their masters during the War of Independence and given service to the British. They had been allowed to live in Preston when peace was made but had finally been persuaded to settle in Sierra Leone.

The old houses in Preston were repaired and new ones built to accommodate the Trelawnys. In September they began to move from Halifax in small parties. Disputes in connection with priority of removal and choice of habitation broke out among them and were kept up for a long time, but in spite of this they were all settled in their new homes by early October.

Clothes and stores had been ordered from England but before they could arrive, the cold weather set in. Consequently, these things had to be bought in Halifax at exorbitant prices which cut deeply into the 25,000 pounds provided by the Jamaican Government to maintain the Trelawnys.

The Governor of the province, who had become very interested in the Maroons, thought that the best means of "civilizing" them would be to begin instruction at once in the Christian religion and in reading, writing and arithmetic. He appointed a chaplain and teacher of the Church of England, with an assistant, to live among them. Their duties were to perform public worship regularly and teach school.

The winter usually lasted seven months in Nova Scotia and it was a time of little labour. All that was required of the Trelawnys at first, therefore, was regular attendance at church and school lessons for the younger ones. The church sermons were taken up, not so much with the Christian religion, but with convincing the Trelawnys that they were happy and that they should be grateful to the people of Jamaica for sending them to Nova Scotia. The parson would also praise the Prince, Colonel Quarrell and Governor Wentworth, and impress upon his congregation that the Governor was their best friend. Some of the Trelawnys would smoke their pipes during the sermons, others would sleep.

The next big civilizing step was to encourage the Trelawnys to get married in church in a Christian manner, and to persuade those who had two or more wives to choose one only and abandon the rest. The authorities did not say how they expected them to make this choice, but they warned the Maroons that if they broke any of the laws of God they would be severely punished in the after-life.

The Maroon men gave a typical answer to all this. They said that since God and Christ were good they could not require them to forsake their wives or any of their children. They then suggested to the parson that he try to persuade the women. The women, however, promptly rejected his arguments about Christian marriage and loudly berated their men for sending the parson to them.

Quarrell was alarmed by the failure of these efforts and came to the conclusion that the only way to get the Maroons to adopt a European way of life was to break up their community and scatter them among the white inhabitants. He wished to spread them in a small settlement as far as New Brunswick and suggested that they be allowed to occupy various unused barracks as a first step. His idea was rejected and Quarrell became so despondent that he began to think of resigning.

Meanwhile, the winter of 1796 arrived early and was turning out to be more severe than usual. From the time the Trelawnys left Halifax to the setting in of cold weather it had barely been possible to get enough fuel to last for even a moderate winter. The Trelawnys soon exhausted their supply and had to burn their pasture fences.

In December the clothes and provisions which had been ordered from England arrived. Potatoes were a major part of the cargo and great dependence had been placed on this item to see the Trelawnys through the winter. Unfortunately, the potatoes were stored in cellars which were not frost proof and were promptly frozen and destroyed.

The grain stores throughout the area were similarly affected and at once the price of flour rose steeply. Halifax was threatened with famine. At the Governor's request Prince Edward sent the Trelawnys a large supply of flour from the public magazines, but as even this proved insufficient, Quarrell sailed to New York on February 23rd to try to buy flour and other provisions at a moderate price. He returned after a month's absence with supplies enough to save the situation from becoming really critical.

Dejected spirits and the unaccustomed confinement on board the transports had undermined the health of the Trelawnys at first. Now, in spite of the hardships and long, severe winter, they recovered their health and much of their old defiant spirit. They began to complain about the cold and said that Nova Scotia was not for them.

The Trelawnys had done such a good job helping to build the fortress at Halifax that several of the inhabitants of Nova Scotia thought that it would be an excellent idea to make further use of their services. They proposed that they be allowed to employ them as indentured servants. The proposal was referred to Quarrell and then to the Governor.

When the Trelawnys were informed, they smiled. Even in this strange country they were very much aware of their proud and independent history which had lasted nearly one hundred and fifty years. They were not about to tarnish

their heritage. So they laughed at the attempt to make
them indentured servants, told the Governor that they
were a free people and requested that they be removed to a
warmer climate.

Apart from those who wished to make use of the
Trelawnys as indentured servants there was another group
who feared that if they became too industrious they might
cause the price of labour to be reduced. Between these two
conflicting schools of thought and the failure of the
Trelawnys to respond to the efforts to civilize them, a general feeling of disenchantment developed in the province,
and the original enthusiasm was replaced by apprehension
and resentment.

In addition, the money provided from Jamaica for the
support of the Trelawnys began to run dangerously low and
the Jamaican Assembly resolved that they would not give
any further support after July 22nd, 1798. They expected
the Trelawnys to be largely self-supporting by that time;
but the severity of the weather and the determination of
the Trelawnys to leave Nova Scotia, were making this goal
impossible to achieve.

Meanwhile, the ground continued to be bound by the
frost deep into the month of May, 1797, and the year was
well advanced before it was possible to do any farming.
When the ground finally lay open for use, however, the
Trelawnys were reluctant to work. This was their way of
protesting against remaining in Nova Scotia and particularly upon the barren Preston land where not even hedges
would grow.

As is so often the case in protest groups, there was a
weak section that was inclined to give in to outside pres-
sures. Some began to plant potatoes but the militant group
promptly beat them up. When this happened, Quarrell
decided to take drastic measures. He removed a number of
families (probably those belonging to the section that
wished to co-operate) to a settlement called Boydville,

about four miles above the upper part of Halifax harbour. There, in spite of the threats of those who remained at Preston, they immediately began to work.

Quarrell next placed the Preston group under the immediate supervision of Mr. Chamberlain, the schoolmaster, and instructed him not to feed them if they refused to work. By this method Chamberlain was able to get one hundred and fifty of them at work by early June.

Believing that he had gone a long way towards solving the problem, Quarrell now decided to resign. He transferred the responsibility for the Trelawnys to the Governor of the province on July 22nd, 1797, and turned over the property which still belonged to the Government of Jamaica to a Captain Howe who was made Superintendent of the Trelawnys.

At first the Trelawnys seemed to be responding positively. On August 4th, 1797, Sir John Wentworth wrote that since Captain Howe had taken over as Superintendent, the Trelawnys had gradually abandoned all their plans, foolishly and wickedly made:

> "not to work, not to plant, not to repair their houses, not to send their children to school, not to go to church, lest these things should keep them here (in Nova Scotia), and frustrate the wild, visionary and cruel scheme of a removal to a warmer country...
>
> They are healthy, increase in numbers and I verily believe, they now weigh two-thirds more than when they arrived... so fat and lusty have they grown."

They were working at clearing land, making hay, driving carts, etc. They made bricks, dug cellars, carried stones and hoed potatoes. The women, boys and girls gathered strawberries and raspberries.

Quarrell spent most of the next nine months settling bills and clearing up the business side of the operation, which had become muddled. When he left, an address was written to him on behalf of the Maroons which was filled with insincere statements, but in which they appealed to him to persuade the Jamaican Assembly to remove them to a more congenial climate.

Quarrell did not reach Jamaica until the end of October, 1798; his departure from America was held up by the threat of French raiders. He was voted the sum of £5,000 by the Jamaican Assembly for meritorious services and to compensate him for expenses and sufferings.

Under Superintendent Howe the situation at Preston began to deteriorate once more. Apparently he was anxious to please the Maroons and gradually they started to neglect their work. Many of them began spending their time in cock-fighting, playing cards and strolling into town where they occasionally earned money doing casual jobs. In this way the rest of the year went by.

The second winter was almost as hard as the first. The amount of snow that fell was more than the inhabitants of Nova Scotia had ever experienced in that region. It was impossible to do any field work and the Trelawnys spent much of the time indoors where they were fed and kept warm at government expense. They played cards a good deal of the time.

Chamberlain continued to teach the youngsters but the older Maroons refused to attend the weekly sermons and made little progress in Christian understanding. The only concession they made to Christianity was to have their children baptized. They continued the custom of polygamy in which marriage was entered into by the simple process of consent; and when a Maroon died he was buried with the old Coromantee ceremonies.

The long period of cold, the heavy snowfall and the tedious confinement renewed the desire of the Trelawnys to leave Nova Scotia. They longed for the sun and the hills and the freedom of movement they had once enjoyed. They grew sullen, obstinate and hard to control, and the

Governor became impatient with them and regretted the day when he had encouraged their settlement in Nova Scotia.

In addition, it now seemed impossible that the Trelawnys would be able to sustain themselves by July 22nd, 1798, the date set by the Jamaican Assembly. So, the Governor wrote to Jamaica asking the Assembly not only to continue their maintenance of the Trelawnys but to vote more money. He was supported by the Duke of Portland who said that the Jamaican Legislature was bound to defray all expenses incurred by the Trelawnys until they could support themselves.

The year 1798 was an unhappy one for all concerned. Chamberlain replaced Howe as Superintendent of the Trelawnys and immediately brought back the policy of withholding food from those who refused to work. Once again the Trelawnys grudgingly set to work but the whole cycle was repeated when the winter again set in. Throughout the cold months they fed their desire to leave and in 1799, before the snow was off the ground, they declared that they would never make any effort to improve their lot or co-operate with anybody as long as they were kept in Nova Scotia. They spent the winter of 1799 in a state of severe discontent and became a dead weight upon the government, costing ten thousand pounds a year.

It now became obvious that the situation was getting worse, and that the most sensible thing to do would be to grant the desire of the Trelawnys and find another and more suitable home for them. People now began to remember the freed American slaves who had lived at Preston before the Maroons, and who had eventually migrated to Sierra Leone. Perhaps Sierra Leone was also the place for the Trelawnys.

Sierra Leone is in West Africa and is bounded on the north and east by Guinea and on the south by Liberia. West lies the Atlantic Ocean. Originally it was divided into

267

many small independent kingdoms or chiefdoms. From the late fifteenth century European traders frequented the place but no European power had any jurisdiction there. Traders settled in the country under the protection of the African rulers who welcomed them for the goods they brought.

A group of freed African slaves went from England to settle in Sierra Leone in 1787. They were sponsored by Granville Sharp, the great English abolitionist, who called the place "the Province of Freedom" and hoped it would become a base against the Slave Trade. A subchief named King Tom gave the new migrants a strip of land, but they were driven out by his successor in 1789. The settlement was revived in 1791 by the Sierra Leone Company, a trading organisation sponsored by opponents of the Slave Trade and with its headquarters in London. They rebuilt the town and named it Freetown.

It was this Company which had induced the former American slaves to leave Nova Scotia and settle in Sierra Leone. Unfortunately the group became turbulent and unruly and were soon a great threat to the stability of the settlement. When the Directors of the Company were asked to receive the Trelawny Maroons, therefore, they were reluctant to do so as they feared a repetition of their experience with the Americans.

It was suggested to them, however, that the Trelawnys could be used to help keep the American group in order, and when, in addition, the Company was told that they would be paid for the actual expense of settling the Trelawnys, they agreed to receive them. The persistence of the Trelawnys had finally brought about the results which they had hoped for. They left Nova Scotia at the beginning of autumn in the year 1800 and arrived at Sierra Leone in October.

They were immediately put to the test. The Afro-Americans had started an insurrection in an attempt to seize power when they heard that the Sierra Leone Company was about to be allowed to establish its authority. The Trelawnys were thrown into the fight and helped to crush the rising. Everyone was suitably impressed by their warlike skill, and it was evident that the years spent in Nova Scotia, playing cards, lounging about and occasionally cultivating the land had not weakened their powers.

Shortly afterwards some tribal chiefs struck a sudden blow at the settlement. The Trelawnys helped to repulse the attack and assisted in forcing the removal of the chiefs from the immediate vicinity of the settlement.

The Company had indeed made a fortunate decision when they agreed to receive the Trelawnys, and the Trelawnys, by willingly risking their lives, had now earned the right of citizenship in their new home. The Afro-Americans were awed by the tough and fearless spirit of the Trelawnys and, paradoxically, looked to the Europeans for protection against them.

The Trelawnys were described at around this time as being "active and intrepid, prodigal of their lives, confident of their strength, proud of the character of their body (community), and fond, though not jealous of their heritage." They all desired to go back to Jamaica at some time in the future and because of this were not easily induced to work towards a permanent settlement in Sierra Leone.

The authorities found it difficult to govern the Trelawnys and almost impossible to force them into the mould of European civilization. No one dared to suppress their practice of polygamy and there was some speculation as to how far they would quietly submit to any restraints of their inclinations and habits by the civil power which was now largely represented by the Company.

Despite all this they were eager to work for wages and many of them showed a great desire to learn handicrafts. Once they turned their attention to these trades, they surprised everyone by the rapidity with which they became master craftsmen. The great hope for their eventual integration into the way of life which the Company was trying to build at Freetown was the fact that they allowed their children to receive religious instructions and formal education, even though they refused it themselves. The Trelawnys never ceased to speak about Jamaica and never lost their deep love for the mountains and valleys which had been the home and refuge of the Maroons for almost a century and a half.

It is doubtful if any of the adult generation of Trelawnys who participated in the conflict of 1795 ever returned to Jamaica; but it is known that towards the middle of the nineteenth century Trelawnys did return, perhaps the children or grandchildren of the exiles.

The Maroons who remained in Jamaica became confirmed in their role as mercenary hunters of runaways and rebels.

They were last used by the Government in 1865, (thirty-one years after slavery was abolished), during the Morant Bay Rebellion, an uprising of small farmers in the parish of St. Thomas against colonial corruption and injustice. The leader, Paul Bogle, who was acclaimed a National Hero in the 1965 centenary celebrations of the rebellion, was captured by Maroons.

A census return for the year 1801 showed that the total population of the four surviving Maroon communities in Jamaica (Moore Town, Charles Town, Scotts Hall and Accompong) numbered only seven hundred and twenty-three, including men, women, children and invalids. It is possible that the census was not accurate, and, no doubt, many of the Maroons had drifted away from their communities. Nevertheless, the figures show that the total population of the four towns was very little more than the single Trelawny group, which numbered about six hundred.

The Trelawnys were perhaps, the most militant and

independent of all the Maroons. They were never really defeated and their spirit was never broken. The genius of Cudjoe, their great chieftain, remained with them, and was passed on in their time of need to such men as Johnson and Smith.

Their love of freedom was outstanding, and their inability to live in harmony with the Jamaican slave society resulted in their banishment, which was the only thing they feared. But even in their exile their love of freedom triumphed, for they were eventually sent to a place which was founded to be a base against the slave trade, and which was called the "Province of Freedom."

The removal of the Trelawnys from Jamaica put an end to the great epic which had begun in 1655, when the Spanish-Africans broke loose and fled to the mountains at the time of the English invasion.

EPILOGUE

THE MAROONS TODAY

Soon after the Trelawny Maroons were transported from Jamaica, barracks were erected on the site of their old town to accommodate regiments of British troops. Soldiers continued to be stationed there until the middle of the nineteenth century. Many of them fathered children from women in the area, as was evidenced for generations in the complexions of some of the inhabitants.

For a while Trelawny Town (or Maroon Town as it came to be called) was headquarters for the troops stationed in the Country of Cornwall in western Jamaica. The headquarters were later transferred to Falmouth, capital of Trelawny which is one of four parishes in Cornwall.

In 1839, a sanatorium for European troops was set up in Maroon Town. Huts were built for the purpose and the 68th regiment was quartered there. During the Crimean War (1854-1856), the troops were withdrawn from the parish and the barracks at Maroon Town fell into ruins. Up to the first decade or two of the twentieth century remains of a loopholed block house could still be seen, among other things.

The Maroon villages — Moore Town, Charles Town, Scotts Hall and Accompong — still survive, and they are still inhabited by Maroons.

The limited treaty lands could not support all the increase of the Maroons and many of them moved away to

272

seek education and opportunity in the larger towns and cities on the plains. Many of today's Jamaicans who have never even seen a Maroon town can boast of Maroon blood, and many of the Maroons who live in the old towns have taken husbands or wives who were not Maroons. So it is that the ancient warrior strain has spread into the population at large and is perhaps, in part, responsible for what is dogged and indomitable in the Jamaican character.

The towns under their elected Colonels still maintain some vestige of autonomy and some unique qualities of their own. The Colonels still try minor cases and have considerable prestige. The old Maroons recite the ancient deeds; some half forgotten, some embellished. The old dances and songs and folk tales still prevail, and some of the rituals are still performed.

The Accompongs can take you to Cudjoe's cave and proudly point out the spot where the treaty was signed, and perhaps show you a copy of the document. The Moore Town Maroons yearn after the legendary Nanny of haunted Nanny Town and speak guardedly of valuable buried papers. You can still hear the sound of the abeng echoing through the hills, and the best jerk pork is still made by Maroons. But the truth is that the strength and spirit of the Maroons are no longer the exclusive property of the mountain strongholds; they belong to all Jamaica.

Printed in the United States
2282